GETTING FROM
TWENTY
to
THIRTY

D0613541

GETTING FROM TWENTY to THIRTY

Surviving Your First Decade in the Real World

MIKE EDELHART

M. EVANS

Lanham • New York • Boulder • Toronto • Plymouth, UK

Library of Congress Cataloging in Publication Data

Edelhart, Mike
  Getting from twenty to thirty.

    1. Young adults—United States—Psychology.
2. Autonomy (Psychology)   3. Life skills—United
States. I. Title.
HQ799.7.E32   1983   305.2'35'0973   82-21007

ISBN 978-1-59077-293-5

Distributed by
NATIONAL BOOK NETWORK

M Evans
An imprint of Rowman & Littlefield
4501 Forbes Boulevard, Suite 200
Lanham, Maryland 20706
www.rowman.com
DESIGN BY RONALD F. SHEY

Manufactured in the United States of America

Contents

Introduction

SOMETIME IN OUR early twenties we move into our own lives. There's nothing to it. Everyone does it. Right? Well, not exactly. It's true that we all, ultimately, move into our own lives and have some sort of separation from our parents. But it's not true that there's nothing to the move. In fact, it's one of the great challenges we face during our twenties. It thrills us and it terrifies us. Bill Geffen was hardly prepared for what he felt as he drove with his father from his family home in New Jersey to his first apartment in New York City.

"At first, when I got out of college I moved into my parents' house for a while . . . until things got rolling. I remember feeling like I was a kid again. For a while I felt really secure because I really didn't know what I was going to do with myself. And my parents sort of took care of me. But after a few months I had a job and I knew that I needed to be on my own.

"I got an apartment with a friend and my dad helped me pack up some stuff and the furniture from my bedroom at home. A small truck took the stuff to the city and I said good-bye to my mother and hopped into the car with my father. And as soon as we started to pull out of the driveway I felt like I'd been hit by a ton of bricks or something. I just got this overwhelming feeling of panic.

"I mean, this was it. A job, a place of my own . . . the whole thing. I wanted to say, 'Daddy, don't make me go,' and get all my furniture back into my bedroom and climb into the bed and sleep until my mother called me down for dinner. But I couldn't. Instead, I let my father drop me off at my apartment, went to work the next morning, and went back to New Jersey for the weekend. And that was my pattern for months."

As we move into our twenties we yearn to be free, independent, on our own—but not entirely. A part of us still looks back longingly at the security of home and school and the wonderful, effortless dependence of our lives as teens. We look forward and leap ahead to a new

1

level of personal independence; then almost immediately glance back over our shoulders and take a couple of halting steps back toward familiarity.

We feel tremendous excitement about what lies ahead of us, but we're a little scared of it too. We know we don't want to remain teen-agers, yet we have deep misgivings about leaving that comfortable part of our lives behind. We hang in the middle of two life paths, and swing from one to the other in uncertainty.

This is the emotional situation we confront as we begin our twenties. We are struck by an anxiety born of our sudden new possi-bilities and our lack of experience in how to approach them. In fact, it is probably unfair to give this initial emotion of the twenties a name; it is too different from what we've felt before, too powerful to be de-scribed by catch words. It is simply the "new emotion," a knockout blend of terror, uncertainty, and giddy joy that whipsaws us around in a blur of unexpected situations and sensations.

What should we do? We still feel real gut attachments to the dependencies of our past. We want to keep them. We want to stay in the warm bosom of family, school, old friends, old haunts. Who wants to go out in the stormy, cold adult world? But we also des-perately need to get on with the work of life.

The resolution of these opposed sides of our lives is the chal-lenge we face at the start of our first adult decade. One by one we must carefully detach the apron strings of the past, never cutting them all, because we need to retain some of the past's stability. At the same time, we cautiously make new attachments on the side of the future—few and tenuous at first, but steadily more solid and numerous.

At first we swing wildly from independence to independence, from being adult sophisticates to being quivering kids. The swings are irra-tional, unexpected, and alarming. It seems that we may flap around forever, but gradually we gain control of the swings. We point them where we wish to land. We slow them. We begin to get our feet on firm emotional ground. And, as impossible as it seems when the twenties open, we eventually stop swinging and begin moving forward toward our goals for an adult life.

We begin the twenties poised on the edge of a cliff. We know we have to jump to get across to the other side. A part of us is determined to do it and certain we'll make it just fine. Another part looks down and can't help but think it's an awfully long way down. The two views war within us as we lean forward on our toes and think: ready, set . . .

1

The Twenties:
Expanding and Changing

THE CHANGES THAT mark our twenties affect us in every role we play in society and touch us in the more intimate confines of our private feelings and emotions. We aren't growing in just one way or one direction. We are expanding everywhere at once, like a balloon.

During our twenties we are at our peak mentally and physically. We have left behind the rules and strictures of adolescence, and have yet become tied down by the choices that have been made, as are people in their thirties, forties, and fifties.

At work the decade of the twenties is our time for testing what we've learned and what we think we want to do. It is the time in which we make valuable contacts, earn credentials, develop skills and support networks. We enter the decade with a headful of dreams about our careers and capabilities; by the time the twenties are over we have tasted failure and success, have measured our competence in the harsh adult world, and know where we want to go in our work and how we can get there.

Our sense of money grows enormously during the twenties. We are still basically the coddled children of our parents and schools when we enter the decade; money is something other people give us and we spend. But quickly we come to learn how much effort stands behind every dime and dollar. Money changes into a measure of our value. By the end of the decade we view money in proportion to ourselves. It has a different value for each individual, a different role in every life.

On the social scene the twenties are the time we move from the heavily patterned crony-hood of our teens toward unique and varied

3

personal relationships defined by our own rules and needs. We find a style that is tailored to us rather than to the crowd of our peers.

Among family members the twenties are a period of shifting positions. The entire pattern of family behavior has to be rechoreographed with you, as a company member, recast from a child into an adult. Family members tend to circle one another during the twenties—dodging and feinting, approaching and retreating as they gauge the danger of their opponent. Eventually, when the battle is finished and the smoke clears, a new relationship emerges.

The twenties bring deep change inside us as well. During this decade we lay the foundation for developing a rich personal sense. We begin to pinpoint what we really want in life and how to get it. We develop our first lasting self-image. We learn who we want to love and what we crave from our partners. The process is something like cooking an egg: At the beginning everything is transparent and fluid, and by the end the individual has defined form. Like the egg, we may not cook evenly, but ultimately everything comes together.

A FOUNDATION FOR SURVIVAL

For many the twenties are a period of scrambling for survival, of learning the ways of the world and attempting to adapt to them. Everything around us seems to be happening so quickly, and with such excitement, that in the end we're left wondering how we ever made it through at all.

Karen Lewis recalls going through her twenties in the late sixties and early seventies. "Perhaps because I turned twenty in 1968, when all the anti-Vietnam and counterculture activities were at their peaks, and turned thirty when all of those activities were at a standstill, I characterize my twenties as years of moral development. The issue I remember thinking most about—more than career, romance, and so forth—was what sort of life values I would have. Vietnam was, for me, a moral issue. The civil rights movement was likewise. And whether I was going to work for love or work for money was exactly (although somewhat naively) the same sort of question.

"Almost everyone I knew at the time was dealing with the same sort of issues. And today, fourteen years after we all turned twenty, we're dealing with the consequences of decisions we made then. One guy I knew was a lawyer—graduated top of his class at Columbia Law

School, Law Review, all sorts of honors. When he got out of law school all the top corporate law firms tried to court him. They wanted him to work for them. If he had accepted their offers he'd probably be a partner today, making well over $100,000 a year.

"Instead, he went to work for legal services—defending people who couldn't afford to hire a fancy law-firm lawyer. Last year he was earning somewhere in the high $20,000s and desperate because his wife was expecting their first baby and they were living in a tiny one-bedroom apartment. Now, with all the federal cutbacks it looks like he'll lose his job and he may actually have to go work for a firm—if he's lucky enough to get hired. They don't look kindly on thirty-four-year-olds who have no corporate experience. Did he make a mistake when he got out of law school? I don't know. On some level he probably would say yes, but I made similar choices and I still feel ambivalent.

"When I began working I was very young and ambitious. Before I'd had my twenty-fifth birthday I was an executive in middle management. I was really hot stuff. When I met the man I was going to marry, who was a writer, we decided to travel—to spend time living in all sorts of places and both do our own writing. Basically, we decided to get off the corporate track and have some adventure. I'm sure the spirit of the times was an important factor in our decision.

"Now, lots of people I used to work with are in very high-powered positions, although we're just making do. We work hard, do things we really care about, and live in crowded quarters with our children. Did we make a mistake?

"I guess that in some ways I did make a mistake, but I honestly don't regret what I did in my twenties. I learned during those years that I was happier working for myself than working for other people. And I really developed a kind of independence that many of my friends who've been on a straight work path for the last fourteen years just don't have. One of them got fired a few weeks ago and she's scared to death. What's she going to do? On some level I came out of my twenties knowing that I could always get by on my talents; and even though I don't earn quite as much as some people, there's something liberating about the independence I feel. The experience of going through my twenties shaped my sense of self."

During our twenties we are happier, freer, less inhibited, and also probably more ignorant than we ever have been or ever will be again. Adolescents still live in a world where parents' rules and values dominate. Adults have learned skills, have made certain choices that define their lives, have chosen a value system for themselves. Our world is different from both. We must reject the illusions of the older generation and create our own sense of life. In the process, though, we toss away the only view we've ever known and face the twenties having to devise a replacement. We start the twenties from scratch.

I remember the first month I was living on my own and earning a regular weekly paycheck. I just couldn't seem to coordinate anything. The beginning of every week I'd feel really flush and go out and buy myself some clothing, which I needed for work, and maybe go to a movie and out to dinner with friends. And by the time Wednesday would roll around I'd be borrowing money from friends to get me through the week. That meant that my next paycheck would already have a good chunk cut out of it after I paid back my debts.

It just never seemed to work. At some point I decided that eating out was too expensive and that I'd start cooking for myself, which usually meant frying a hamburger in a pan and eating it while I was standing up in front of the stove. Given that style, meals usually took about ten minutes and I'd be left with time on my hands, not feeling very satisfied, and ready to go out and meet some friends at a bar, which meant more money. And there I was again with the same problem.

It was all pretty funny for a while, but once I got beyond the novelty of it—after I'd been going that way for nearly a year—it became very depleting and I knew I'd simply have to go back to step one and learn how to live like a normal human being.

The problems of our twenties come in two types. Some represent eternal constants, those that have faced young adults since time immemorial. Other problems are specific to our times. The difference between them is important. The long-standing, traditional trials of the twenties will tend to be very much the same for most of us. And the timeless questions ultimately hold greater import.

The more specific problems of the decade, of which there are an infinite variety, call for immediate coping. Handling them well can smooth the rough spots of our development, can help us succeed in the current situation. But they lack the connection with our vital humanity that would bring about real maturity.

Because these two kinds of problems are so different, and have such divergent impacts, we will discuss many of the situations in this book through both frameworks. The universal questions will form the background for the more immediate concerns. Keeping them separate helps maintain a balanced view of what is happening during the twenties, and what counts most in the long run.

In the 1960s the milieu faced by twenty-year-olds was nearly as pleasant as their parents' protection. The economy boomed, apartments were cheap, and social relationships relaxed to the point of insouciance. The world was the twenty-year-old's oyster. He/she could choose from industries pleading for his/her services, or rebel in the cushioned comfort of a middle class with more money than it could spend.

The 1980s, on the other hand, are an arid desert when compared to the rich sixties. The economy stinks. Help is almost nowhere to be found. Twenty-year-olds face a grim struggle to find jobs, a plodding search to locate affordable apartments, scant hope for loans at exorbitant rates. We have to hunt for companionship in a social scene that is fast regaining its rigidity. Our families may be in the throes of financial hardship, and if we want to protest the work ethic we can starve along with our good intentions.

The difficult climate of life in America today makes the passage through the twenties far harder than it was twenty years ago. The fears are heightened. The importance of every decision is increased. The punishments for poor planning or performance have escalated.

That's why I feel this book is so timely. Sailing blindly through the twenties may have worked in the past, but I've seen too many victims in the seventies to advocate that course today. These are treacherous waters you are entering, and your best bet is to be prepared. Getting from twenty to thirty might be rough, but you can make the best of it—and this book will show you how.

THE THREE STAGES

The trials of the twenties break into three distinct layers. Like the skin of an onion, each layer is much similar to the others, yet entirely unique. This book is structured in three major sections, each covering similar areas of concern—love, work, family, money—while the problems and challenges each presents are entirely different.

The first section deals with the "breaking away" years, those after college, the army, etc. These are the years of creation. During them twenty-year-olds feel panic. We rush about trying to find something—anything—that will give us some hope of a fulfilling career. We pass through the difficulties of establishing a new social life that follows the easy days on campus. Or we slam into the wall of adult responsibility in a young marriage. Everything about this period is turbulent and unsettled. We may move about a lot, looking for a nameless something we feel we need but can't put a tag on. We may try on a number of faces, both in our personal lives and in our careers, hoping to find out which one fits best in the real world. We may cling to our dreams in the face of harsh realities in the real world.

Money is so rare during this period that it becomes almost an object of veneration. Shelter is a phobia. Family and friends turn inscrutable. Life is at once a vast challenge and an enormous burden.

The early twenties can be a time of "dissatisfaction, constant turmoil, internal turmoil," as Jane Wise remembers. "I didn't know if I wanted to travel, but I had this insatiable desire to find something out. The problem was that I didn't know what that 'something' was. For a while I thought I'd find *it* from other people, so I started hanging out with the strangest assortment of people imaginable.

"And I had different clothing for my different worlds. I had straight clothing for my straight friends. And I had long flowered skirts for my hippie-type friends. And I had some really sophisticated things for an older group of people I knew. I think, in fact, that I wanted to be all of those people."

To some degree, the first stage of the twenties involves finding a way to be, see, and do "all of those people." But, like all procedures that involves choice, in order to *be* one thing, we have to let go of others.

The second stage focuses on the years of the middle twenties. During this time we have created a place and are busy evaluating it. Our careers have begun, but are they good ones? We have friends, but are they the right ones for us? Are our apartments too big? Too small? Did we get enough schooling? Do we need more experience? Do we need to chuck our current lives and start over before it's too late?

We confront our dreams. Does it look like we are moving toward achieving them? If not, do we let them go or hang onto them and change our lives?

We have a little money. How much do we need? How great a motivator is it for us? What kind of life can it begin to build?

The second stage is marked by the presence of real choices. We begin to realize that every opportunity carries with it a limit. Every choice we make eliminates dozens of other choices we could have made. Our lives are winnowing down, becoming more confined, more compartmentalized. Either this process is willful—the elimination of things we don't like or want in favor of those we have chosen—or it is involuntary—the disappearance of possibilities through confusion, failure, or a lack of clear objectives.

This second stage of the twenties runs less turbulently but deeper than the earlier passage, like a rapid that races through a narrow stretch without rocks. It is no less vital or difficult, just less frenetic. If the first layer is the establishment of our physical lives in the twenties, this is the settling of our internal lives.

While the second stage of our twenties is characterized by the idea that rebuilding our lives piece by piece would, in the end, produce the perfect life for each of us, the third stage brings with it the realization that much of what happens in the world—and subsequently to us—is beyond our control. So in the third stage we begin to embrace life in all of its dichotomies, difficulties, and absurdities. At the same time, we begin to sense ourselves as survivors, as vital personalities, and we begin to have faith in our power to control the things that are within our realm of influence.

Many of us entering the third stage find within ourselves a gnawing sense that despite our tinkering with the externals of our lives—apartments, partners, careers—there is something else lacking. Many begin to yearn for an inner sense of self that has been lacking since adolescence. What is happening is that we are, in a sense, "coming home" again, and the third stage becomes a process of consolidating the youthful figure we left behind in the college dormitory with the adult person we have been working on the last ten years or so.

Learning to listen to our inner selves in the late twenties takes many forms. One of the most easily seen is the attitude toward friendship. At this age we begin to stop examining our friends for their flaws, for the things they do that might hold us back from being the ideal self we imagine, and begin appreciating them for their more enduring qualities. We find that we can be forgiving of their faults, and more appreciative of their loyalties, their senses of humor—the qualities that made them friends in the first place.

This third stage is a tricky one, because it runs counter to all of the pressures for material security and success that marked the early twenties. But, like all of the stages of growth, if we don't meet the challenge when it arises, we'll eventually meet the repercussions. The inability of people to rediscover themselves in their late twenties produces that legendary "turning thirty anxiety." Many of us, when we turn thirty, begin to wonder who we are, where we've been. The age of thirty is, in many ways, an imaginary wall we've built, but the questions are very real ones, and often linger from the age of twenty-seven, twenty-eight, or even earlier.

While I can't promise that the advice I've collected in the third stage of the book will make for a joyous passage into your thirties, I do feel that you'll be more aware of the questions that crop up at this time.

The key to getting through the twenties isn't just self-understanding. The changes we undergo derive from shifts in the practical aspects of our lives—in our jobs, surroundings, finances, personal relationships, and family ties. If these basic elements of our lives are out of control or beyond our understanding, the psychological impact on our development will be devastating.

However, the crux for action lies not in the psychology but in learning about and controlling the practical aspects of life. If the central elements of our lives respond to our thoughts and plans, if we have a solid grasp on where we stand with them, then the psychological impact of life in the twenties should be extremely positive.

In each of the three stages of the twenties we have to reexamine our performance in these crucial areas and look forward to what we can anticipate in the stage that lies ahead. By planning and understanding we can rein in the components of existence and use them to help us grow, rather than simply letting them batter us about at will.

Without preparation for the real world we're terribly vulnerable to its vagaries. Mike Engels, who turned down a job working with his father because he wanted to venture out from the security he'd always known, was hit hard by reality when he had to confront attitudes and morals quite different from his own.

"I guess I just found the real world very shocking. I really did. Growing up in the North Shore of Chicago, I wasn't exposed to a lot of things. I guess my life was sheltered. All of a sudden I'm working with people who don't think the way I do. They didn't have the same kind of morals as mine. I don't mean to sound prissy or anything, but it just wouldn't occur to me to lie to someone on the telephone, or to take a friend out to dinner and put it on my expense account.

"I guess all of those things aren't terrible crimes, but I never really thought about any of it before I was thrust into the business world. I was terribly disillusioned for a while, but then I just decided that I'd do things my way and other people could do things their own way. I just couldn't take it all to heart. I had to make it on my own terms."

THE PRICE WE PAY

The process of change we undergo in the early twenties has its price: sadness, a sense of separation, a loss of well-loved patterns of the past. It can be a touch depressing to see so much we have clung to in life swept away, even if we realize that a better, more adult set of life circumstances lies ahead.

Many of us begin to feel that we must offer up our dreams as the price we pay for our emerging adulthood. We begin to sense deeply that every decision closes off another option, another alternative. We feel that the many new responsibilities of our lives will slowly rob us of our cherished images of the future. And, in many ways, that feeling is quite justified—in the face of the first years of the twenties, the real world appears all-powerful and ominous; our dreams frail and weak. But it is important to hold on to those dreams because these days of struggling and scrambling for survival will pass, and we'll need to return to what is truly important to us. In the midst of this difficult first stage, it's good for us to remember what we are dreaming of, what we want to make of our future, against all of the odds.

It is in competently handling the everyday traumas that we gain the knowledge and insight that lead to the vital personal growth of this decade. By overcoming them as we pass through these three stages, we grow into our adult shape. We are not "finished," like some piece of statuary—change never ends during life—but the basic form of the person who will live out the rest of our days has been defined.

I hope that this book, by delineating the pattern of our change so that we can recognize what is happening to us, and tracing the lives of contemporaries who have just been through the process, can help make the path through the twenties clearer and less threatening. If we can begin our twenties the tiniest bit less ignorant, perhaps our experience can be richer, more controlled, more thoughtful, and the person who emerges at the other end can be better defined, more self-aware, more secure at work. In short, a person who is, in all ways, more successful.

Part 1

Breaking Away

The Ties That Bind

WHEN WE REACH our twenties most of us are overwhelmed by a feeling that we have to get away. Our parents' home seems maddeningly restrictive. Our parents themselves appear as intransigent fogies, barriers to our self-expression. We can't understand them, don't like them, don't want to be with them. In short, we want out—fast.

We are born as members of a family. Our lives orbit around the center of that unit, the adults. About the time we enter our twenties, the centrifugal force of our own development requires that we tear free from our old familial orbits and soar off in search of paths of our own; not entirely under control, perhaps, but at least free.

At the same time, our home represents a haven against the outside world, a fortress of familiarity in a suddenly unfamiliar landscape. We want out of it, but we don't want the gate shut behind us. Or we would like to be able to exist within its confines as independent agents—that is, we'll take the protection but reject the rules that come with it.

Here, as in so many areas during the early twenties, the basic confrontation is between our warring needs for freedom and dependence. Many of us can't just walk out on our parents and slam the door. We want their approval of our departure, we need it as a sign that we are doing the right thing. We also don't want to hurt our parents, who obviously have mixed feelings about both our staying and going. They don't want to hold us back but they don't want to shove us out either.

The situation varies widely from family to family. The possible problems are so complex and so charged with emotion that any set of general guidelines, such as those given here, can only serve as a backdrop for personal action. We each must take the time to think through our own family's situation before we choose a course of action. We should feel our way forward to a plan that seems right for us, rather than accept the absolute necessity of damning the torpedoes and blasting our family to smithereens. Remember that while we want our family to change, we don't want it destroyed. We want to achieve freedom of movement but we don't want to face the wintery cold of today's society totally cut off and alone.

These feelings are what explode into most of our families when we hit our twenties. Our relationship with our parents undergoes a deep change. In some houses the process is merely uncomfortable. In others it can be a wrenching, even violent, confrontation of intransigent opponents. In all cases it is a necessary transition from our status as children to our development as true adults.

This time of shifting is as upsetting for our parents as it is for us. Our emergence as adults is a tangible sign of their aging. For two decades they have nurtured feelings of protection and control over us, and dropping them can't happen instantly. For us, we want freedom, but we shrink from the thought of losing the cushion against the world our parents have always represented. We don't want to lose everything that is familiar.

The tension of this pushing and pulling from both sides builds up throughout our teens. Eventually it must manifest itself in a shift of everyone's lives, usually when we move out. This move, said psychologist Daniel Goleman in *Psychology Today,* "is a symbol of a longer and more complex process that lies at the very heart of what it means to be an adult."

For our generation the attainment of this vital symbolic release from our parents will be harder than ever before. Studies have shown that leaving home is becoming both physically and psychologically harder to accomplish for each succeeding group of twenty-year-olds. Since 1969 the proportion of young Americans between the ages of twenty and twenty-nine living at home has increased by 25 percent.

The economy is one obvious cause. Leaving home today costs so much more than it used to that many of us simply can't afford to leave in our early twenties. The only way we can see to gather a grub stake for our own lives is to postpone departure until the money builds up or our wages catch up with our needs.

In such an uncertain atmosphere how are we and our parents supposed to know if we are handling this rite of passage well? How can our folks know if they are clinging, holding us back? How can we know if we are hiding too long behind the skirts of our parents, instead of getting out there and facing the cruel world?

Our society certainly doesn't help much. Other cultures have fixed and recognized ceremonies or markers that establish the time to leave parents behind. Marriage, the traditional marker in this country, isn't the clear-cut rite it used to be, and nothing else augments it to a significant degree.

Recent research indicates that there are ways to tell when the home situation has gone from being uncomfortable to being unhealthy. The crucial element is how what happens in the family affects how the young adult functions outside the home. "Some people don't want to get married," says a psychologist in *Psychology Today*'s study of leaving home, "and they stay with their parents until the parents get old, and then they care for them. If these people are working and doing something that they like with their lives, it's perfectly reasonable. It's when someone stays at home and is chronically inadequate, always failing—and the parents are always worrying about them and taking care of them—then it's pathological."

In other words, our parents' home may be a reasonable place to rest while we cope with the harsh outside world, but it isn't a safe haven. Even if we are within the physical confines of home, we must develop as separate individuals from our parents, responsible in our own right.

How do we know if we're too closely tied to our folks?

"One sign is that you are overly concerned with what your parents think," says Dr. Howard I. Halpern, a New York psychotherapist and author of *Breaking Loose*. "Other signs are if you feel that you are holding yourselves back for them; or if you have not formed new relationships that are in some ways as important as your relationships with your parents; or if you feel guilt for thinking or doing something that is not what your parents would have wanted for you; or if your parents' anger still sets off childhood feelings of terror."

As marvelous as it would be to sit down with our parents on our twenty-first birthday and instantly talk over life and our problems as mutually understanding grown-ups, it is, in the fullest sense, impossible. We shouldn't replace our youthful visions of perfect protector-parents with an equally unrealistic picture of perfect pal-parents. It won't happen that way.

Stripping off the layers of behavior built up over years leaves raw patches and scrapes that won't vanish instantly. Our changing awareness hasn't exactly settled down yet either. So, for the early part of our twenties, the most likely pattern of intercourse with our parents is usually wary give and take. We test each other, experiment with new ways of behaving toward each other. Parrying and thrusting, we set up new boundaries for behavior.

The heart of this skirmishing lies with us. We are the ones who have suddenly changed. It is our new sense of ourselves and the world that is forcing the family to reexamine itself. Our parents don't have much say in the matter. We are ready for change, our lives demand it of us.

But what about them? They may not be ready; they may not have spent the past decade building up this decisive confrontation as we have. The situation may smack them between the eyes, leaving them shocked, bewildered, and hurt.

They may not know how to react. They want us to grow up, but they don't. They want us to be independent and successful, yet they want us to remain dependent and need them totally. They are proud of our new capabilities and they resent them too.

We must remember that we are not going through this shift alone. We are dragging our parents through it with us. So while it is a necessary transition, we should strive mightily to make sure that it doesn't grow into total family confrontation. The greater sensitivity to the issue should be on our side, because it is our impetus that brings on the crisis. We should follow strategies that can speed the changeover to a new family arrangement without destroying the fragile web of existing relationships in the process.

Gail Jones, now in her mid-twenties, was compelled to face the most painful sort of separation from her mother. It is an extreme but revealing example of the difficulties of this change.

"My mother is a sort of Scarlett O'Hara character. She comes from a very, very wealthy family in Georgia and she grew up as a kind of queen of the manor on a cotton plantation. It galled her to think that she might ever have to provide for herself and her two daughters, and when my father left home for the last time, my mother just sort of dropped her financial burdens in my lap.

"For years my sister and I each worked two jobs while mother did nothing. I was baby-sitting, working at a McDonald's, and packing groceries . . . all the time just assuming that this was what I had to do. I did it for three years, until I was twenty-two, without realizing that this was a total role reversal, and it was crazy. I just didn't think about it. Maybe I was too tired to even think.

"But around that time lots of kids I'd been to high school with were graduating from college, and I began feeling depressed. I was smart in high school. I got good grades and I loved school. I took a few night courses in a community college when I graduated, but I couldn't manage it with all my work, so after a while I quit.

"But when I saw my friends getting out of college with degrees and moving on to good jobs I began to realize that I was screwing up my entire future. Everything that I always wanted for myself was going to be sacrificed so that I could take care of my mother, who was perfectly capable of taking care of herself.

"In a very unusual move for me, I just decided that 'It's me or her.' And I picked up and left home. It was extremely difficult. In fact, I'd say it was the hardest thing that I've ever done in my life. My mother did everything she could to make me stay. She told me I was abandoning her and that she was going to die without my care. But I knew that the issue I was facing was one of survival. It was me or her. And I had to choose *me*. Any other choice, and I would have died."

At its root the adjustment between us and our parents is an internal shift and a personal one. So the best practice for understanding and coping with what is happening might be nothing more elaborate than sitting down and thinking about it.

We should put ourselves in our parents' situation. We are facing our greatest time of opportunity; we are breaking out. But they aren't going anywhere. We are leaving them behind. We don't need them as much anymore. They have to change their lives to cover the empty place our adulthood leaves. They not only have to readjust to us, they have to readjust to each other without us in the middle.

We are old enough to be considered grown and young enough to be excited about it. They are old enough to be worried about time's passage and its effects on them and young enough to feel regretful and reminiscent about their own passing adulthood.

They also feel fearful about our newfound power and—in their eyes—our excessive hopes and enthusiasm. They've been through the wars. They know—or at least think they know—the disappointments and troubles that lie ahead for us. They wish they could protect us, but deep down know they can't. They wish we could understand life as they do, but know that is impossible. They know we aren't prepared for what lies ahead for us, but they want us desperately to be. They want us to soar and succeed, but they wonder if we'll forget them. Now that we don't need them, don't depend on them, will they shrink to some distant corner in our lives?

We can't just think about our own changes as we try to work through the crises that afflict our parents and ourselves in the early twenties. We must think of them too. We must try to help them see life through our eyes. We must keep talking no matter how difficult relations become. It has been at least twenty years since they stood where we are. A lot has changed since then that they may not be fully aware of, including themselves. We must draw them a picture of our world, and keep redrawing it for them until they can see it as clearly and as undeniably as we can.

Sometimes this involves really climbing inside our parents' world and seeing things through their eyes, before we can help them see things through our own. A friend of mine lived at home during college and finally, at age twenty-two, felt compelled to move out and make a home for herself. Her parents just couldn't cope with her leaving.

"There were lots of times in college when I wished that I weren't living at home . . . when I wanted to stay out until four in the morning but knew my folks would be climbing the walls with worry if I did. It's not like I even wanted to do anything they wouldn't approve of, but I just needed to test my wings, and I couldn't do it while I was living under their roof.

"Before I graduated I started preparing them for the fact that I was going to move into the city, but they just closed their eyes and ears to me. Sometimes they'd say guilt-inducing things like, 'Are you embarrassed about us? You don't want your friends to meet us?' Or, 'What will people say about a young girl living on her own in the city?' This was years ago and they just didn't know any twenty-one-year-olds who lived on their own. Most of the young women—or 'girls' as they say—got married right out of college and moved in with their husbands . . . and that was fine.

"Finally I got an apartment and the moving truck came, and it was probably the worst day of my life. My parents looked ashen. My grandmother kept telling me that I was killing them. But I moved, and for nearly a month they would barely talk to me. Finally I just couldn't stand it. I tried to think a lot about where they were coming from and I went out to see them and have it out on a Sunday.

"As soon as I got to their house I began talking about all the things they'd taught me. I learned a lot about the value of a home from my parents . . . by which I mean a home in the emotional sense. A place you think of as your own; where you can relax, make dinner for friends, be a host or be alone if you want to. I asked them what they saw as my future if I never married. Did they think that if I never married I should be deprived of having my own 'home' as well?

"It was painful for all of us, but when I left I think they understood that I was trying to be the kind of person they had raised me to be; and that I couldn't do that while I lived with them. Of course, things didn't magically get better. There were problems for years and years about my having rejected them, but I honestly think they're proud of me now. I think they feel like they learned something from me about growing up . . . something their own parents had never learned or allowed them to learn."

A NEW VIEW

Whether we can physically move out or are forced to stay with our parents during the beginning of our twenties, our view of them is transformed. They have always represented crucial goals to us. They weren't so much humans as examples. We endowed them with the qualities we felt were important for life. Either positively or negatively they pushed us toward the values we have come to call our own.

Then, with dizzying swiftness, our emerging adulthood shifts the focus of our view, and our parents become merely people, a man and a woman with gaping holes in their personalities, with huge frustrations, failures, uncertainties that make them merely normal but seem incredible to us. At this moment we confront ourselves in a new way, and we see our parents in a totally new light as well.

Sometimes this confrontation can make us recoil, almost as though we'd been tricked by them. In order to show that we have been totally dominated by these fallible mortals we suddenly see before us, we may go on a binge of total independence, often bordering on the ridiculous. It is a purgation of our childhood fantasies about both our parents and ourselves.

Often we have no control over whether or not we can hang on to our "fantasy parents." Jerry Franks was in his mid-twenties when his parents got divorced, and the facts of the divorce were unavoidable.

"I grew up worshipping my father. I wanted to dress like he dressed, do the kind of work he did, sound like he did . . . the whole thing. I think—as weird as this may sound—that I never really examined the extent to which I idolized him until my mother left him.

"I was dumbfounded when she called and said that she and my father were splitting up. I thought they were perfect together. As it turns out, my father had been having an affair for almost ten years, and my mother knew about it for most of the time. When my little brother went off to college she figured she didn't have to live with the pain anymore, and she asked for a divorce.

"For more than a year I couldn't talk to my father. He was everything I respected and I felt like he'd done something terrible to me. Never mind my mother . . . it all felt like a dirty trick on me. He pleaded with me to talk, but I just couldn't.

"Finally the time came when I was ready, and we talked for hours and hours. I can't say that I condone what my father did, but I came out of the whole thing feeling sort of sorry for him. He's down about twenty notches in my opinion, but maybe that's better. The thing is, I think he really loves this other woman the way I thought he loved my mother. And the reason he stayed with my mother for all those years was that he didn't want to hurt me and my brother. It doesn't make sense, and I don't think it was the best way to handle it all. But I also think he genuinely loved me and wanted to do what he thought would be best."

ASKING FOR OUTSIDE HELP

One of the best things we and our parents can do is blow off steam and search for fresh ideas by working with outside arbitrators. These can be a professional therapist, our best friend, or our father's oldest buddy—anyone with whom any of us feel close and comfortable.

The importance of outside arbitrators arises because as family members we can't take an objective look at our own behavior and our own lives. We are too intimately entwined with the situation. The very patterns of behavior we and our parents are trying to modify limit our reactions to each other and circumscribe the possibilities we will imagine for dealing with our problems. The real issues between us can become lost in power struggles and family rituals.

Elaine Tilson found an uncle of hers to be just such an arbitrator, even though his advice, ultimately, was more akin to that of her parents' ideas than her own.

"At some point in college I decided that I really wanted to go to art school, and I applied as a transfer student. It was only after I got accepted that I presented the whole thing to my parents, and their reaction really set me into a tailspin. My father just listened to what I had to say and said, 'No.' As blunt as that. I started carrying on and he asked me if I could name him one woman artist. I couldn't. All of my heroes were men.

"My father's an educator and very into testing, and all through my childhood he tested me to see where my aptitude really was. And my aptitude was in math and science. So that's what he wanted me to stick to. I didn't hate the idea of being a scientist—in fact, I liked science. But I really wanted to be an artist. Finally, after a lot of arguing, my father and I agreed that I would talk to an uncle of mine who was an artist.

"I adored this uncle. He was a real bohemian, a real romantic character. I talked to him about my feelings and he said that I should never take an art lesson or attend an art school. He said the only thing that would happen is that I'd start drawing like whatever school I attended.

"So I respected his judgment more than my father's interpretation of my test scores and I decided to continue with science but pursue painting on my own. It was a good way to handle it because I didn't feel like it was just a matter of my father forcing his will on me. It wasn't a power trip or anything. My father and I both felt pretty good about the outcome."

In Elaine's case her uncle managed to defuse a very explosive situation. No one should feel uncomfortable or shy about asking the help of a trusted outsider during the turbulent, difficult times of change in the early twenties.

A CHAOTIC TIME

If all this has given you the impression of a madly chaotic, uncontrolled period, that's a fairly accurate picture of what happens much of the time. The essential tool for reducing the confusion and avoiding the turmoil is talk. But a different and far more difficult kind of talk than we've ever had with our parents before.

Until now, we and our parents have always talked from an unequal footing. We were the receivers and they the transmitters. We were the inexperienced ones and they were the holders of all necessary knowledge. No matter how friendly and open our families were, this basic difference was there. They talked to us, with some justification, as if we were kids.

That has to change. All those rules of proper conduct in the household must be junked in favor of a new set that recognizes that we are adults and should be spoken with as people who have a full measure of worth. On our part, we must get past the tumultuous, guilty feelings growing from our childhood and learn to talk with our parents as people. It's not their fault they aren't the demigods of our creation; they never claimed to be. It was our need, not their own, that created that role for them, and it is our responsibility to reconcile the role's disappearance. Overall, we find that our parents aren't the autocratic gods we were dealing with before, and we must build a new image of them and begin dealing with them as real human beings.

Barry Posen recalls one day when he noticed that there had been a shift in the dynamic of his relationship with his parents. Even though he could recognize that this shift was inevitable—even healthy—it made him uneasy.

"I'd always really relied on my father for support: everything from 'Gee, I need fifty dollars' to just calling up and talking about how well or poorly I did on a test. In other words, a little moral encouragement. But lately I think things have shifted from them providing me with that sort of support almost to me providing it for them. I've talked about it a little bit with them.

"Basically what's happening is that they're treating me as an adult. They use me as a sounding board for their ideas about where they're at and what they're going to do with their lives now that they're retired. Suddenly—I guess not so suddenly, but I've just noticed it—I'm the strong one who can come in and hear what they're saying and offer some advice.

"Sometimes I find this whole new role I'm in kind of draining. I get irritated by the responsibility of sorting out things with them. At the same time I really appreciate that they're facing big changes. I can't just ignore them. Where I used to rely on them, I think now they're starting to rely on me, and, you know, I have a weird sense of obligation to them. In some respects I feel really good about being there for them."

Barry's parents are still *there* for him in many respects. To some degree, the fact that they're allowing—even asking—him to help them is a confirmation for him of his real status as an adult. Barry, his mother, and his father are all going to be the richer for acknowledging the fact that their relationship can survive change.

More Than Nine to Five

THE SINGLE MOST important task that faces us as we enter the twenties is finding an occupation. Not only do we confront a financial imperative—we now must work to live—but psychologically we need to establish a structure to build our lives around. For the overwhelming majority of us, a job is the heart of that structure.

The work we select is far more than a decision about what we'll do from nine to five. The entire character of our lives is molded by the varying pressures, confines, and expanses of the kind of career we select. Our job will affect the kind of people we meet, the area where we live, how we dress, even what attitudes we form about life.

It is the first crucial decision of adulthood, and as a result is one of the greatest crises in our lives. Today, unfortunately, the task of choosing a profession is more difficult than ever.

Even those who are willing to start at the bottom are experiencing problems. Deborah Johnmann never expected to have any trouble getting a job in advertising, because she had what she considered to be a very realistic attitude.

"How was I to know that there were thousands of college grads, from better schools than I, who were willing to start from the so-called bottom? The fact is, I didn't even know what 'bottom' meant. I spent six months going to all the advertising agencies, telling them I could type, I would file, I was an English major who graduated with honors, and all that stuff. The people in the personnel departments just looked bored and told me they'd keep my résumé on file . . . which I figured out after not too long meant a lot of nothing.

"All during those six months I was living with my parents, which was really hard to do after being away for college. I just wasn't used to having anyone keep track of my comings and goings. But what could I do? I had no money to get an apartment. Finally I just decided to do temporary work, and I went to one temp agency that's managed to keep me pretty busy. Now, I'm sharing an apartment with two other girls—a one-bedroom apartment with three beds in it—and I figure that one of these days when I'm working as a temp in an ad agency I'll do something to catch someone's attention.

"If that doesn't happen I don't know what I'll do. I'll tell you, my sister is eight years older than I am and she didn't have the kind of problems I'm having today. It's pretty dispiriting, and the way the economy is going I don't know when things will get better."

Twenty-year-olds a decade ago faced all the psychological troubles we do. They had to adjust to their new adult selves while trying to fit into new work and life situations. They had to face rejection at job interviews and a sense of being lost when starting a first real job. They had to shift from being big shots in school to being the youngest, most ignorant members of a work staff. So do we.

But they had a leisure to search and select their job opportunities many of us do not. In fact, quite a few twenty-year-olds today don't even get the opportunity to try becoming adjusted to life in their field of work because they simply can't find a job related to it. Twenty-year-olds today stand ready to accept the responsibility of starting forward on a career, only to be shoved aside by a society that doesn't have enough jobs for existing workers.

John Marshall went on from college and actually got a Ph.D. in political science. He was twenty-six when he began looking for a job.

"I must have sent out a hundred letters to colleges in big towns and small cities all over the country. I thought for sure someone would have something for me. Obviously I was deluded . . . probably from spending too many years in school. After a few months it became apparent that no one was hiring anyone. In fact, teachers without tenure were out looking for jobs, and there was no way I could compete against all these unemployed Ph.D.'s with more teaching experience than I.

"Then an odd thing happened. A friend of mine with a little kid asked me if I was interested in subbing at his kid's daycare center. He knew that I loved kids and figured at least I'd be making something to pay my rent . . . just barely. I said sure, I was game for anything, and now, two years later, I'm hooked. I work there full time. It's damn hard work and I know that a Ph.D. in poli-sci isn't really doing me a hell of a lot of good, but I'm finding it more gratifying than anything else I've ever done.

"Of course, there's a problem about money. The field just doesn't pay a living wage, and I wouldn't mind getting married and having my own kids at some point, which I could never do on what I'm earning now. But I'll worry about it another time. For all I know the world could blow up in five years from now. At least I'm having a good time with what I'm doing. And I've got all these little kids climbing on my lap every morning telling me that they love me."

Many of us, then, must face the double problem of trying to start our adult lives while being forced to postpone the step that is supposed to anchor the process. Or we are required by economic necessity to make choices about our careers that used to come much later. We may have no choice but to abandon our original career plans before we ever get a chance to test them. This increases the frustration enormously; we begin to feel we've been cheated of a fair start.

It would be wonderful to be able to supply a pat method for avoiding these problems, but there isn't one. This section contains much advice about selecting, finding, and handling the first job, but in times like these some of us will get burned no matter how well we approach the problem. However, it is imperative that we keep in mind that having a rough time when we start out in our twenties is not the same thing as failing at life. Just because we are frozen out of our job field at twenty-one, doesn't mean we should abandon it forever. We should look upon our early twenties options as a way to test possibilities we might not have considered before. If we wind up liking what we have—good. If we don't, we still have years in which to work our way back to the field we originally desired. We are never locked in during our twenties. There is always some room for change. So we needn't despair if getting started proves a frustrating experience.

Also consider that many of us who breeze right into our chosen fields will leave them soon after, disillusioned by the gap between what we expected and what we found. John Shingleton, placement director at Michigan State University, recalls talking to a young woman TV journalist and asking her how she liked her job. "I like it fine," she said, "but the hours are killing me."

"She had found out that 'all that I thought I wanted isn't all that I really wanted, because I can't live this life,' " Shingleton says. "Some people want to be engineers, and they get on the production line, with all the noise and union crap, and they think, Holy Toledo, this isn't what I thought engineers did."

Susan Lessner never doubted for a moment what she wanted to do. She'd decided by age five that she wanted to be a teacher, and after her first year of college she knew that she wanted to teach English literature to high school kids.

"Rather than start work right after college I decided to go on for my master's in English at the School of Education at NYU. Teachers' salaries are higher when you have a master's, and since my parents were willing to support me for another year it seemed like a good idea. And, of course, I loved school. The problem came when I began teaching.

"Basically I never had a chance to teach what I wanted to teach. For one thing, the kids were horrible. Well, maybe they weren't so horrible. Maybe it was my fault for not being able to control them. But whoever's fault it was, my classroom was like a zoo. There I was, five feet tall, standing in front of a room filled with kids who were bigger, louder, and stronger than I, who couldn't have cared less about William Shakespeare.

"And aside from the kids, the curriculum I had to follow was unbelievably boring. In some respects, I don't blame the kids for being so uninterested. If I had to read the stuff they were supposed to have read I wouldn't have been interested either.

"The whole experience was an incredible crisis for me. I'd literally never thought about doing anything other than teaching. I'd come home from work every day and cry for hours. It was like starting out at base one. It was more than I could handle myself so I went to a career counselor and worked with her to try and figure out what I wanted. I loved books and the idea of sharing them with kids and began to explore the field of library science. It involved getting another master's degree, which my parents had no intention of paying for, but I decided to take the plunge. So I took out loans and went back to school.

"I'll tell you, it was pretty scary. I was putting myself into hock this time, and some part of me kept asking, 'How can you be sure you're going to like this?' But things turned out well. I loved it. Now, I'm second in command at the library of a small college near New York, and I feel very excited about my career. I was lucky."

Since we have virtually no real life experience when we emerge into our twenties, all we have to judge careers by is a dream, our fantasy of what life will be like. In this light, our inability to get exactly the job we wanted at the start may not be as bad as it seems; the available alternatives may turn out to be far more to our liking than the reality of the job we dreamed about.

The goal of our first job is to *learn*—about the business we are in, about ourselves, about the way offices work and workers interact. It is the ultimate practicum, a real on-the-job learning experience.

We can achieve lasting triumphs in this first campaign in the job wars. Our career choice can be ratified and our confidence bolstered by success at this basic level. Our view of the future and our role in it may be richly deepened by what happens to us on the first job, making everything that comes after much smoother and more certain. At the same time, we must beware of the pitfalls of our new working state. We must avoid becoming trapped in a job or field that doesn't work for us; we have to be ready to confront disillusionment or failure. We have to beware the venality, the backbiting, the unreliability we are likely to find in the corporate jungle. We have to avoid allowing our hopes to rise so high that the reality we find at work dashes them and leaves us without a goal and energizing expectations.

In short, we are being presented with our first opportunity to experience, participate in, and prove ourselves in the real world.

BEFORE YOU GO LOOKING

Where do students go for advice?

"First of all, go to competent placement officers," says John Shingleton, placement director at Michigan State, "and I say competent because there are a lot of incompetent counselors. There is a tendency in academia to put the wash-outs into counseling spots. Secondly, talk to the people in a given field. If you want to be a doctor, talk to a doctor. If you want to be a lawyer, talk to a lawyer. Third, work in the environment and the type of job you want to pursue, as an intern or volunteer—that may be the very best way of finding out.

"The best thing is to know yourself. That is the single most important thing: knowing your attitudes, what turns you on, your motivation, where you want to be located—if you know that, I almost guarantee you can get a job. The problem is that most people don't know where they're going, where they've been, or where they're at," Shingleton said.

The second biggest problem? "Most students don't spend enough time job hunting. They'll spend more time picking out a stereo set than they will looking for a job."

One way of finding out about your chosen field is by working in it over the summer, or in a part-time job. Ben Good had always been intrigued with the idea of becoming a journalist. Toward the end of his sophomore year in college he decided to test the waters and wrote to nearly every newspaper in the city asking if he could come and work for free during the summer.

"I got a whole bunch of letters of rejection but most of them were from people pretty high up . . . like the city editor. Somehow my letter worked it's way through the ranks. Someone at the *Herald Tribune* must have thought, Here's a gutsy kid. He's got initiative. Let's give him a shot. So along with all my letters of rejection I got one acceptance—which is, of course, all I needed.

"God, that was a strange and exciting time. While I was at the *Herald Tribune* all of my idols were working there. People like Tom Wolfe, Jimmy Breslin, Dick Schaap. It was an incredible experience. Nobody knew my name. I was just 'boy.' I was there and watching and confused most of the time. Nobody took the time to explain why I was doing things or what was important. I did the functions without always understanding why they needed to be done. But it was a kind of cementing for me of my idea that I wanted to be a journalist."

How can you get a feel for who you are? I have always favored a game I call "I am." To play this game you should pick a quiet time and place. Sit down with a blank sheet of lined paper, and at the top write: "I am . . ." Then write different completions for the phrase on each line of the page. You end up with a mosaic picture of yourself.

Long before you start looking for a job, you must also start thinking about what job you'll look for. You need solid information about what jobs require, what skills are necessary, and what jobs are available.

THE THREE KEYS

Richard Bolles, in his marvelous book *What Color Is Your Parachute?* lists three keys to create a foundation for finding the right job:

Key No. 1.   You must decide just exactly what you want to do.

Key No. 2. You must decide just exactly where you want to do it, through your own research and personal survey.

Key No. 3. You must research the organizations that interest you at great length, and then approach the one individual in each organization who has the power to hire you for the job that you have decided you want to do.

Bolles's prescription works, and his book has sold hundreds of thousands of copies as a result. But like any truly valuable tool, it requires work. It means much more than merely typing up and mailing out résumés. It demands hours in the library researching communities and companies. It means asking questions of everyone around who might have a useful nugget of information. It takes raw courage to step forward and face a person who can make or break all your plans.

But in these times that kind of dedication is what it takes to get started where you want to. Nothing comes easily anymore.

"The person who gets the job is not necessarily the person best qualified for it," John Shingleton says, "but the person who works the hardest for it."

A friend of mine bought *What Color Is Your Parachute* when he lost his job. He'd never really liked what he was doing and decided to capitalize on the fact that he'd been fired. His plan was to collect unemployment and really work at finding his "parachute." A week after he began the book, however, someone he had once worked with who'd moved on to another company called and offered him a job. The money was good, so even though he loathed the work he accepted. Two months later he quit and returned to the project of the John Bolles book.

"I cannot believe the work involved in finding a career," he told me a few months later. "For the last three months I've been spending days in the library, talking to friends about how they see me, writing my autobiography, and thinking about what I really want for myself. I'm just at the point where I'm ready to contact people at corporations that interest me . . . and I fully expect that whole process to take another couple of months.

"It's lucky I have some money put away. The thing is I don't feel like I'm unemployed. I just wish there were some way of getting paid for career searching. This is a full-time job in itself, and I haven't even reached the point where I have to deal with rejection. It's bound to happen."

EMPLOYMENT AGENCIES

If every advantage helps, what about turning to an employment agency as a professional ally in a job search? The personal approach is far preferable, but if you feel totally at sea, an agency might help redirect your efforts. Here are some considerations to make when working with one:

1. When you're working with a counselor you need to be clear on what his/her job is, and what your job is. His/her job is to sell you on a job. No matter how aggressive or nonaggressive the counselor is, the goal of his/her work is to get you to take a job. Your goal, on the other hand, is to find *the* job you want. In order to accomplish *your* goal you've got to keep a clear head and not be swayed in your pursuit.

2. If you're unhappy with a job your counselor has found you, go back and say so. His/her job is to find you a job you want. If you feel stuck in something you dislike it means that your counselor's work isn't done. When you report your dissatisfaction you can be perfectly pleasant about it (after all, anyone can make a mistake) but you aren't required to compromise your professional happiness to make your employment counselor happy.

3. If you're unhappy on the next job he's/she's placed for you, find yourself another counselor. There are lots of employment agencies and only one you.

4. Talk to your employment agency about the issue of "exclusivity." Chances are that you can have three agencies trying to place you instead of just one. And if they know they're not the only one you're working with they may feel an extra motivation—competition.

5. Don't overburden yourself with too many referrals at one time. You'll only end up being overwhelmed. It may be easier for an employment agency to give you a list of fifteen people to contact and see than it is for them to take it one by one with you; but it's not your job to make their life easy. It's your job to find a career.

6. Monday is the worst day for job hunting. After the Sunday paper most employment agencies are swamped by phone calls and applicants. Despite what your inner voice of desperation may tell you, the jobs will still be there on Tuesday . . . and you'll stand out from the crowd.

7. Try to learn about openings in small companies or in the

creative fields through your employment agency. Many such companies use agencies in place of a personnel department.

8. There's no getting around the fact that a visit to an employment agency will take hours and hours . . . before you even meet with your counselor. The best way to get through all that waiting is to wend your way through a stack of magazines. About a month before your appointment, stop reading your favorite periodicals. You'll have plenty of time to catch up on them while you wait.

9. Go prepared with half a dozen copies of your résumé.

10. Before you sign an agency contract read it carefully. Who is required to pay the bill? It should be your employer. (And if you're offered a job double-check with the employer's representative: "I want very much to accept your offer but since I'm coming from an agency I have to be certain that it's your policy to pay the fee.") Also, make certain that the agency gives a prorated refund if you quit or get fired within a month or so. They should.

11. If an agency sends you to see someone you've already contacted on your own (by telephone, personal contacts, direct ad, or whatever) make it clear to him immediately that you're already pursuing that possibility. Neither you nor the contact you've made should pay the agency a penny if you get that job. In fact, you might call up that independent contact and let them know about your involvement with the employment agency. They'll be pleased to hear that you think in terms of saving them money.

Keep in mind that if you can get to employers without an agency you're better off—no matter how hard employment agencies try to convince you otherwise. Employers are delighted to save themselves a fee.

12. If an employment agency sends you out on an interview, make it a point to call them as soon as it's over. Some feedback never hurts, and they'll be pleased to see how honest you are.

13. Even if an agency offers to make up your résumé, make sure you approve of it before they send it out. Résumés written by agencies can be pretty standard and boring. Since you're the commodity on the shelf, it's your job to make sure that you're properly packaged.

14. Send any complaints about your treatment by an employment agency to: Chairman, National Employment Association Ethics Committee, 2000 K Street NW, Washington, D.C. 20006.

15. Finally, if you possibly can, find a job some other way.

THE INTERVIEW

The end result of any career-searching techniques, says Richard Bolles, is to present the interviewer with a pleasant, low-stress interview. If he/she finds the encounter enjoyable, the interviewer will be much more likely to remember you favorably. This is particularly important on first interviews, where the initial impression you leave is so vital.

Bolles calls the attitude you need window shopping. Don't be looking for a job, come in search of information. Actually converse with the interviewer. Be interested in what he/she says and ask questions based upon a sincere desire to know more. Don't perform or attack, interact and probe.

Remember that interviewers are hassled and stressed all day long. Any hint of genuine, reasonable human contact they glean from a meeting will be a big bonus in your favor.

Relax. Consider Zen, which says that the one who pursues the goal least avidly, is surest to attain it.

On the more prosaic and practical side, if you were impressed with a company during an interview, follow up. Call after a couple of weeks to see if there is anything else they need from you. Let them know that you are seriously interested in them. If you don't get a job and still remained interested in them, check in regularly. People sometimes get picked up by a company only after months of persistent, polite nagging.

Alex Cole was very tense about his first job interviews. He came from a family with very little money—not enough to support him for even a short time after college—and he had debts to begin paying off. He would have liked to pick up his diploma on Friday and begin work on Monday, so the time spent looking for a job added to his tensions.

"I remember walking into my first interview and feeling like my entire body was trembling. All I wanted to do was get down on my knees and plead with the interviewer to give me the job. And the interviewer seemed like he was a real elder statesman, about eight feet taller than me.

"I remember that my eyes kept darting around his office. I didn't even know why . . . probably because I was too nervous to look him in the face. But all of a sudden I noticed a book in his briefcase. The briefcase was opened on the floor next to his desk and the book was

Sophie's Choice. I had just finished reading the book the night before, so as soon as we shook hands and said hello I said that I couldn't help but notice that he was reading *Sophie's Choice.* He smiled right away and we talked about the book for a few minutes.

"The thing is that even though we didn't dwell on the novel, as soon as I found something to relate to him about other than the job, he became a regular person to me. And from that moment the interview went like gangbusters. It was a great experience. And I got the job to boot."

No other single aspect of job hunting is as important as the interview. It overshadows, by far, the impact of any résumé. An unimpressive résumé can be overcome by a dazzling interview; and a résumé that categorizes years and years of experience can amount to nothing if it doesn't hold up to the scrutiny of an interviewer.

So, how do you make the most of an interview? Probably the best advice is to be prepared. And the first step of preparation involves learning about the many different forms an interview can take. There are at least seven different kinds of interviews and they each call for a different kind of participation on your part.

THE PUT-DOWN INTERVIEW

The put-down interview is a good place to start, because as unpleasant as it invariably is, it requires the most simple, clear-cut behavior on your part. In the put-down interview, the interviewer's goal is to create as much stress and make you feel as uncomfortable as possible. All the questions will be designed to make your palms sweat. Many of them don't have right answers: in other words, whatever you say will be wrong.

The following example of a put-down interview begins with a question from the interviewer:

"I see that you're applying for a job with us selling insurance despite the fact that your own father owns an insurance agency."

"Yes. I'd like my first step into the business world to be on my own."

"Rather make your mistakes somewhere that won't cost your family money?"

"Um. . . er . . . No. It's not that. I'm not planning on making mistakes. But I want some independence.

"Pretty sure of yourself, aren't you. Don't you think you can make mistakes?"

"Of course. Everyone can make mis——"

"Doesn't your father think you're mature enough to handle a job with his agency?"

"He does. In fact he'd be delighted to have me come and work for him but I thought that in the beginning it would be better . . ."

"How long are you planning on staying with us before you join up with your dad?"

GETTING THROUGH THE PUT-DOWN INTERVIEW

In case your stomach is already in knots just reading about the put-down interview, rest assured, it needn't be. You have a choice of responses. You can say, "I find your behavior rude," and get up and walk out; or you can get up, without saying a word, and leave. No one is obligated to sit around and be abused. The goal of an interview is to get a job offer, and you probably wouldn't want to work with anyone that treats you as poorly as a put-down interviewer.

THE PSYCHIATRIC INTERVIEW

There are times when interviewers think of themselves as psychiatrists. Such interviewers aren't necessarily bad people; they're just confused. And it's up to you to set them straight. Consider the following.

"I see from your résumé that you worked summers in your dad's insurance agency."

"Yes. My father, his father, and his grandfather were all in insurance and I always had an interest in insurance as well. I figured that the summer was a good time for me to get a realistic sense of what the work entailed."

"I'll bet it was. Tell me, did you always feel that your father wanted you to follow in the family tradition and sell insurance?"

"Well, I suppose I always knew he'd be pleased if I did."

"And you always wanted to please him?"

"Well, it's always nice to please a parent, but I wouldn't say that that's the only reason I chose insurance."

"Are you an only child?"

"Yes."

"So it really is on your shoulders to carry on what your great-grandfather began. That's quite a burden. Keeping dad happy and making him feel like his life work is worthwhile. . . ."

GETTING THROUGH THE PSYCHIATRIC INTERVIEW

Unless your interviewer is, indeed, a psychologist and you're ready to open up your soul to him/her, you might help him/her get back on the track by a subtle turn of the tables. When the interviewer asks if you always wanted to please your father ask him/her something about his/her own father. "There were times I loved pleasing him, and other times I loved getting under his skin. How about you. Was your father in personnel?"

If the interviewer comes back with something like, "We're not here to talk about my father," you can apologize pleasantly and suggest that it might be more profitable not to talk about fathers at all. "I'd be perfectly delighted to talk about myself and my aspirations and talents."

If the interviewer doesn't let up on your psyche, you'd probably do best to cross him/her off your list and assume that he's/she's done the same.

THE CIVILIZED INTERVIEW

Most interviews are neither psychiatric nor put-down. In fact, they're usually quite pleasant and civilized. The civilized interview is structured by the interviewer, who sets up and leads you through a discussion. He'll/she'll ask questions about what you've done in the past, and listen not only to *what* you answer but to *how* you answer. If the interviewer senses that the questions are too specific, he'll/she'll generalize them to make your part easier. If he/she senses that the questions are too general and you're floundering, the interviewer will help you focus in on what he's/she's looking for.

Most of the time the civilized interviewer will ask questions that can't be answered by a simple yes or no. Rather than say, "Did you like the insurance field when you worked for your father?" the interviewer will ask, "What did you like about the insurance business when, as a youngster, you worked for your father." And as soon as you've finished your answer, he'll/she'll segue into the next question.

GETTING THROUGH THE CIVILIZED INTERVIEW

A civilized interview is actually a discussion. And the best way to get through it is to regard it that way—as a conversation. If you need help, your interviewer will give it to you. If you need direction, or are worried about gaping silences, they'll all be taken care of for you. All you have to do is relax enough to listen, and tell yourself that you're talking to a friendly, interested stranger.

THE MAPPED-OUT INTERVIEW

Some interviews literally follow a map. The interviewer will read questions from a sheet of paper, which is usually placed somewhere on his/her desk just beyond your view. Although the history behind these mapped-out interviews is well-intentioned (they were supposed to insure fair and objective treatment of all applicants) they are inevitably stiff and disconcerting.

The questions actually don't differ that much from those you'll hear in the civilized interview—Why do you want to work in this field? Why did you leave your last job? etc. The fact that they are being read to you implies that you're not really being heard, and that your interviewer is maintaining an uncomfortable distance between you and himself/herself.

GETTING THROUGH THE MAPPED-OUT INTERVIEW

Your best bet, if faced with a mapped-out interview, is to act as though you were in a civilized interview. Listen to the questions and answer them as thoughtfully as you can. If you notice that your interviewer starts scribbling on cue cards, you should feel perfectly comfortable taking out your own pencil and paper and making some notes for yourself. Fair is fair.

THE "TELL ME ABOUT YOURSELF" INTERVIEW

You're twenty-two years old, fresh out of college, and sitting across a desk from your first real job interviewer. You shake hands, introduce yourselves and lean back, poised for the first question. It goes like this:

"So Peter. Why don't you tell me about yourself."
What do you say? Where do you begin?
"I was born in Brooklyn. I don't eat meat. Last summer I went canoeing. I've always wanted to be an administrative assistant."

If you ramble on for too long, you'll probably notice your interviewer squirming . . . or sleeping. If you answer too briefly there may be an interminable silence. There's nothing harder than an interview where the interviewer abnegates control to you. At best, it takes twice as long as necessary.

GETTING THROUGH THE "TELL ME ABOUT YOURSELF" INTERVIEW

The best thing you can do when you recognize that you're having a "tell me about yourself" interview is think about what you want to convey and convey it. Say it all, so that you don't walk out thinking, I should have told him . . . , and when you're finished just sit back and look friendly. The silence—if there is one—won't get to you if you're prepared for it. Think pretty thoughts . . . or ugly thoughts . . . or whatever works best at making time fly for you. If your interviewer asks if you have anything to add just say, "No. Thank you for your time. It was good meeting with you," and leave.

THE PANEL INTERVIEW

There are occasions where you might be interviewed by more than one person. It could be a panel of people, or it could be only two. Some firms train their personnel staff by allowing them to sit in on interviews that are conducted by experienced interviewers. Whatever the reason, these interviews can range from pleasant to torturous. You can feel like you're on the witness stand or you can feel like you're talking to a group of interesting professionals. It all depends on you and how well you do with groups, and on the interviewers.

GETTING THROUGH THE PANEL INTERVIEW

If you can relax and respond to one question at a time, you can get through a panel interview as easily as a civilized interview. If you find it impossible to relate to that many people at once—and if the ability to relate to small groups isn't a prerequisite of the job you're hoping to get—just say, with as much assurance as you can, that there's a great deal you'd like to say but you're finding yourself inhibited by the number of people you're facing. If they don't set you at ease or suggest an alternative, you can go on to ask if you might talk with them on a one-to-one basis.

THE FIFTY MOST POPULAR INTERVIEW QUESTIONS

Frank S. Endicott, retired director of Northwestern University's Placement Center, has compiled a list of questions most often asked during interviews with college seniors. Better than anything else, it tells you what a job interview is like.

1. What are your long-range and short-range goals and objectives? When and why did you establish these goals? How are you preparing yourself to achieve them?
2. What specific goals, other than those related to your occupation, have you established for yourself for the next ten years?
3. What do you see yourself doing five years from now?
4. What do you really want to do in life?
5. What are your long-range career objectives?
6. How do you plan to achieve your career goals?
7. What are the most important rewards to expect in your business career?
8. What do you expect to be earning in five years?
9. Why did you choose the career for which you are preparing?
10. Which is more important to you, the money or the type of job?
11. What do you consider to be your greatest strengths and weaknesses?
12. How would you describe yourself?
13. How do you think a friend or professor who knows you well would describe you?
14. What motivates you to put forth your greatest effort?
15. How has your college experience prepared you for a business career?
16. Why should I hire you?
17. What qualifications do you have that make you think you will be successful in business?
18. How do you determine or evaluate success?
19. What do you think it takes to be successful in a company like ours?
20. In what ways do you think you can make a contribution to our company?
21. What qualities should a successful manager possess?

22. Describe the relationship that should exist between a supervisor and those reporting to him or her.
23. What two or three accomplishments have given you the most satisfaction?
24. Describe your most rewarding college experience.
25. If you were hiring a graduate for this position, what qualities would you look for?
26. Why did you select your college or university?
27. What led you to choose your field of major study?
28. What college subjects did you like best? Why?
29. What college subjects did you like least? Why?
30. If you could do so, how would you plan your academic study differently? Why?
31. What changes would you make in your college or university? Why?
32. Do you have plans for continued study? An advanced degree?
33. Do you think that your grades are a good indication of your academic achievement?
34. What have you learned from participation in extracurricular activities?
35. In what kind of work environment are you most comfortable?
36. How do you work under pressure?
37. In what part-time or summer jobs have you been most interested?
38. How would you describe the ideal job for you following graduation?
39. Why did you decide to seek a position with this company?
40. What do you know about our company?
41. What two or three things are most important to you in your job?
42. Are you seeking employment in a company of a certain size? Why?
43. What criteria are you using to evaluate the company for which you hope to work?
44. Do you have a geographical preference? Why?
45. Will you relocate? Does relocation bother you?
46. Are you willing to travel?
47. Are you willing to spend at least six months as a trainee?
48. Why do you think you might like to live in the community in which our company is located?
49. What major problems have you encountered and how did you deal with it?
50. What have you learned from your mistakes?

INTERVIEW QUESTIONS YOU SHOULD ASK

A job interview doesn't necessarily have to be a one-way street. While in reality an interviewee doesn't have any bargaining power, you can at least present the impression that you do. You can ask questions of your own. This lets the interviewer know that you consider yourself a person of substance and dignity, who won't just take anything (even if you actually would). And, of course, it allows you to glean some information about the job and company that is important to you. You may even get a feel, through your questions, for the impression you made on the interviewer; it may not help you with him/her, but it will aid you in improving your performance the next time.

Save your most detailed questions for later interviews. Your potential boss is the person to ask about the downside of the job that may influence your decision—its tedious aspects, the extra hours or shifts you will be expected to put in, the risks of your not working out in the position.

Be sure to satisfy yourself about these issues before you make a decision:

- What exactly the job is—its title, responsibilities, the department or boss you would work for.
- How the department job fits into the company structure—its purpose, its budget, the other departments with which it works.
- Your opportunities for advancement.
- Whether there have been any recent organizational shake-ups.
- What your predecessors in the job moved on to.
- Whether the position can be upgraded as your responsibilities grow.
- How long the position has been open.
- How job performance is measured.

Just as answering and asking questions intelligently at an interview are absolute musts, there are some absolute mustn'ts for job interviews as well.

Never, but never:

- Yawn.
- Talk with your hands covering your mouth.
- Complain about a professor or a former employer.

- Swear.
- Say you plan on going back to school in a couple of years, even if you are. Employers won't hire somebody they know plans to leave.
- Talk too much or try to overwhelm the interviewer. Let him/her lead.
- Try to keep the interview going when you see he/she wants to end it.
- Ask about vacations, holidays, retirement, or other perquisites of the job. Stick to questions about work itself, not how much time you'll have off from doing it.
- Demand a certain salary. Let the interviewer tell you what the company offers, and then use your listening response, affirmative nod, to show you're satisfied.

LEARNING TO WORK WITH PEOPLE

One of the greatest lessons a first job can teach us is that we cannot operate alone. Whatever field we are in, we must work in concert with other people on many different levels. The most natural relationships we will establish early in our careers are networks of support and commiseration with our peers, a subject that is covered in detail in Chapter Nine. But the most vital set of interpersonal experiences will be with our superiors.

Bosses, foremen, vice-presidents, supervisors will determine the character of our first career experiences. They can be our biggest allies or our worst enemies. Because they were around first, we have to assume that responsibility for achieving a positive relationship rests with us.

John Shingleton agrees, "The most important thing a worker can have on the first job is a supervisor who is supportive and can nurse him or her through the first promise."

The first supervisor is the most important one you'll ever have, Shingleton says. "Hitch your wagon to his or her star."

Most people are underemployed, especially in the early stages of a career. The crucial point is to demonstrate what you can do in a crisis, under the eye of those who count in the organization, Shingleton believes. "You must have respect for the work ethic," he says. "People get a job, and they slip into things like abusing sick leave, and they think it goes by unnoticed. It doesn't."

George Buskirk, a UCLA placement expert, feels you should strive to impress your superiors: "When they see someone who's got something on the ball, they stand up and salute, believe me. There just aren't that many people who have got things on the ball. Most of the people you meet are losers."

How does one become a winner? "A winner's got to want to win," Buskirk states. "Most people don't want to win. To win, you've got to put forth effort. To lose, you don't have to do anything.

"I can go out and play Ohio State in football. If I'm not going to hit anybody, I'm not going to get hurt. But if I go out there to try to win, hey, I'm going to be hurting.

"Most people want to be losers. They won't admit this, but down deep they don't want to pay the price.

"The first thing you must do is make up your mind that you really want to win. Another thing is to accept responsibility. You show me a loser and I'll show you a guy who's always blaming bad luck. There's no shortage of alibis for losers.

"A winner knows if he's going to win, it's going to be his doing, and if he loses it's his fault."

Buskirk believes winning is a learned behavior. Most people have never seen a winner operate and so don't know how to be one.

"You've got to get with a winner and observe." Buskirk advises that there are politics in any situation; the new worker should keep his/her eyes and ears open, and check things out; see who has power. "Ask around and see what the power structure is," Buskirk says, "and then crack it."

GRIDLOCK ON THE FAST TRACK

For anyone who went to a top business school in the last decade the prescription for success seemed self-evident. Tie yourself to the millstone to get through it. Upon graduating secure a job with a hotshot managing consulting firm or with a *Fortune* 500 company and play it for all its worth. After a couple of years change positions, firms, make your mark, and break into the wonderland of "general management." Because at the end of that rainbow—as M.B.A.'s in their twenties and thirties were led to believe—was a whole world of big bucks, stock options, super perks, and, of course, "career satisfaction."

Today's M.B.A.'s are discovering, however, that like any wonderland, the streets (and corridors) of the giant corporations are no longer paved with gold. Hundreds of thousands of bright young men and women, equipped with prestigious degrees, the right uniforms, and a legacy of optimism, are finding it necessary to readjust their expectations downward. The wisdom of the trade has always held it that if you don't make management rank by the time you hit forty, you probably never will. That outside limit of forty is getting lower every year, so that by now if you're not with a company in your early twenties, you may never be. Some of the biggest employers of M.B.A.'s report that incumbents are remaining longer in entry-level positions at the second and third levels thereafter.

Human resources personnel at top corporations have cited several reasons for the "slowdown" of the "fast track." Primary among these reasons is, of course, the *recession*. The recession has made it harder to even hire expensive M.B.A.'s. This is no longer the era of go-go growth and diversification. Rather, this is the time to sell off marginal businesses, invest in high return securities, lie low.

One of the first areas to be pruned in this new time of pulling belts in is the management structure. The 1980s promises fewer rungs on the ladder. Accompanying this trend is the dreaded phenomenon known as "salary compression." Starting salaries for top M.B.A.'s are as much as they ever were but have not been adjusted for inflation. Taking this into account, starting salaries for Harvard M.B.A.'s have not increased at all from 1970 to 1980.

The disappointments in the marketplace go hand in hand with the creeping anomie that, according to human resources experts, is infecting the baby-boom M.B.A.'s. Today's new crop of M.B.A.'s seem to have some difficulty *bossing* anyone. They are good at nurturing those under them, but they seem to lack the tenacity and survivalist techniques of yesterday's organization men.

The decay of the market and the personal difficulties faced by today's young M.B.A.'s call for new answers. One response may be that today's M.B.A.'s must simply forego the dreams of power, money, influence, and endless pursuit that was the birthright of yesterday's hotshots. For those talented M.B.A.'s who won't be running their company's board of directors by the time they're thirty-five, there may be some satisfaction in using their training and skills to work out the problems of a local charity or civic organization.

The ideal of having one's own business is also becoming a subject of interest for many of today's M.B.A.'s. Business schools across the country report a marked increase in student interest in entrepreneurship. The fact that this is the worst time since the depression to start one's own business is another matter.

The ultimate answer may be a total discard of yesterday's concept of *the* career. Career change is the new rallying cry of today's economy. Many of today's M.B.A.'s will go through two or even three careers before finding the satisfaction that they were promised when they entered business schools in the first place.

TAKE THIS JOB AND . . .

Whether or not we find a perfect mentor, whether or not we fall in among a cadre of corporate winners, we should always remember that our first job is a test, not a life sentence. We can't know when we start if our expectations will be fulfilled. So, we shouldn't be crushed if we find ourselves disappointed after we've settled in. It isn't us, it's the job.

The important point is that we learn something from what we've experienced. Where does our disappointment come from? What aspects of the job get us down? What parts of the job still excite us? We should ask questions about every part of our work lives, trying to build a picture of the situation that would suit us better than our present one. Then, we must begin research to find that position.

Even if our first job turns out to be an unmitigated disaster, remember that it served at least one purpose—it got us started. No matter how rotten it was it at least lifted us from the ranks of the untrained and unemployed and set us among the working adult population. Now we can move on from there in better shape than when we had nothing at all behind us.

While we are on a first job that doesn't seem to loom long in the future, we ought to concentrate on building up our general skills for the future. Every task we master, every ability we acquire could be vitally important somewhere down the road. We mustn't let an uncomfortable job tear us down; rather, we must ignore the worst aspects and focus in on building ourselves up any way we can. We must think like the convicts who use their enforced leisure to lift weights or read great literature. We can derive some positive benefit from the worst situation.

Still, with so many of us starting at the very bottom of the career ladder or off it altogether, it is inevitable that many of us, despite our best efforts, begin the twenties suffering from real-world shock. The vast gap between where we are and where we expected to be yawns before us as a depressing chasm. Our self-esteem falls into the gap. We have attempted our first test with life and we flunked. We are obviously unfit to be adults. We should throw in the towel before more humiliation is heaped on our heads by life.

Nonsense. Even a wrestling match allows three falls. And the problems faced in getting started don't reflect so much on our personal worth as on the information we were working with. We probably didn't realize what it would be like out there. We didn't research enough or work hard enough to figure out an effective way to confront this distressing situation. Now, we have much better information. We can focus more clearly on what our situation is. Having been bounced once, we can get up and do the job better the second time around.

HIRING YOURSELF

The early twenties are probably too early for most of us to step out on our own in business. But it's not too early for would-be entrepreneurs to use these years for on-the-job study in the field in which they eventually want to own a business.

The potential business owners among us can soak up the details of their chosen field on someone else's payroll during the early twenties. They can become familiar with the milieu of the business and learn about common pitfalls and shortcuts.

It is never possible to know too much before starting a business. The practical education gained early in the twenties could provide the difference between success and failure further down the road.

Throughout the process of getting and beginning a first adult job the sensation most of us feel is one of playacting, a certain unreality. Down deep inside we haven't changed too much yet. We still feel the same way we did in our teens. We're still kids—free, wild, loose, unfettered. But on the outside now, we are adults. We dress grown up. We talk grown up. We sit at desks or stand in factories like grown-ups do. People react to us as they would to a grown-up.

We know that it's a sham, however. We're like a new character that has been dropped into the middle of an ongoing play. We go along with the action, but our lines still don't come naturally; we feel apart from the action.

But, truly, it is this total immersion of our personalities in the acid bath of adult behavior that stimulates the growth that sets our twenties off from other adult decades. We aren't really faking it as we start the twenties; all the components for feeling adult exist within us. But we haven't committed ourselves to accepting them yet. We're trying on the suit, but we don't know if we want to buy.

The first few years of the twenties are spent staring at ourselves in the mirror, getting used to the suddenly adult reflections we find there.

Finding a Place of Your Own

THE FIRST APARTMENT is your escape from the world. It is a hole in the wall. It is the place where you first stretch your wings and live your own kind of life. It costs so much every month that you are forced to choose between two kinds of Campbell's soups for dinner. We can furnish it, decorate it, fix it up to your heart's content. The landlord won't let you drill holes in the wall. It is everything you have ever wanted. You want to go home.

If the first years of the twenties are filled with the confrontation between our adolescent dreams and the real world, then the first apartment is one of the primary fields of battle. Practically everyone has a horror story, or has a friend who has lived through a horror story, about the first apartment. And the punch line to every one of these stories is: "I loved it there." The first apartment is really your first world of freedom—it is all yours, warts and all.

The rush to freedom that accompanies most moves in the early twenties can sometimes bring about unnecessary hardship. This chapter will show you how you can avoid some of the most common pitfalls in finding and living in your first apartment.

HUNTING FOR AN APARTMENT

The apartment hunt is one of the first tough jobs you'll face in your mid-twenties. With today's housing mess, you have your work cut out for you. Here's a checklist of things to do.

1. *Decide.* First of all, decide what your first apartment must be and must not be. You have to realize that now that you have to be at work at nine every morning, you can't live over the local disco. Decide *where* you want to live. How close to your work would you like to be? What kind of neighborhood suits your tastes? Target several alternate places, and begin your search there.

2. *Dig.* Don't look just in the obvious places. Sure, the local paper is a good source of leads, but check out other sources, such as bulletin boards in local supermarkets and laundromats. Tell everyone you meet you're looking for an apartment, because you can never tell who might have a friend who just told his/her landlord he's/she's moving out. It's not a bad idea to ask local barbers, butchers, or other local merchants if they know of any apartments to rent. Even if they don't know of apartments, they may be able to tell you about the neighborhood, and indeed their reaction may tell you a lot about how you'd fit in to the neighborhood.

3. *Advertise.* Take out a classified ad in the newspaper. List your needs, how much you wish to pay in rent, and a bit about your personality. The personality bit will screen out roommate seekers who are completely incompatible. If possible, list a newspaper box number, not your phone.

4. *Hit the Streets.* Check out your preferred neighborhoods, and look for more than For Rent signs. Look for indications that someone is moving or has moved out. Keep an eye peeled for moving vans or rented trucks, and also for apartment windows with no sign of life.

The sight of workmen in a building may be a sign that the building or an apartment in it is being fixed up.

If you see a building that looks nice, is well-maintained, and is in a good location, talk to the super, or call the rental agent for the building. Again, it doesn't hurt to ask, and if they don't have a vacancy there, they may be able to steer you to one.

5. *Look Neat.* When you inspect an apartment, look nice, clean, neat, and responsible. We all know that under that purple Mohawk you're very responsible, and that you plan to start bathing at least once a week. Unfortunately, landlords don't have the time, the means, or the interest in discovering the real you, and they will judge you as a tenant by the way you look. Again, don't be a phony, but try to make a good impression. It could be the difference between getting an apartment and sleeping in the train station.

6. *See a Realty Office.* Often they handle only higher-priced, singles-type apartments. If that is what you're looking for, give them

a call. They may have a bargain. Again, ask around and see which local realty offices have good or bad reputations.

7. *Check Out Rental Agencies.* Agencies that charge a fee to sec their listings before you get an apartment are almost always ripoffs. If you're really desperate, at least check out such places with other apartment-hunters, with the Better Business Bureau, and with any tenants' rights groups.

Agencies that charge a fee to look at listings should not be confused with legitimate real estate brokers, who will charge you a fee for actually renting an apartment. The time was when any resourceful young person could find an apartment on his/her own. In today's housing market, especially in big cities, the brokers may have you where they want you. If you're sleeping on a friend's couch, you start a high-pressure job Monday, and you just can't find a place, it may be worth your while to see a broker.

Again, ask around and see if you can find a broker who has treated people fairly. Find out what you're paying for, and don't sign anything until you understand it thoroughly. If you feel you're being pressured or if you feel uncomfortable, politely thank them and leave.

You'll do best if you go through an agency that will charge a fee only when you actually sign a lease on the apartment they've shown you. Be prepared to pay up to two months' rent for the convenience, however.

8. *Consider a Temporary Place.* Taking a sublet for six months or a year can be a good way to settle, especially in a strange city. A sublet can give you a secure base of operations in your apartment hunt.

Most big cities have residential hotels and many cities have residential hotels just for young women. Not only are these often quite comfortable, they can be less expensive in the long run than paying a broker or getting a lousy apartment. Most cities have YMCAs and YWCAs that offer clean and reasonable, although rather small and bare, rooms.

If it is practical, you might want to see if friends can put you up for a while; or you may have to swallow your pride and live at home with the folks while you're looking. In both cases, share the rent and other expenses and be nice to everybody.

9. *Be Patient and Persistent.* Don't give up and move back home. The majority of people do find someplace to live. At the same time don't get so desperate that you pick a place that is totally unsuitable. Be patient. If a prospective apartment has no heat in the winter, or is in a neighborhood where you are sure to get mugged, or

is simply so ugly and dreary that it will drive you bonkers, your mental health and your work will suffer. Besides, you'll probably just move out in a few months, minus your security deposit, and have to start all over again.

Don't just grab a place—check it out. New York freelancer Jim Tinen was filling out an application for a grungy sixth-floor apartment in Manhattan's garment district when a tenant came through the lobby. Tinen asked her how she liked it. "Well," she replied, "the elevator's always broken, there's no heat in the winter, and they've raised the rent three times in sixth months." Living in such an apartment is worse than any apartment hunt.

10. *Don't Spend More Than You Earn.* How much should you pay for your apartment? The old rule of thumb said you should pay about one-fourth of your income for housing. Today's housing shortage may have changed that. You might take one-fourth as your ideal; you might take rent equaling one-third of your income as your upper limit.

It's a good idea to ask how much your friends are paying, and it's a better idea to observe how well they're faring. If you live close enough to walk to work or in a city where good public transit enables you to get along without a car, you might be able to invest a bit more in your apartment.

Remember, while you're probably not ready for a penthouse, it's a tough world out there, and it's worthwhile to spend enough so that after a hard day at work you can come home to a place that's fairly comfortable, secure, and cheery.

THE LEASE

From before the day you move in until the day you move out, perhaps the most important aspect of your new apartment will be the lease. The lease is a written contract spelling out the rights and responsibilities of tenant and landlord. Generally, most leases give landlords the rights and tenants the responsibilities. Don't assume anything. Read every word of the lease. Insist that your rights are spelled out in writing. Don't hesitate to add to or change the lease: Most leases are printed up to favor the landlords overwhelmingly. For instance, many standard leases specify "no pets"; if your landlord has no objection to pets, a clause stating that pets are okay should be added to the lease. Here are the most important considerations:

1. *Subleasing.* Say you're offered a great job in another city, but your lease has six months to run. Under subleasing, you shift the right to live in your apartment to another tenant without breaking your lease. Subleasing is also a way of going on a long summer vacation while making some money on the apartment.

The exact nature of a tenant's right to sublease varies from state to state. Since subleasing is a common source of conflict between tenants and landlords, it is very important to put in the lease what your rights to sublet are.

If you sublease, go to a stationery store and buy a sublease form, a standard form that will sound much like your own lease. When you sublease, keep paying rent to the landlord and collect rent yourself from the subleasing tenant. This is the best way to avoid conflict with your landlord over a sublease.

2. *Rent.* Except for the rare areas with rent control or rent stabilization, such as New York City, a landlord can charge whatever he wants. If the landlord charges more for two single men than for one single woman, you can't do a thing about it.

3. *Rules.* The lease should fully explain the rules for making the rent payments, including the due date, how many days after the due date the tenant has to make the payment without being charged a penalty, when such a penalty will be charged, and how much the penalty will be. In this, leave nothing to chance or oral agreements.

4. *Condition.* The lease should ensure that the apartment is turned over in fully livable condition, conforming to all building codes and health codes, and that it is the landlord's responsibility to keep it that way.

If appliances come with the apartment, their presence and condition should be noted on the lease.

Anything else should be spelled out. Inspecting an otherwise nice renovated apartment in Brooklyn, Jim Tinen foolishly assumed that a toilet seat was standard equipment in apartments. "Sorry," the landlord told him, "that's your responsibility."

5. *Fixing.* Make sure the lease specifies who fixes what, who pays for it, and how. If the landlord is out of town and the stove breaks, can you fix it and send him the bill? The repair clause of the lease should say that the landlord has to reply to your requests within a set period of time and cannot refuse reasonable repairs without a written explanation.

6. *Beefs.* If your landlord balks at making repairs, try to steer a

middle course between being impatient (if the problem is minor) and being flexible. On one hand, have you ever been tardy about handing in a term paper or returning a borrowed book? On the other hand, you have a *right* to a dwelling in good repair. Be polite but firm, courteous but insistent.

A reminder sent with the rent check often helps. If that doesn't bring action, send a business letter to the landlord—and send it registered—informing him that if he doesn't respond to your complaint, you will write to the building inspector, the health department, the consumer services bureau, the real estate board, the district attorney, and his mother. He can't evict you for complaining, and often such a letter is enough to get a lazy landlord off dead center and into his handyman togs.

7. *Changes.* A lease may be impressive, but by no means is it an original of the Declaration of Independence. Make whatever changes you feel are necessary.

8. *Signing.* Make sure you get a signed copy of your entire lease. This is crucial. Legally speaking, if the landlord doesn't give you one, then all you have done is applied for the apartment. You aren't responsible for the rent until the landlord signs the lease and gives you a copy.

9. *Deposits.* Security deposits are probably the most common bone of contention between landlords and tenants. Make sure the lease spells out how big a deposit you have to pay, where the deposit will be kept, how much you'll get back, and how soon you'll get it back. Keep your apartment in good shape, and when you move out, clean up, even the oven. Nevertheless, don't count on that money for repaying a loan shark. Stealing deposits is the favorite indoor sport of landlords.

10. *Responsibilities.* Keep up your end of the deal. Pay the rent on time, keep the place clean, try not to knock down the walls. If your landlord is a reasonable fellow, you want to give that behavior positive reinforcement. Even today (and even in New York) good tenants are hard to find, and any sane landlord will try to make cooperative tenants happy.

11. *Fight.* If you feel a landlord has gypped you, you can fight back. A landlord has more clout than a tenant, but you have rights too. You will have to realistically judge the effort and the costs of a legal battle against your chances of winning, how much you might win, and how satisfying winning would be.

Some housing beefs can be taken care of in small claims court or, in some cities, in a special housing court, where a lawyer is not needed. Anytime you step into court, however, having a lawyer at your side helps tremendously. You can bet your security deposit the landlord will have one.

Unfortunately, good housing lawyers charge fees up to $150 an hour, which obviously can eat up anything you might win from a landlord. Also, cuts in governmental spending have cut legal services. See if your city has a tenants' right group that can help.

You *can* beat the landlord. Before you try to do so, get help from a lawyer, a tenants' group, or other knowledgeable sources, and make sure you understand what you're doing.

You can rent an apartment without a lease, and in many areas outside the big cities it is the common practice. It has its advantages and disadvantages. If you think you may be moving on at some indefinite point down the road, then renting without a lease can be helpful. But without a lease you have no guarantees of service, response, or availability. You have the right to stay in the apartment for the period covered by the latest rent payment. After that, the landlord can throw you out. By renting without a lease, you trade freedom for protection. Since a lease protects you, it's worth having.

If you're in a town where renting without a lease is the rule, you'll have to size up the landlord pretty accurately. If you have the feeling you don't trust him, or just don't like his face, walk away.

If it's any consolation, the renting-without-a-lease situation seems to prevail in smaller towns, where people are a bit more forthright than in big cities, and where the landlords are a bit less rapacious.

MOVING IN

Finding a place is only half the trauma. Moving in is the other half. Moving is considered one of life's most stressful experiences. One way to make the stress of those first hectic hours in your new place more bearable is to prepare a survival kit. You might include:

- An alarm clock or clock-radio. You'll need it the next morning even if you haven't unpacked by then.
- Coffee, coffee pot, and a frying pan (or tea, if you're a tea fancier).

You have to start the next day with food and drink, even if your belongings are all still in boxes.

- Something to munch on during the hard work of unpacking.
- A book or magazine to read during your first night.
- Your pillow.
- A change of clothes.
- Grooming and toilet articles. You can't assume the previous tenant left toilet paper.
- Pen and paper for making notes about all the little things you'll have to get.
- For smokers, cigarettes and an ashtray.
- Light bulbs. Prior tenants often take theirs with them.
- A plate and a set of silverware.
- Your personal phone book so you can tell friends and family you've moved in.
- An object that symbolizes home to you. Perhaps a favorite plant or piece of artwork. Putting it up right away gives you a greater sense of belonging.

Put the survival kit on the front seat of your car when you move so you know it will be with you through the whole process. The kit can make settling in to a bare, new apartment a much easier experience.

MOVING OUT

When you move out you might as well give yourself the best possible shot at recovering your security deposit. The landlord has a legal right to collect a deposit as protection against ordinary wear and tear on the apartment. Ah, but what is ordinary? There's the rub. The landlord wants to charge you for every scrape and knick, and you insist the sink would have fallen in even if your St. Bernard hadn't sat on it. Here are some tips that might help you rescue your security deposit from the landlord's clutches.

1. *Take Photos.* If the landlord is uncooperative, or you find a serious problem after you've moved in, take photos. The date on the print will show that the problem existed well before your move out.

2. *Set up Rules.* Talk to the landlord and lay down the ground rules beforehand. For example, do you have to defrost the refrigerator? Clean the oven? Putty up any holes you make in the wall?

3. *Start Early.* Start cleaning well before the day of your departure, and completely clear as many rooms as possible. Ask the landlord to come inspect the apartment with you a day or two before you are going. If you have your original list of defects, bring it with you. If not, go through the apartment and jot down the things he thinks should be charged to your deposit. When you both are satisfied the list is fair and complete, sign it. He should send you the bills for the agreed-upon work, with what is left of your deposit.

4. *Clean up Anyway.* If it's obvious the landlord intends to keep your money, clean up anyway, and make any reasonable repairs. Once you've cleared out, take photos of the apartment. The photos may convince a small-claims-court judge that you deserve your deposit back.

5. *Write.* If the deadline for the return of your deposit passed, write a forceful tell-all letter to the landlord describing your efforts to leave the apartment clean, your evidence, and stating your determination to get your money.

6. *You Can't Hide.* Don't think you can hide damage. 'Fess up and offer to fix it. If you've turned your apartment into a pig sty, don't fool yourself into thinking you'll get your deposit back. Someone has to clean the stove, scrub the floors, and plaster the walls. In such a case the landlord has a right to spend your deposit to fix his place.

7. *Leftovers.* Most of us, in the course of living in our first apartment, accumulate a variety of worldly possessions. If you want to leave behind a sofa or a dresser or something else that won't fit into the trailer, ask the landlord. Here's an area where good relations with the landlord helps.

ROOMMATES

Times are tough, and more of us are starting our twenties while still living at home than has been the case in decades. One alternative may be the artificial family: roommates. The benefits are obvious.

Your rent is cut drastically.
You get instant companions.
Roommates bring their own supply of books, furniture, records, and kitchen supplies, cutting everyone's outlay for housekeeping.

You won't have the whole responsibility for the lease and for the upkeep of the apartment.

On the other hand, starting out with roommates has its drawbacks.

After college finding roommates may be difficult. In college not only are roommates plentiful, but you start out being similar in your basic routines and occupations, no matter how you differ otherwise. In the real world it may be harder to find compatible roommates.

You won't be totally in control of your life. Other people will have some say in what you do.

You won't get the full experience of being independent. Your roommates will act as buffers between you and experience.

You may not like your roommates. Strangers may turn out to be people you loathe; friends may turn into enemies.

You may have to make due with less space than you would if you had your own place or even your own room.

You will lose privacy. Your problems and foibles will become grist in the mill of your roommates' gossip. Also, having a date over can become a group experience.

Roommates can become great friends or vicious enemies. When you're prospecting for a place to share, try to give a good impression, but be honest. If you're a bit of a slob, and you move in with the other half of the Odd Couple, the results will probably involve more agony than comedy.

There aren't many hard-and-fast rules about which setups work better than others. Jim Tinen was one of five roommates in the first apartment he had after college. He hadn't met his four roommates before moving in. (Each tenant rented a bedroom separately, and they all shared living room, kitchen, and bathroom.) It worked out beautifully: Tinen found all of them to be friendly and easy to live with.

Having got lucky once, Tinen next moved into an apartment with the same setup. One of the other tenants turned out to be an outpatient from a mental hospital. This fellow had a habit of smoking in bed, and flicking the ashes and butts onto the mattress. Aside from the danger, the fellow was sleeping next to a mound of ashes and butts. Soon his floor was littered with dirty clothing, empty food jars and cans, and dirty kitchen utensils, all of which in turn was covered with greenish gray stuff that was either lint or fungus. The smell became overwhelming, not only in the apartment but down the open-air hallway. Pleas and threats failed to make any impression on this man.

To avoid such disasters you should inspect prospective roommates as carefully as prospective apartments—perhaps more so. Some white paint will cheer up a drab apartment, but it's unlikely you'll be able to easily renovate the roommate who likes to practice his bassoon at three in the morning.

Moving into a household with established roommates has an advantage in that the roommates have already gone through a shakeup, and have things running somewhat smoothly. The disadvantage is that they may be set in their ways and expect you to go along with a routine that doesn't suit you.

It can't be long before roommates begin signing formal agreements, but even in our legalistic society, a roommate contract seems a bit much. It is a good idea, however, to sit down before you agree to be a roommate and hammer out the specifics of housekeeping. The questions you should answer include:

Who cleans what? The variations are endless. Do you clean your own dishes, or take turns? Do you all get together to clean house every Saturday or is each person responsible for separate areas?

Who pays for what? Some sharing is inevitable—unless you want to keep track of how many paper towels each of you uses.

Who cooks what? Are communal meals feasible? If you take turns cooking, you spread out the cooking chores and get a greater variety of foods. The obvious drawback may be your roommates' cooking ability; a less obvious drawback may be coordinating meal times.

Discussing these points may save a lot of grief later on and can tell you more about your prospective roommates.

Inevitably your roommates will have flaws. In another test of adulthood, you'll have to challenge the flaws that infringe on your rights and tolerate those flaws that are tolerable. An otherwise perfectly nice fellow may utterly ignore the mound of dirty dishes in the sink, no matter what; the young woman who is like a sister to you may not be able to keep a secret. Some bad habits you can change; others you have to live with or leave.

By the way, we guarantee that you—yes, you—have some trait, habit, or characteristic that will sometimes drive your roommates crazy. Remember that before you try to improve the people you live with.

Work it out. If one roommate is a lousy cook, make him permanent dishwasher. If one roommate shirks her turn at doing the dishes, make each roommate responsible for his/her dishes. If one roommate doesn't take care of his assigned cleaning job, make cleanup a group activity, so that the chore can't be sloughed off.

RENTERS' INSURANCE

When I was just starting out—about twenty-two—I was convinced that I had no possessions worth insuring. I rented a neat little house in Knoxville, Tennessee and filled it with my trinkets. About a month after moving in the place was ransacked. I suddenly realized that among my worthless goods were a camera, a tape recorder, binoculars, radios, and much more. I couldn't replace any of it. I should have been insured.

Renters' insurance is cheap and flexible. You buy it in multiples of $1,000. Figure out the cost of your important possessions and add ten percent for the things you inevitably forgot. Then go out and price policies that cover unspecified personal property, that is, those that don't require a list of exactly what you own. Make a list for yourself, though, and include serial numbers of any goods that have them.

Make sure your policy covers all possibilities: theft, fire, vandalism, rain, etc. If floods or earthquakes are a worry where you live, make sure you get special coverage for them, because they aren't included in standard policies.

Ultimately, the first apartment is everything that is great and terrible about the first decade in the real world. But after you've dealt with the landlords, settled matters with your roommates, moved your books onto shelves and put some pictures on the walls, nothing can beat the feeling that comes from sitting back with a cup of coffee, on your own couch, in your own room—*on your own!* You'll live in a number of different places over your lifetime, but this experience is truly unique.

Becoming a Consumer

ECONOMICS TEACHES THAT money enables us to exchange value for goods. We are paid a certain amount of money for the value of our work, and in exchange we pay out a certain amount of money for the things we want.

All of that would be simple if we didn't live in a world of extremely complicated markets. Everywhere we look there are manufacturers and producers competing for our money. A simple walk down the street leads to a barrage of pleas for our hard-earned cash. One of the most difficult lessons to learn in the early twenties is how to control the amount of money we have going out. There are ways of getting the things we really want with what we get paid, and our first years in the real world opens up those ways to us.

This chapter looks at the world of the consumer. We'll consider the ins and outs of smart shopping, from buying food and clothing to purchasing an automobile. Of course, this is an exhaustive subject, and many other books have been written about any one of these topics. What I am basically trying to show here is how that first rush of freedom that we feel in our early twenties often makes it difficult, if not impossible, to remain open to the wise, intelligent decisions that can be made by a consumer who will take time, shop carefully, and plan ahead.

BUYING FOOD

After I'd moved all of my furniture and belongings into my first apartment I was hungry. I walked into the kitchen, opened up the refrigerator and all of the cabinets and was dumbfounded by the obvious. They were empty. I needed to fill them. I was no longer in my mother's house, where shelves were lined with everything from paper goods to relish, and where a basement cupboard was generally stocked with an inventory much like that of the corner grocer. I had to shop.

Shopping, which may seem as easy as strolling down an aisle with a cart, requires, in fact, a great deal of skill. We have to learn what the basic minimal requirements of a kitchen cupboard are. Then we have to find the right place to buy them: a place where the prices and quality are consistently good. We have to learn what to buy in quantity, and what will languish and grow moldy in the back corner of the fridge. In fact, there's so much to learn about food shopping that we'd best take it step by step.

Once a week we should do a basic shopping. This saves a great deal of money and time. I remember being invited to someone's house for dinner and arriving early. He was still cooking . . . chicken paprikash . . . and as he came to an ingredient in the cookbook he didn't have he'd grab his coat and say, "Be right back." Two minutes later he'd return with a little paper bag.

Buying things as we need them, every day, usually means shopping in little stores that are open odd hours. And shopping in little stores usually means paying unnecessarily high prices. In order to do a weekly shopping we need to keep track of our requirements. One of the best ways to do this involves taping a piece of paper to the refrigerator door every Monday, and making a note of things that are running low.

We can complement this list by planning the week's meals. For example, if you're going to be eating at home seven mornings and five nights, you should write down seven breakfasts and five dinners, and check to see that you have everything you'll need. Planning meals ahead of time that way makes the week's cooking, as well as the shopping, much less hassled.

In addition to once-a-week shopping, it's important to know what kinds of food give us the most for our money. I, for example, didn't know a thing about buying meat. I had some vague recollections of going to a butcher with my mother or grandmother and hearing them ask for specific cuts—other than sirloin and porterhouse. My grandmother used to ask for some neck meat ground in with her chopped meat, and told me that it made her hamburgers sweeter.

Although I never mustered the nerve to ask for neck meat—in fact, I still haven't gotten beyond picking up a prewrapped package of chopped meat—I learned very quickly that I couldn't afford to blithely buy the meat I was accustomed to eating at my mother's house. Lamb chops, for instance, were just beyond my budget. The steak that's best for eating, turns out, economically, to be best for eating at someone else's house. At my house I eat a lot of stewed meat. Because it cooks so long I can buy cheaper cuts of meat. And I can make twice as much as I need and freeze away a second night's dinner. I also find that it just isn't necessary (or all that healthy) to eat red meat every night. Chicken is cheaper and better. And even though my mother would be shocked at the thought of my having tuna fish for dinner, it's healthy and filling.

Vegetables, which are cheap and can be a dinner in and of themselves, should always be bought in season, and whenever possible they should be bought fresh. If fresh vegetables aren't available, the next choice is frozen; and it almost always pays to buy the store brand rather than a name brand of frozen goods.

One of the key things to remember when shopping is to stay away from prepared foods. I had a great-uncle who owned a Jewish appetizing store. He sold herrings, lox, all sorts of smoked fish, and bagels. I loved everything in the place and he used to enjoy sitting with me and lecturing me on the business of appetizing. Nova Scotia salmon was very expensive, but it wasn't his prime money-maker. He made the greatest profit on his salads: chopped herring salad; macaroni salad; potato salad; lox salad. All of the ingredients of these salads cost him pennies. (The herring in his herring salad were the odd little pieces that he couldn't really sell.) Yet he could charge a good price for the salads because they had required some time preparing, and because people liked serving them.

The point of this nostalgia is that prepared foods usually cost twice as much as if we were to prepare them ourselves. Frozen string beans that come in a sack with their own butter are expensive. Cooking plain string beans and allowing the thirty seconds or so for some butter to melt, is cheap. TV dinners are convenient, but for the money spent we could roast a turkey, carve it up, pack it away in plastic bags in the freezer, and eat well for a month.

The ultimate extension of buying prepared foods is, of course, eating out. The facts are simple: Unless we're ready to budget the bulk of our income to food, we'll have to curtail visits to restaurants. We could probably cook an entire roast beef dinner for four at home, for what such a meal would cost for one at a reasonably good restaurant. Those of us who haven't yet considered how much money we drop at restaurants should go back through the calendar for a month and jot down our eating-out expenses—including tips, cabs, etc. It'll be a shock—there goes the money that might have bought you a new winter coat.

There are certain foods we should never buy. Soda and candy are two good examples. Most of us discover that we eat what we have. If we have a huge bag of chocolate covered M&M's peanuts, somehow, over the course of a week, those peanuts will find their way into our mouths. Soda, which has very little nutritional value but costs quite a bit, really should be replaced by juice . . . and a remarkably thirst-quenching, startlingly inexpensive drink called water.

COUPONS AND SPECIALS

Not too long after I was married my sister-in-law began talking to me about coupons. I listened politely to everything she said, and snickered all the way home. Coupons! Who had the time to sit and clip coupons? It seemed like the ultimate bourgeois preoccupation. Ten years later my wife and I eagerly turn the pages of magazines and newspapers looking for bargains and cutting coupons. Why? More to the point, why not? If some manufacturer is putting money in my hand you can be sure that I'm going to accept it . . . graciously.

As we move into our twenties we begin to realize that we have to work hard for our money. Lots of the things we took for granted in our parents' home cost more than we can now afford. And if we have any aspirations for attaining those things, we're going to have to be aware of where our hard-earned pennies go. If something is on sale and it's the sort of thing that will keep, buy it in quantity. If local stores have certain days that they double the value of coupons, make sure to get there and cash in. We must look at prices and, whenever we can, buy cheap without sacrificing quality.

All the money we save from shopping wisely is money we can spend elsewhere. And as we assume more and more adult responsibilities there will be more and more "elsewhere's" for that money to be spent.

BUYING CLOTHES

"I remember meeting my mother for lunch one day while I was still working at my first job out of college," Karen Lewis says. "We met at a midtown Manhattan restaurant. She was wearing a suit and a silk blouse. I was wearing baggy Dee-Cee overalls and basketball sneakers. She looked at me as I approached the table and her jaw dropped.

" 'That's the way you go to work?!'

"I launched into a dissertation about how in publishing people didn't judge you by what you wear. What they care about is how smart you are, not how well you dress. What can I say? It was 1969. I believed what I was saying.

"But the fact is that my mother was absolutely right. The people I worked with thought I was a terrifically smart kid, with a capital *K*. My responsibilities were limited to those of a kid. When promotions came I got the ones that kept me in my office, rather than the ones that would have expanded my contacts in the industry. I didn't get to take people to lunch. Nor did I get to be taken. I didn't go to conventions and cocktail parties."

While it may be true that on some level lunches, conventions, and cocktail parties aren't the be-all and end-all of a career, they are, in many respects, important. They are the occasions that widen our horizons. They are the places where we meet people who might offer us jobs. And people that don't dress appropriately—that is, people who look like kids—don't get to show or be shown around town.

One thing to keep in mind is that worn-out Dee-Cee overalls and basketball sneakers are inappropriate for virtually every line of work. And beyond that cardinal rule things do get a bit more specific.

Everyone's dress style is somewhat different. The way we put ourselves together should reflect something about the way we see ourselves. But there are certain parameters within which most of us conform. Depending on the kind of work we do those parameters can become wider or narrower. Bankers, for example, usually dress more conservatively than people do in the creative industries such as film, records, publishing, advertising. One of the first jobs *after* landing a job should be to look around and see how people dress. And it's always a good idea to look up: How does the person whose job you'd like to have in five years dress for work? He/she is the one you want to be identified with; not the guys or gals in the mailroom or the secretarial pool.

Unfortunately, if the high-powered people in your office have their jackets custom tailored at Dunhill's, your pocketbook is going to limit you. Still, it almost always pays to buy good-quality clothing. In fact, it's better to have fewer good clothes than closets full of cheap things. The rule of buying *good* is particularly true when it comes to shoes and bags. Cheap leather goods invariably look cheap. Fine shoes and a fine handbag or briefcase can often overshadow a less than extraordinary set of threads.

Once you've developed a sense of what sort of clothing goes in your office, you'll need to go through your drawers and closets and reasess what you have. The first thing to do is put all of the denim in one corner—the "after work" side of the closet. Then start casting aside anything that looks significantly different than what you've seen on the job. That's not to say that a blue shirt with yellow stripes should be trashed because you saw only yellow shirts with blue stripes. Rather, it means that the casual jacket you wore in school, or the double-knit leisure suit with six-inch lapels, should either go to Goodwill, or your parents' basement until they become fashionable again.

After you've emptied the closet of all the definite "no-goes" you can begin to think about what you need. Always lean a bit toward the conservative look if given the choice. Trendy things are expensive, and go out of fashion as fast as they come in. Classic-styled clothing is just as expensive but can be worn much longer; and when you're buying something as expensive as a winter coat, you want to be certain of getting several winters out of it.

The rule about conservatism also applies to color. If you have to go out and buy three turtleneck sweaters, three blouses or shirts, three skirts or pants and two blazers, planning the colors ahead of time will give you dozens of extra permutations for outfits than would have been possible if you bought it all willy-nilly. The key to a versatile wardrobe lies more in the planning than in the actual quantity.

Where does all this good clothing come from? If you can possibly arrange it, the best time to buy clothing is out of season. As summer clothing begins to make its way onto the racks, winter clothing is reduced. And bit by bit the reductions grow. The best stores have the best sales, and while the selection is usually somewhat limited, the buys can be spectacular. But buying out of season can be something less than great fun. It's hard to get enthusiastic about a winter coat in

June. It's equally hard to look at sandals when your toes are still numb from cold. Don't despair. There are alternatives.

Nearly every city has discount stores, and many of them come through with everything they promise. Shopping at these stores is usually less pleasant than shopping at better stores—a young man I know described the communal dressing rooms at the discount store he frequented as smelling like a men's locker room . . . after the game, before the shower. But the clothing you bring home is more important than the ambiance of the store. And if you don't have much money the sacrifice is well worth the discount.

Those who live in a large city, like New York, have an additional option for buying clothing. Many manufacturers open their factories to the public on Saturdays, and if you can find out where they are, the savings can be phenomenal. A friend of mine emerged with a particular designer suit for half the price he'd seen at a swank department store.

Once you've acquired all of your clothing you will have assumed a new responsibility. Clothing requires care, and the more attentive you are to the things you wear, the longer they'll last. Don't wait until a suit or dress is speckled with stains to have it dry-cleaned. Things should be cleaned regularly—before it's too late to get them fresh-looking. Sometimes the dirt accumulates so evenly that we don't even notice that a once-beige raincoat is now a deep brown. But if we have it cleaned every six to eight weeks it will never change color.

Shoes also require regular attention, and given their cost these days it pays to keep an eye on heels and soles. Don't let them wear down beyond repair. For one thing, shoes that need lifts don't look good. For another, they don't last long. Leather also should be oiled or polished regularly. It needs the moisture if it's to remain supple. When leather is neglected it begins to crack, and cracked, aged leather doesn't gain in character.

The whole issue of clothing—what to buy, where to buy it, and how to care for it—is very much a part of everything we're discussing about the twenties. Most children don't worry about their clothing. Their mothers lay it out for them every night and they put it on. Their drawers are magically replenished with clean underwear. Their shoes don't fit them long enough to have the opportunity to wear out.

Part of being an adult involves assuming responsibility for our own backs and the things we cover them with. Dealing with this responsibility is as important an issue as personal hygiene. People who dress inappropriately for the lives they aspire to might just as well go to work each morning without brushing their teeth.

BUYING A CAR

Some us may have bought a car when we were in our teens, but it was probably a clunker, or our folks helped us with the purchase. Now we may need to go out and get a car on our own, and it will have to be a vehicle we can depend on. No clunkers, please.

Buying a car always has been a significant purchase. These days, though, the purchase of a car approaches historical significance. Cars today cost about the same as the houses we lived in as children probably did. And we can finance the purchase at a mere 18 percent over four years, leaving us wth the debt of a small Eastern European country.

What, then, can we afford? Less than we think. The sticker price of the car is shocking, to be sure, but it represents only part of the car's true cost. The real costs of owning a car start with the purchase price and loan interest and go on from there. We must include all costs to see how much we can afford—if any car at all.

For instance, what will it cost us to run our car every day? We'll need gas, oil, tires, spark plugs, tune-ups, wiper blades, and more. Obviously, a big gas-sucking monster costs more than a small car to fuel. But what about repairs? Does one offer a better maintenance plan than the other? How long can either go between oil changes and tune-ups? Might we be able to handle standard maintenance ourselves? All these factors could affect the cost of owning the car.

Then we must consider depreciation, a kind of hidden cost. How fast will the car we are interested in lose its value? Some cars sell for almost their original price after three or four years; others are hard to give away. Guessing which will be which is tough, but we can look in the automotive Blue Book at the library to see how the prices of similar cars have held up in the past.

A slowly depreciating car costs less than one whose price drops quickly, because the car's resale price can offset some of our expenses and make our next car less costly.

What about repair costs? They vary enormously. Once, in order to get a starter motor for a Peugeot I owned that broke down in Colorado, I had to fly to Chicago to pick up the part and fly back to

Colorado to put it in the car. The distributor wouldn't ship it for weeks. That part cost me hundreds of dollars. Hopefully, you will think ahead more effectively than I did.

Last, but not least, don't forget insurance, title, and taxes. They have to be figured into the total cost of owning the car.

For detailed information on figuring the cost of a car, write for an excellent pamphlet from the AA Auto and Travel Club of Boston, called *Cost of Car*. Send a stamped, self-addressed envelope to AA Auto and Travel Club, 888 Worcester St., Wellesley, MA 02181.

Once you've looked over the financial situation, do you still really want the blinking vehicle? If you do, there are some strategies for trying to get the price down as far as possible.

BUYER BE WARY

New. When we go out to buy a new car, we face a salesman who is expert at selling cars. We must be at least semiexpert at buying cars to match him. Otherwise he'll roll right over us. Try some of these ideas:

1. Shop when business is off. After Christmas and through the winter car buying tends to slump and you may get a better deal. Same goes for late summer when the new models are coming in. You can get a good deal on the current edition. However, note that the new car you buy in August becomes one-year-old in September when the new cars hit the racks. That doesn't affect you or the car, but it does instantly decrease the car's trade-in value one full year's worth, even if you've only been driving it two days.

2. Use the list price only as a beginning point for bargaining. Never accept it immediately. Never work under the delusion that you'll always get a break on the sticker price either. Try to get the price down, but—especially if you are looking for a small car with good gas mileage—don't be surprised if the dealer hangs tough. On small cars, dealers get a much smaller markup than they do on big ones. So, they have less room to maneuver. And the little number usually can be sold quickly. If not to you, then to someone else. The dealer doesn't need to bargain to sell, so he won't. With a compact the dealer isn't likely to make back in expensive options what he gave up in sticker price.

3. If you are in a small community, you may get a better selection and better deal, by shopping in the nearest high-density, high competition area. If the Chevy man has a Volkswagen dealer across the street, a Renault shop two doors down, and a dozen other dealer-

ships within a few miles, he is going to work harder to sell to you than someone who owns the only shop in town. He is also likely to have higher volume, which means he can shave prices a bit and will have more cars on his lot we can choose from.

4. If a dealer doesn't have a car on the lot that thoroughly pleases you, order one. I know: you've chosen your model and you want the car *now,* but buying a car that isn't exactly right is a mistake. You'll have to wait a month or more for an ordered car, but you'll be driving it for years, and at those prices you should get your dream-mobile.

5. Most dealers offer their own car financing. Don't jump at it. Banks almost always offer lower loan rates than the dealers do. Try a bank first. (For more on shopping for loans, see Chapter Six.)

6. You may be offered a special rust-proofing for the car after you have signed the papers to buy. This isn't entirely a sucker play, but it's not quite fair either. You've just emptied the piggy bank for a precious vehicle and the salesman tells you that it will rust to pieces in three years without a $200 protection job. If you are in an area that salts roads heavily in winter or if you plan to take the car through very dusty, dirty areas (like a construction site) these treatments may be worth the money. The system does protect a car from rust. It also adds measurably to the car's weight and cuts down slightly on gas mileage. If you keep the underside of your car reasonably clean, you can probably skip the expensive process.

7. If you have a trade-in, come armed. Look in the Blue Book for the wholesale value of your trade-in. This is the minimum the dealer should offer in trade if your car is in good shape. If he offers less, insist that he explain in detail why you aren't getting "book" for your car. If he tells you that the dealership can't unload your particular model, that's nonsense. Huge auto auctions exist for no other purpose than to allow dealers to unload trade-in cars they don't want to sell themselves. They can get the wholesale book price for your car at the auction—if it's in good shape. If your car is in particularly good shape or has special extras, point them out to the salesman and insist on getting trade-in credit for them. Tape decks, racing stripes, fancy wheel covers don't qualify as special extras. They limit the resale potential of the car, rather than help it.

Used.   When buying a used car, we contend with two problems: the owner and the owner. In one case the owner will be ignorant of the car and won't be able to give an accurate picture of its condition. In the other, the owner will know all about the car and will do his/her best to give a falsely glowing picture of its condition. Ignore the owner except when you have specific questions. You aren't buying an owner, you're buying a car. Keep your attention there. Check the beast yourself.

1. *Rust.* Go over the car body for rust, especially along chrome strips, under wheel wells, and inside the doors. When painted over, rust appears as a slightly rough spot on the surface. A place where the paint seems dull has probably been sanded and repainted because of rust. Assume there is still rust underneath. Rust doesn't mean you shouldn't buy a car, but should significantly lower the price under the book value. If you get a rusty car, sand away, reprime rusty parts, and paint the body immediately.

2. *Exhaust pipe.* An exhaust pipe is like a car's tongue. It tells a lot about a car's health. Any black smudgy or runny deposit on the exhaust pipe indicates oil burning. This means that the engine seals haven't been properly cared for or the engine hasn't been tuned for a long time or that something major is wrong inside. Bad sign. Serious rust on the exhaust pipe denotes an owner who hasn't paid much attention to his/her car. Expect problems with the engine in general. If the exhaust pipe vibrates a lot while the car is idling, the timing is out or the engine isn't tuned, again signs of poor maintenance, which may rebound on you.

3. *Shock absorbers.* Lean all your weight against the car just above one of the front tires. Let go. The car should rise just above normal height and settle gently back down. If it bobs up and down, the shocks are shot and will have to be replaced.

4. *Engine.* Only someone with auto experience can pick out the good and bad nuances in an engine. Unless you are buying a super-cheap clunker, demand the right to have the mechanic of your choice inspect the engine. Say you are going to stop by your favorite mechanic's while taking a test drive. Invite the owner along. If he/she balks, something is definitely wrong. If he/she comes, the mechanic can tell both of you authoritatively what is (or isn't) wrong with the engine. It's worth the $10 it costs to avoid buying a lemon.

5. *Transmission.* If the car has automatic transmission, test shifting by turning the car on, putting a foot on the brake, and shifting through the gears, pausing for a two count at each gear. Shifts should be made fast and smooth. A jerk, a clunking noise, a long pause be-

tween gears, a whine-slap sound, all indicate transmission trouble that will cost money.

6. *Radio, etc.* Don't assume anything works. In July turn on the heater. Check all the lights. Check the radio, turn signals. If your state has car inspections make sure the car has a current inspection sticker.

7. *Brakes.* Brakes are hard to set rules for. Basically, if they don't make noise and they stop the car in a reasonable distance, fine. The pedal shouldn't feel spongy when you press steadily. However, just what spongy means is tough to define. The pressure you feel as you hit the brake should be satisfying, not terrifying, that's the best I can do. Now, going slowly, with room on both sides and no traffic, take your hands from the wheel and steadily tighten the brakes. Does the car veer toward either side? This indicates the brakes will need to be adjusted. Also have your mechanic check the master cylinder for brake fluid level and color.

8. *Your impression.* How does it steer? How does it feel in traffic? Are the blind spots over the driver's shoulder uncomfortably large? How is the pickup? Can you read the dials on the dashboard? Are the seats comfortable? Basically, do you like the car as a moving environment?

9. *Records.* Ask the owner to produce his/her repair and maintenance records. If you have any suspicion that the mileage shown is not accurate, insist on having him/her sign a paper stating that the shown mileage is correct. If the owner won't produce records, it's probably because he/she doesn't have them or has had work (such as accident repair) done on the car he/she doesn't want you to know about. Bid the owner good day and give back the keys. There are too many fish in the sea to take a chance.

10. *The sting.* Once you're satisfied the car is the one for you, pretend you are a merchant at a bazaar. Try to get the price down. Use lines like: "Well, I think you may be able to get $500 for this car eventually, but I'll give you $450 cash for it right this minute." Or: "Keeping the ad on this car another week will cost you $20, give me $20 discount and you can sell it right now." Or my favorite gambit: After looking over everything, get a slightly distasteful look on your face a la a French maitre d'. Then, as if you didn't know what the price was, you should ask, "What did you want for this?" Sometimes the uncertain owner will knock a few bucks off the newspaper price, or will say, "I *want* $750," a sure sign that he'll/she'll take less than that.

ON TWO WHEELS–BUYING A MOTORCYCLE

Basically, the rules for buying a motorcycle are the same as those for a car. New buyers should look for slow periods and high-volume dealers and should come equipped with facts and a deep reservoir of skepticism. Used buyers should check the merchandise over for themselves as thoroughly as possible; in the case of a cycle check the chain, engine, tires, and gear shift.

Some additional facts to keep in mind when cycle hunting:

1. Motorcycles come in different types. Street and highway cycles are for riding on pavement. Highway bikes have engines of at least 175 cc.'s and can be used on city streets. Smaller-engined street bikes may not be safe on the highway.

Dirt bikes are designed for trail riding and other off-road pursuits. They're used more as recreation vehicles than as transportation.

Touring bikes are the big ones with good shock absorbers, weight, and strong engines for long trips at high speeds. They can be bulky for stop-and-go traffic.

The type of bike you buy depends upon how you want to use it. No matter what dealers say, no single motorcycle works well in all situations. Every model is better in one of these areas than any other.

Mopeds are miniature motorcycles entirely for short in-town trips. They get almost no power, top speed is about 25 miles per hour. But they get 100 miles per gallon and are extremely cheap. One step up from a ten-speed bicycle.

2. Motorcycles are measured by engine size. A 250 Kawasaki has a 250 cc. engine. Work up from small engine sizes to larger ones. Begin with the smallest sizes available and keep on testing cycles until you reach the engine size that just produces the power you want. The power available from similar-sized models of different companies can vary, so experiment at each dealership.

3. You may have trouble with insurance. You may have to pay as much for your cycle as a car owner pays, even though the bike costs much less. Theft coverage will be especially dear. Try to get insurance with a company that specializes in motorcycle coverage. They will compute your premium on the weight and speed of the bike, for as much as a 90 percent savings over the other insurers.

4. You may have trouble with loans too. Since cycles are

vulnerable to small accidents and relatively easy to steal and for years have had a downbeat tough-guy image, lending institutions shy away from cycle loans. When loans can be obtained, interest rates will likely be more than for a car.

5. Sixty percent of cycle accidents occur during the first six weeks of ownership. Learn how to properly operate your bike and you will save yourself much grief, possibly even your neck. Some dealerships offer free courses. Or practice by yourself in an empty parking lot. Avoid big streets and highways for the first few weeks.

CAR MAINTENANCE

There's no excuse today for a car's early deterioration. Either you or a professional mechanic can handle simple service maintenance. Here are the services that will save your car's life and prevent future problems if done on a *regular* basis:

Tune-up. You should have your car tuned up once or twice a year. This process essentially involves readjusting the carburetor and the ignition system. In addition, you will probably have to replace a few inexpensive parts, such as spark plugs, points, and condenser. A garage mechanic conducting a routine tuneup should generally do the following:

Check all fluid levels.
Clean the battery and terminals.
Examine and if necessary replace the pollution control valve and air filter.
Replace and adjust breaker points using a dwell meter.
Inspect the distributor cap, rotor, condenser, and spark advances.
Set break-point gaps.
Check ignition timing.
Check automatic choke.
Replace fuel filter.
Adjust engine idle.
Run a compression check on the engine.

With a few moderately priced tools (check your owner's maintenance manual) and a little mechanical skill you can perform the tune-up yourself. If you prefer to have a professional do the job, an independent garage is the cheapest and most reliable choice. A tune-up costs about $25.

Lubrication. The car's frame is supported by a number of bearings and close-fitting joints that require greasing at regular intervals—like every time you get a tune-up. Consult your owner's manual and mechanic for exact time specifications. Even the most inexperienced mechanic can perform a lube job. With a grease gun and a supply of the proper lubricant, you can finish the job at home in about a half hour. Most service stations also handle this simple chore for a relatively low price.

Tires. Car wheels are precisely aligned, but this delicate alignment can be changed by any forceful blow to the front end of the car (such as hitting a curb or driving rapidly over rut-filled roads or across railroad tracks). This alteration in tire alignment can ruin a set of tires (especially a new set) in a matter of weeks. Check the tread on your tires periodically. If you notice any uneven wear, have the wheel alignment checked immediately and corrected in a garage or wheel specialty shop. Rotating the tires at recommended intervals (check your manual) also will distribute wear more evenly and extend the life of your tires.

In addition, you should check tire pressure weekly or at a garage when you fill up with gas. Since pressure gauges on service-station air pumps are often inaccurate, it wouldn't a bad idea to buy a reliable pocket gauge and keep it in the glove compartment. Take readings only when the tires are cold, since tire pressure can increase as much as six PSI (pounds of air per square inch) during driving. The owner's manual should state the correct PSI for each car's tires.

Oil. Checking the car's oil level and changing the oil at regular intervals are among the best preventatives against engine problems. You should have the oil level checked every time you stop for gas. Better yet, check it personally and save money by buying oil at a discount store and pouring it into the crankcase through a simple kitchen funnel.

Oil should be changed at the intervals specified by your owner's manual or by a reliable mechanic. You'll probably find that oil (especially in the newer economy cars) should be changed more frequently than your manual states—particularly if you drive mainly in city traffic and through a lot of dust and dirt. Every 2,000 or 3,000 miles or every two or three months (which ever comes first) is a good rule for compact and subcompact cars. Larger cars can go for 4,000 to 5,000 miles or four to five months. Your car's oil filter should be replaced with every second oil change.

Brakes. Since you use your car's brakes constantly, you should inspect the brake drum lining at least every 20,000 to 25,000 miles. An unnoticed thin lining may put too much pressure on the brake drum and mean a costly repair. Also check the wheel cylinders and return springs every 40,000 miles and the brake drums every 100,000 miles.

With patience and care (and a good self-service manual), you can perform an adequate brake job. Those who prefer to have an expert do it, should expect to pay about $80.

Clutch. If your car has a manual transmission, the best self-service advice is *never* ride the clutch pedal. Driving with the pedal partly depressed (and thus partly in action) will wear the clutch out very rapidly. And a sure way to ruin the clutch is to ride it while sitting on an ascending hill at a traffic light. Instead, depress the pedal completely so that the clutch is disengaged, and hold the car with the brake.

Radiator. The level of antifreeze and water mixture (called the coolant) in your radiator should be checked every month or two. It should be one and one-half to three inches below the bottom of the filler neck. Many owners and service stations add plain water when the coolant level gets low, but a better practice is to add a half-and-half mixture of antifreeze and water. This will keep the fluid in the radiator from becoming diluted. You can make up this mixture in advance and keep it for months in an old antifreeze container with a tightly closed cap.

Other fluid levels to watch include the battery electrolyte (check monthly in winter and weekly in summer), brake fluid (should be one-quarter inch from top of master cylinder), power-steering fluid, and automatic-transmission fluid.

WHEN YOU GET TAKEN

Even the most careful consumers sometimes get ripped off, and when that happens, we complain. Griping about bad service or shoddy work isn't whining, it's a necessity if we want to protect ourselves and keep businesses honest. As consumers, we have three inalienable rights, which we should defend vigorously:

1. *Information.* We have the right to receive accurate complete information about what we buy. We deserve honest, understandable answers to our questions. Giving us all the information we need to use a product safely and effectively is the manufacturer's and store's responsibility, not ours. We aren't private detectives or newspaper reporters who should have to ferret out the facts.

2. *Safety.* Products should do what they say and shouldn't expose us to unexpected dangers. When an unforseen danger pops up with a product, the company has a responsibility to inform us and make restitution for the product.

3. *Arbitration.* When we and a company disagree about a product we purchased, we have the right to go to court or any other concerned body for an impartial decision on who is in the wrong. If we bought on credit, we can withhold payment until the argument is settled. We cannot be harassed or threatened for doing this. No third party can try to take back our merchandise while we are fighting about our purchase.

In theory these rights are marvelous, in practice they must be backed up by grit and backbone on our part. We must never shrink from asserting our rights as consumers. We are just starting out in life and have enough problems without getting stuck with defective or worthless merchandise.

If you feel you've been taken, you should go first to your original salesperson and see if you can get him/her to respond to your problem. Usually he/she will. If you get rebuffed, go to the store manager. If again you don't get satisfaction, you must put your case in writing and send it in a letter to the manager and his/her boss at company headquarters. (You can usually get a name from the local library, city commerce department, or simply by calling up the company office and asking who the boss is.) In the letter you should state that you will write every agency that touches on their business about your shabby treatment if they don't get reasonable. And if they don't follow through on this threat. If those letters don't work, talk to a lawyer about going to court, if the situation has enough money involved to make that practical. Or you can go to small claims court on your own simply by going to the local court clerk's office and signing up.

A FEW LAST WORDS OF ADVICE

Our lives from the early twenties on include innumerable purchases that will become headaches if we don't shop effectively. Here are some solid general rules you can institute at the beginning of your twenties that will help you be a savvy shopper for years to come:

Buy only from established, reliable stores. If they aren't well-known or liked in the neighborhood, go elsewhere. You want to know they'll be there next month when the device they sold you breaks down.

Always shop around to compare prices before committing yourself to a purchase. Compare credit terms, too, before charging a purchase.

Don't merely compare price. Look over the whole package. Will one shop pick up and deliver the sewing machine for repairs when another won't?

Ask questions. Make the salesperson work. This lets you know whether the store has a well-trained knowledgeable staff. It also gives you an impression of the operation. An honest salesperson doesn't know everything but looks up what he/she doesn't know. A dishonest salesperson is totally glib; he/she doesn't have to look anything up because he's/she's making it up as he/she goes along.

Do homework. Look in consumer testing magazines and books to get an idea of what brand and models you are interested in before going to a store. The more you know, the less chance you'll be disappointed in what you get.

Read everything you sign in full. You don't want to get stuck with hidden charges or surprise exclusions of the store's responsibility.

Never sign anything you don't understand. You should ask to take the documents with you to check them out. If the store won't let you have a copy of any document, there's something fishy going on.

Get all warranties, extras, and repair agreements in writing. Oral arrangements don't stand up.

Ignore all adjectives in ads. Stick with the numbers. *Reduced, wholesale, discount* mean nothing anymore. One store's retail price may be less than another store's discount super ultra wholesale price. And remember there is no free lunch in buying. A store that offers a camera for half of what other stores do, should raise your suspicions, not your hopes.

Never buy anything other than what you planned to buy when you walked in the door. Bait and switch is a major ploy of unscrupulous stores. They will advertise a sale on a popular item, say a Sony Walkman radio. But when you get there, the Walkmen have all hoofed it out the door. Instead they try to convince you to get a much more elaborate gizmo that is also "on sale" at a much higher price than the advertised special. Forget it.

Handling Money

WHEN WE GET out on our own, the earning and spending of money becomes a primary concern. If you have borrowed to get through school, the bills have piled up and you must face the double burden of setting up your life and paying for your education. If your parents have helped you out, now is usually the time they shake your hand, pat themselves on the back for a job well done, and tell you to take it from here.

This abrupt shift causes a money myopia in some of us. We are so overwhelmed by the intrusion of fiscal fears that we can't see beyond them to any other needs. Until the money situation is settled and calm, we literally can't relax. This is priority number one and there is no number two.

Others don't get quite so agitated by money's new character in the twenties, but for all of us the change requires adjustments across the board in how we handle our lives. We are forced to break new ground in terms of personal responsibility and realistic appraisal of ourselves and our situations. The impact of money in the early twenties goes far beyond our pocketbooks. The stringencies of coping with this rare commodity toughen up our psychic muscles all over. Coming to terms with money as a new adult is a large part of coming to grips with our new lives.

When I first got out of college and went to work, I was stunned by the sudden importance of money. I'd worked during school and had felt quite independent. I thought that once I graduated, my preoccupation with money would fade in the face of a regular paycheck. I was dead wrong.

I found, instead, that I thought about money almost constantly for the first several months I was working. I had so many things to buy. My planning was so poor my paychecks never seemed to last long enough. I was always running to catch up with myself. My first reaction was fury at the cruelty of fate. My second response was disgust at my inability to make life perfectly smooth. My third reaction, and the only useful one, was a resolve to sit down and keep figuring my life out until some sort of tenuous financial balance emerged. I found a friendly banker and threw myself at his feet for advice. That was a significant turning point in getting my life started.

In our twenties, for the majority of us, the buck first stops at our desks. We make the money and spend it ourselves. We generate the bills. We sign the checks. We open the accounts. And we have to listen to the angry calls of unpaid creditors. If we scrape together enough money we can buy what we want; if we don't we can't. For the first time ultimate responsibility for the basic stuff of our economic lives rests with us. This is sobering.

We come to grips with money at the same time life is jostling us elsewhere. Our first jobs, and what we get paid for them, bring on a sense of financial deflation in which every dollar suddenly becomes enormously valuable, because we receive so few of them. There may be too few to go around, a unique and shocking experience for those of us from middle-class homes. We realize suddenly why promotions, careers, and raises were so important to our parents. We don't merely want money; in our early twenties we see what it is to truly need it.

With the responsibility of our own money comes the avalanche of paperwork every consumer faces—warranties, statements, invoices, tax forms, leases, and dozens of other densely packed documents that we have to read, comprehend, sort, and store. We may sometimes feel like the Renaissance king of Spain, who, in the midst of the world's most alluring and illustrious kingdom, spent his entire life indoors, sorting the bills he had to pay to maintain it all.

Every facet of this chilling dive into fiscal waters is made more difficult for us than for previous generations of twenty-year-olds by today's downtrodden economy. We have the misfortune to tiptoe into adulthood at the moment when inflation-swollen prices remain, while recession-level wages are being offered.

We are the generation that marks the end of the economic easy times in modern America. We begin work at the time when unions are canceling wage hikes and every industry is trying hard to consolidate its costs.

This means that many of us will have to tighten our belts more than the previous generation. Our starting salaries will be a little harder to swallow. The creation of a livable financial structure for our early twenties will be harder to accomplish and will require more imagination and nerve than ever before.

MAKING A BUDGET

Nobody likes to make budgets, and still fewer of us like to stick by them. However, today's most unlivable economy makes the maintenance of a livable budget more essential than ever. This is an unforgiving time, and if we lose control of our money now, it may take the better part of the decade to get straightened out again.

Now, while our financial stakes are smaller than they will be later in life and our resiliency in life is greater, is the best time to get into the habit of financial planning. The mistakes we make today, even if dreadful, will only leave small scars later on. A decade from now, similar mistakes could be disastrous. Accepting the burden of budgeting in our early twenties can prevent innumerable financial woes as our financial lives grow more complex in the years ahead.

A working budget, however, doesn't imply the need for an all-encompassing, rigid, incredibly detailed document that rules our every penny. While a total control budget might be a worthy goal in theory, it simply won't coexist with the lives that most of of lead. A budget that is too complicated or constricting will not last; when the problems grow too great we'll junk it rather than submit to its stricture, and that doesn't help at all.

In the early twenties, when our financial problems tend to be straightforward and immediate, we should set up a flexible, general budget, an elastic guideway that keeps us from running amok but lets us stretch a bit here and there. It should keep us cognizant of what we intend to spend and where the money to cover those expenses is coming from. It should remind us that an increase in any area of our expenditures requires a reduction somewhere else or a guaranteed increase in our overall income. In short, it should be a constant reminder that, financially speaking, there is no free lunch.

A budget begins with income. Use the following list to figure how much you make. Don't include a penny of income that isn't guaranteed. If you are a salesperson working on commission, include only your guarantee and perhaps a reasonable expectation of other earnings. If money from your parents comes irregularly, don't include it in your budget. The day-in, day-out pattern of your financial life must be based on dollars you know will be there.

PERSONAL INCOME
Salary (take-home pay only, don't include taxes)
Parents or other benefactor
Other (tips, piece work, etc.)
Total

Once you have a clear idea of how much money you make, put together a list of your anticipated expenses. Include every expense you should face on a regular basis, don't try to hedge. If your budget doesn't reflect reality, it is worthless.

MONTHLY EXPENSES
Rent
Utilities
Transportation
Food
Clothes
School or office supplies
Entertainment
Savings
Loans and other debts
Miscellaneous
Total

Obviously, if the total of your expenses is larger than your income, you have a problem. Something must give. The crucial thing to keep in mind is that what gives is entirely up to you. Can you pare your expenses? What about eating less meat to save on food? Can you walk instead of drive to work? Can you survive with less entertainment? Be hard in perusing your expenses, but don't be unrealistic. It is foolish to reduce your food cost on paper to a level so low you can't comfortably live. And it is useless to fool yourself into thinking you'll do something you really can't; if you crave a movie a week, let yourself have it in the budget, you'll do it even if the piece of paper doesn't list it.

What about raising your income? Can you handle a second job? Maybe something on the weekends? Is it time to get on your knees and ask your folks for one last infusion of cash? Or should you consider a roommate to reduce the fat monthly rent bill?

Whichever path you choose, it is essential that your budget balance. If you can't get your life in order on paper, you'll certainly never do it in reality. In fact, your neat balanced budget is merely the first step toward getting your money under control. Once you have the piece of paper, you must monitor its real-world performance carefully. Making the budget is the easy part, keeping it is what takes guts.

The problem with projected budgets like this one is that it is all but impossible to stick to them. Life is usually more complicated than any list can reflect. So think of the paper budget as a tool with which to craft a working sensibility of your money flow that can help you react to unexpected realities that lie ahead.

For three months keep a running record of expenses and compare it with your budget expectations, month by month. Some of them will run consistently higher than you expected, others will be lower, some will jump all over the place.

Use the basic budget form with columns for each month's contributions to each category. On each line you'll be able to see how your expenses in that area compare from month to month and how the pattern conforms to your budget predictions.

Keeping track of expenses is drudge work, but necessary if you want to get a handle on your money. I recommend spending a few minutes before you go to sleep each night jotting down what you spent that day in each budget category. At the end of the month, total it all up and compare it with your plans. How close have you come?

The comparison of your expectations and your real expenses can tell you whether you need more money overall, or must exert greater control over specific expenses. It can reveal areas where you may have severely underestimated and others where you seem to be handling things rather well. After three months of comparing, make up a new budget and expense sheet based upon the realities you have observed. This projection should be different, much more useful than your original.

But it is still just a model. A budget's real worth isn't as a barrier but as an exercise. It forces us to think about where our money comes from and where it is going. It forces us to become familiar with the pattern of our financial lives, so we know where we have a little leeway and where we don't, where we have problems and where we don't. It is elastic. It can't tell us whether or not to buy a color television set. It can only provide the framework for us to make our own decisions. It can remind us that the TV money must come from somewhere. All the budget can do is point out the realities of our situation, so we can move around among them to our own best interest.

CHOOSING A BANK

While we may have established a relationship with a bank in school, it becomes a necessity rather than an option when we get out on our own. The bank provides security and convenience for our money handling, but more importantly it is a financial ally we may need in order to get over the rough spots in our twenties.

No matter how meager your financial situation, you should definitely have a checking account. It helps keep track of your money and gives you a permanent record for budgeting. But most importantly, it begins that vital relationship with a bank that may prove so important later in the decade.

All checking accounts are not the same, so you shouldn't simply pick blindly when you open one. The particular variations offered by different banks may make an especially big difference to someone just starting out who doesn't keep very large balances.

For instance, some checking accounts charge a fee per check written, usually between 10¢ and 25¢, while others charge a monthly fee based upon how much is in the account, usually between $2 and $4 if the balance drops below $500 or so. Now if you don't plan to write too many checks and don't have too much cash, the first kind of account would suit you much better.

The best checking account of all is a free one. These are becoming ever harder to find. Keep an eye out for new branch openings and mergers that often provide the occasion for free checking specials. Also, you should check with the bank where your employers keep their money to see if they have any special plans for workers. And there's nothing wrong with wandering around town, checking out different banks in person; this has the advantage of giving you a sense of how friendly the place is in addition to the hard facts of doing business with them.

BALANCING YOUR CHECKBOOK

Fill in below amounts from your Checkbook and Bank Statement

Balance shown on bank statement	$ _____	Balance shown in your checkbook	$ _____
Add deposits not on statement	$ _____ _____ _____ _____	**Add** any deposits not already entered in checkbook	$ _____ _____ _____ _____
Total	$ _____	Total	$ _____

Subtract checks issued but not on statement
$ _____
_____
_____
_____
_____
_____
_____
_____
_____
_____

Subtract service charges and other bank charges not in checkbook
$ _____
_____
_____

Total	$ _____	Total	$ _____
Balance	_____	Balance	_____

These totals represent the correct amount of money you have in the bank and should agree. Differences, if any, should be reported to the bank within ten days after the receipt of your statement.

Make sure, with any checking account you get, that you receive statements monthly; some banks still send out quarterly statements, which is too far apart to keep on top of your budgeting. Take a look at a sample statement, too; make sure it's clear and understandable.

Most checking account statements include a form that you can use to balance your checking account. Those whose statement doesn't, though, or who find it hard to follow, should use the method that follows to make sure the totals in the checkbook agree with the bank's figures.

Three kinds of institutions offer savings accounts. The most common is the commercial bank—The First National Bank and Trust, for example, which means it is affiliated with the Federal Reserve System. It provides a full range of banking services, from checking to savings to loans. The second type—a savings bank or savings and loan association—specializes in different types of savings accounts and in making large loans, such as mortgages. The third type of savings institution is the credit union, which is a cooperative group of employees or other people with a common interest who pool their money. The organization they create pays interest on deposits and provides loans for members at rates lower than commercial banks.

Which institution you use depends on several factors. The credit union can be the friendliest and easiest to get a loan from, but the interest we receive on our money there may be lower than elsewhere. The highest paid will be at the savings and loan association, but the broadest relationship and range of services is at the commercial bank. So which is for you? If you plan to have several accounts, the full service bank probably makes the most sense. If you plan to buy a house in the near future, the savings and loan relationship makes sense. The credit union might provide an excellent backup to accounts at other institutions, or, through a payroll deduction plan, might make savings easier for you than the others.

These and many other intangibles go into the choice of a bank and a specific type of account. You should evaluate them according to your particular situation. But one way to compare just about any savings account precisely is by interest rate and method of payment:

1. Get interest rate quotes from local financial institutions.

2. Compare how often the bank compounds interest and what kind of balance the bank uses for interest computing.

Compounding means the addition of interest due to an account.

Five percent compounded weekly is more than 5 percent compounded annually, because in the first instance later payments will include the money already added onto the account from earlier compounding. The more frequent the compounding, the more any given rate of interest will accumulate. Daily compounding is best, and many banks now offer it.

Balance determination can be made in several ways, which can change how much you receive at any interest rate. Some banks pay interest on the smallest balance maintained during any day of the interest period, so if our account drops down to $50 for a single day that is all we receive interest on. Other banks use an average of the balance at the end of each business day, and pay against that. The best arrangement is when the bank compounds daily against the actual daily balance. That way you get credit for your money every day it's in the bank.

3.   Ask about any penalties or charges for use. Some banks will charge for withdrawals or will charge after a certain number of withdrawals. Others will charge if the balance falls below a certain level.

A final consideration: overdraft accounts. If you have good credit, many banks will now let you get a kind of backward savings device— the overdraft account. In this arrangement you receive a line of credit from the bank, tied to your checking account. If you write checks for more money than is in your account the bank will draw from the line of credit to pay them. You won't bounce any more checks. And, in an emergency, you will have the line of credit to draw upon. However, for all its convenience this kind of account can't replace real savings. After all, you have to pay the credit account back. It's a bill, not a nest egg.

USING CREDIT

Credit can be a great liberator or a callous oppressor during the early twenties, depending upon how we get it and how we use it. Surprisingly, in the face of high interest rates and the tight economy, some kinds of credit are still easily obtainable by young adults, particularly college educated ones, who form a prime slice of the consumer market. Unfortunately, the kind of credit most readily available to us is in the form of credit cards, so-called revolving credit because it can be repaid in a flexible fashion. However, it can also mean a revolving door of depressing payments and collection notes if we aren't careful with it.

Credit cards are handed out to young adults with aplomb by

stores, banks, and others eager to stimulate us as new consumers. However, these same institutions are much stingier in the way they dole out the less dangerous, more formal kind of credit—installment loans. Installment credit requires a fixed schedule of installment payments from the day the loan is made until it is paid off. Once we get the money, we know exactly how much we'll owe and when. It is much harder to abuse installment credit than revolving credit.

However, paradoxically, it is also harder to get. This is probably because revolving credit profferers want to sell goods or services, while installment credit usually involves a bank giving actual cash money. And financial institutions are much less enthusiastic about giving out money than stores are about handing over merchandise.

Even if we've used credit before our twenties, it was almost certainly based upon our parents' income and reputation, not our own. Now we have to go about establishing our own bank credit, not an easy task in this period of high interest rates and financial paranoia.

Financial institutions these days aren't exactly awash in money they can lend. That is one reason why interest rates are so staggeringly high. As a result, they can be incredibly choosy about who they give credit to. Not only that, but the high interest rates make payments much larger than they would have been for similar loans in the past, and banks want proof that credit customers can handle those increased costs.

All of this adds up to a difficult situation for young adults who are trying to obtain installment credit for themselves. The only way to break through is to present ourselves to the bank as their kind of people; those they can trust to pay their money back with aplomb. What do they look for? Here are some of the attributes credit institutions like to see in customers:

Stability. They want to know we'll be around to pay them back. They like steady jobs, local connections, kids.

Age. Since recent refugees from adolescence are extremely unreliable by the gray-haired standards of most credit institutions, we have to prove we are more responsible than years might indicate. Banks see the under-twenty-five set as the causes of a preponderant number of car wrecks, and the devotees of a morality that is not exactly tied to commitment. We have to let them know we aren't among the young and the restless.

Income. We need to have assets we can use to pay back what we borrow. If we don't have a trust fund or other cushy financial support, our wages are our only hope for repayment. The bank has to be convinced that we make enough to pay them back.

Expenses. The costs of getting started in adult life can be high. Credit institutions ask about our current bills before they hand over any cash. If it looks to them like our income is too heavily encumbered with bills, they won't want to join the crowd. This is one of the strongest reasons for making and tending a budget.

Credit record. If we have paid for what we have bought on credit in the past, we'll probably do it in the future. So, credit history weighs heavily in a bank's decision to lend money. Unfortunately, many young adults don't have a history. Being a regular customer of the bank helps. Paying off school financial aid promptly would help even more. Knowledge of us as individuals can offset suspicion of our lack of credit background; that's why getting to know a bank or dealing with a credit union on our jobs are among the best ways to establish initial credit.

Other ways we can overcome a lack of credit history include:

Put down a big down payment. By showing we have cash on hand and by making our own investment in the purchase a big one, we can convince the bank we are solvent and will protect interest in the merchandise.

Get a cosigner. If we can convince someone with a solid credit history, such as our parents, to promise to repay our loan if we fail to, the bank will be happy to give us money. It's a big favor to ask, though, and one we should only try if we know we can afford the loan. If we flop, the cosigner must pay off our debt.

Find out why we didn't get credit. We are entitled to an answer about a credit turndown within thirty days, if we request one. By discovering the reason we can work to alleviate it.

There are different kinds of credit. In installment credit, we receive a set amount of money which must be repaid in monthly installments. We are charged based upon the length of time we hold onto the money and the speed with which we repay all of it. The basis for comparing installment loan charges is a figure called the APR (annual percentage rate), which compares these two factors.

Whenever we ask about a loan, we must find out what the APR is. This is the only satisfactory way to compare the costs of loans. Here is the way APR can affect the cost of a typical loan:

HOW LENGTH AND ANNUAL PERCENTAGE RATE (APR) AFFECT A $1,000 LOAN

Annual Percentage Rate (APR)	Length of Loan (Months)	Monthly Payment Rate	Finance Charge	Total Cost
9.25%	6	$171.19	$ 27.14	$1,027.14
	12	87.57	50.84	1,050.84
	24	45.80	99.20	1,099.20
	36	31.92	149.12	1,149.12
10.5%	6	171.81	30.86	1,030.86
	12	88.85	66.20	1,066.20
	24	47.07	129.68	1,129.68
	36	33.21	195.56	1,195.56
13%	6	173.04	38.24	1,038.24
	12	89.32	71.84	1,071.84
	24	47.54	140.96	1,140.96
	36	33.69	212.84	1,212.84
15%	6	174.03	44.18	1,044.18
	12	90.26	83.12	1,083.12
	24	48.49	163.76	1,163.76
	36	34.67	248.12	1,248.12
18%	6	175.53	53.18	1,053.18
	12	91.68	100.16	1,100.16
	24	49.92	198.08	1,198.08
	36	36.15	301.40	1,301.40

One thought to consider if you have trouble getting installment credit during your early twenties is: If the bank is unwilling to lend you money, are you in strong enough financial shape to lend it to yourself by using a revolving charge card? Can you afford with a credit card what the bank feels you couldn't with a loan? Probably not, so proceed with great caution, a feat hard to achieve in today's plastic society.

Revolving credit is enormously convenient, but it is about the most expensive form of credit available. Charges run about 1.5 percent on the unpaid balance every month. If a cardholder is paying in small bits, the interest charges can become breathtaking. Because it is so costly revolving credit should never be used for large purchases. However, revolving credit cards, because of their unmatched convenience, work superbly on trips, for gasoline, and for meals. They allow us to carry small amounts of cash and give us a record of what we have spent.

If you have no credit cards, the best way to get one is through the bank where you have your account. The requirements for a card are much like those for any loan. You should expect to receive a low limit for your credit line, which you can raise after a few months of getting used to the cards, as long as you pay your bills promptly.

Ah, there's the rub. Buying things with charge cards is so simple, and paying for them is so hard. Always remember that credit cards represent not one nickel of money. We must have the money from some other source, or we can't presume to be able to pay for what we buy on our credit cards. We must resist the almost overwhelming urge to splurge with our newfound commercial power.

Money and credit can work as a kind of intoxicant. Many people just starting out seem to stop thinking when they begin buying. Consider Alex Schoenberger:

"I worked hard in law school for one reason—I wanted a great job when I got out. And my plan worked. I was hired, fresh out of law school, by one of New York's top firms. And my starting salary was close to $40,000 a year. That's twice as much money as my father made when he died. I felt like I was loaded and I went berserk. First thing I did was to get a super apartment. Then I began furnishing it: color TV, stereo, Betamax—the works. After all, on the kind of money I was making I figured I could afford whatever I wanted. Clothing. Vacations in the Caribbean. I really OD'd on buying.

"Unfortunately, there were things I didn't figure on. Like how much $40,000 a year is after a single person's taxes. And how much the interest came to on all of the things I had bought on credit. By the end of the first year I felt incredibly pressured. Basically, I was having trouble paying all of my bills. People always joke about how the more money you earn the more you need . . . or the poorer you feel or something like that. Well, it's true—or at least it was true for me. I never dreamed I would really earn as much as $40,000 a year, and I never felt as poor before."

There probably isn't any major problem with splurging a tad when we first get out on our own, as long as it doesn't wipe out our ability to handle the basics of life. Our budgets, which we discussed before, can tell us how far to stretch our new buying powers without breaking us. However, far too often recent initiates into the twenties have trouble turning off the splurging spout.

INSURANCE

Previously, we may have insured a car, but more likely our driving machine was covered under a family policy, as, most likely, was our health insurance. And our possessions were insured as part of our family's trove.

Now, however, whatever protection we garner for ourselves must come from our own efforts. And few financial arenas are as confusing and frustrating as insurance. It's a maze.

First, let's introduce some of the basic terms of the trade:

A *policy* is the legal document that spells out what the insurance company is insuring and under exactly what circumstances and limits.

A *premium* is the amount paid to keep the insurance in force.

A *rider* is an addition to a policy that specifically includes or excludes a situation or object from coverage.

A *binder* is an understanding that comes into existence when we pay for insurance and provides us with our policy's full coverage from the instant we sign the check until the day—often weeks later—when the official policy document shows up.

A *deductible* is an amount of money that is excluded from insurance coverage. If our costs don't exceed this amount, we aren't covered.

A *claim* is the request we make of the insurance company to pay us for a loss.

Every kind of insurance has its own special quirks and problems. We never simply buy insurance. We buy a particular kind. Let's start with the kind we are probably most familiar with, auto coverage.

AUTO INSURANCE

We will probably pay high premiums for auto coverage during our early twenties, because we are considered high-risk drivers until we pass age twenty-five. But exactly what we pay varies with numerous other factors, including our grades, whether we've taken drivers' education classes, our sex (young men are considered more dangerous), marital status (married folks are more careful), and where we live (country people have less to run their cars into).

In addition, the costs for car insurance can change depending upon exactly how much we cover. The minimum amount of insurance we can get away with in most states is liability-injury coverage. This pays the expenses of people we harm in an accident we cause. Liability is sold according to sets of three figures, 10/25/5, for example. This means we are protected for $10,000 for one person's injuries; $20,000 for the total of injury in any one accident and $5,000 for property damage. Most states set minimum standards for liability, but don't automatically assume that you should merely get the minimum. The amount of coverage goes up faster than the premium, and minimum rates are usually grossly inadequate to cover the costs of a full-scale wreck.

Going from 10/25/5 to 50/100/10 may only raise the cost 20 percent. So you should consider how much protection you really need and how likely you are to be sued if you aren't protected fully enough. If you have no assets and nothing to lose if accident victims sue you, the minimum may suffice. If you have possessions you don't want to lose, cover yourself more thoroughly.

Liability insurance doesn't cover us or our cars at all. Those of us who aren't driving clunkers should think about adding collision coverage. The premiums for collision coverage vary with the market value of the car and its style. Today's policies typically carry a $100 or $200 deductible and then cover the real costs of getting our cars fixed and back on the road. Check out the method by which this is determined, however. Some companies let us take our cars anywhere and submit the bill. Others accept bills only from approved repair shops. And still others want us to bring the car to them for an official estimate of what they'll pay before we can get it fixed. Judge your policy on the basis of its flexible provisions for repair.

Comprehensive insurance fills in the gaps in other coverage. It protects against theft, fire, lightning, vandalism, even running into a deer. You only need comprehensive insurance if your car or its contents has particular value. A typical used, young-adult starter car probably doesn't demand this much protection. Some companies, however, offer attractive comprehensive package plans that are affordable, so don't forget to ask.

No-fault insurance follows the same pattern as other kinds except that the basic costs of paying for any accident remain the responsibility of our insurance company no matter who caused the accident. This affects rates somewhat, but doesn't alter the basic insurance needs we have.

As much as possible, you should try to get car insurance through a well-known, reputable insurance company. If an agent offers coverage with a firm you don't know, go to the library and check the company out in *Best's Insurance Record*. Stick with A+ or A rated firms.

HEALTH INSURANCE

The most important kind of insurance we need as we start out the twenties is health insurance. With medical costs going wild, any serious illness or the aftereffects of an accident can bankrupt us or our families. In school and in our parents' homes, health insurance was something we could take for granted. Now we must make sure some kind of adequate coverage continues.

The best kind of health policy is a group plan. The odds are that our employers will provide some kind of group coverage. Since at any given moment most of the members of a group are healthy, rates can be lower and coverage better than with individual policies. Payroll deduction to pay for the insurance and employer payment of some or all of the premium makes it even easier to fit into the budget.

Those who aren't lucky enough to get insurance at work should be prepared for a major financial wallop. Individual coverage could easily cost $50 a month. The best bargain will probably come from Blue Cross or a similar public health insurance plan, rather than from a private company. As an alternative to the high cost of individual insurance, look into joining a health maintenance organization. These co-ops provide full medical care in exchange for a fixed annual fee. Instead of paying insurance members hire the medical care itself. This new variation has become extremely popular lately, as medical costs have driven insurance premiums even higher.

Health insurance comes in various forms. Hospitalization policies cover only expenses billed by a hospital, not doctors' or lab fees.

Medical-surgical policies pay the doctor and his assistants but not the cost of the hospital stay. Major medical coverage is a smorgasbord that offers some protection in most areas, according to a schedule of deductibles and fixed fees or percentages. Disability plans provide basic income protection if an illness makes it impossible for us to work.

No health insurance plan is likely to be perfect. Compare the specific provisions of each very carefully. How big is the deductible? When can the policy be canceled? How does the schedule of costs compare—will one policy pay more for surgery than the other? What about limitations for length of hospital stay, length of time at home, private nursing if needed? Finally, what about inclusion of psychiatric and psychological consultation? After trying to cope with the insurance muddle, we may need to use it.

In most cases you will be asked to answer a series of medical questions when you apply for health insurance. These will delve into any past illnesses, family conditions or habits that might affect your current or future health. Generally, you won't be asked to take a physical, unless there is something suspicious in your answers to the questions. The rate you will be charged for health insurance will be based primarily on your age and area of residence, since these determine your likelihood of illness and the likely medical costs for treating you, respectively. Any serious chronic medical problem you might have will kick your rates upward sharply.

LIFE INSURANCE

Life insurance is another of those uncomfortable financial topics many people would just as soon ignore. To discuss life insurance is to discuss our own mortality. However, considering the enormous cost of everything today—including dying—life insurance is a necessity for those of us with families during our early twenties, and highly recommended for the rest of us. It costs less now than it will when we are older, and provides a worthwhile sense of solidity to our lives.

Life insurance fills the financial gap caused by a death. It is an investment in the sense that we deposit money on a regular basis over the years and our estate reaps a benefit.

In order to entice more people to use life insurance, some policies offer investment benefits to subscribers while they are still alive. These are the so-called whole-life policies, which build up cash value and/or incorporate cash payback plans for retirement. The more straightforward type of life insurance, where the company pays a set amount on the subscriber's death, is called term life.

Eventually, a solid life insurance plan uses both types of coverage. The family's basic standard of living should be maintained by a whole-life policy. If this is taken out before middle age, it offers low premiums, cash value, and the minimum necessary protection.

As family income increases after the twenties, term insurance can be added to increase the protection. Later, when children are grown and needs reduced again, the term insurance can be dropped while the whole-life protection remains. Finally, the whole-life can be used as an income source during retirement and, of course, as a financial cushion for the surviving family members when the inevitable occurs.

There is a formula for figuring out how much life insurance you need. You should first sit down and decide what income level would be necessary to maintain your life-style if and when you have a family. Don't be unrealistically conservative. You may think your spouse could greatly simplify life and reduce expenses; but families tend to lead the same kind of lives after a breadwinner dies.

With this figure in hand, total up any benefits that would automatically come into play upon the death of a breadwinner. Possible sources include: Social Security, pension plans, military benefits, trust accounts for children, life insurance through employers, etc. If you and your spouse work, figure up lists for each separately and for both together. Figure your insurance needs on the list that provides the biggest financial gap.

The gap between these two figures is how much the family must come up with to keep from losing its life-style if a breadwinner dies. Can the remaining spouse earn this much? If both spouses die can the children produce this much income?

In most cases the answer to these questions is no. This means the family must have some way to come up with the difference. The safest way to insure a steady income level is to have sufficient capital in the bank to provide the income as interest or dividends.

Figure how much capital it would take to fill your family's needs with this equation: A is the amount per year your family will need; X is the amount of capital required: $12\% \ (X) = A$.

Twelve percent a year is about what capital generates in insured long-term savings accounts. It also approximates return on stocks and bonds (under good circumstances). When you have found X, add to it a liberal lump sum to cover "final expenses." These include possible costs of a final illness, funeral charges, estate and inheritance taxes, and a sum to cover expenses while the financial affairs are straightened out.

Those who have major assets should subtract their value from the sum above. Such assets might be a house, stocks, bonds, investment property, and jewelry. Their value is subtracted because they could be sold to protect the family, if need be. Now you have finally ascertained the gap in your family's finances if a breadwinner dies. You should be insured to cover this gap.

How much life insurance can you afford? You might think that figuring this out would be simple. Just look at your household budget and determine how much you can spare for insurance.

Unfortunately, the picture is much more complex than that. Life insurance comes in many forms, which vary enormously in protection, price, and cost. Protection is how much, and under what circumstances, the policy will pay off. Price is the cash amount paid for the policy.

Cost, by far the most important factor, is the expense of the policy with all outside factors taken into account. For instance, cost takes into consideration the interest lost by putting money into insurance premiums rather than into a bank.

This brings us to the golden rule of buying life insurance: You want the most protection for the least cost at a price you can afford. Now, the question is how do you go about reaching your protection goals at a reasonable cost and a fair price?

First, you must choose the type of life insurance you want. Here are the two major types:

Whole-life. (also called cash value insurance). The name stems from the fact that this type of policy remains in force until your death. The price you pay is based upon your age when you buy the policy. Once set, the price remains the same as long as the policy is in force. The older you are when you start a whole-life policy, the higher the price will be.

The price also includes an added amount that gives the policy cash value. As the years wear on, your extra payments build up a cash reserve through the policy. It is a kind of forced savings, although it doesn't pay interest. If you wish to terminate your policy at any time before death, the cash value is paid to you, or you can borrow a portion of it at favorable interest rates from the insurance company. However, any cash value taken before you die is deducted from your ultimate death benefits; you can't get both full death benefits and cash value.

The costs of whole-life include the interest you lose by paying extra money for cash value that could be in a bank and the fact that your premiums remain the same even though the insurance company is making money investing your cash value premiums at no risk. In other words, if you have paid $5,000 in cash value payments and receive $20,000 in death benefits, you are actually getting only $15,000 of the insurance company's money, a little less than that, in fact, because they've made interest on your earlier payments that lowers their share still further. This raises the real cost of the policy.

On the other hand, a whole-life policy forces you to save through your payments. The negative cost factors of whole-life policies assume you'd put any money saved by buying cheaper insurance into a savings account, and many people simply wouldn't do it. If they didn't put the money aside through insurance they'd just spend it.

Term insurance. This type of policy provides insurance coverage, period. No cash value. The coverage lasts for a fixed number of years, the term of the policy. At the end of the term the policy can be renewed for a new term at a higher price, which reflects your increased age.

When you reach sixty-five or so you won't be able to keep term insurance but, in many cases, you will be able to convert a term policy to whole-life. The big advantage of term insurance is its price. A term policy may have a price one-third that of a whole-life policy of the same amount taken out at the same age.

Assuming you put all the money you saved by buying term insurance in the bank, term would be a better insurance buy than whole-life. Your money would earn interest (it doesn't with whole-life) and you could use it at no charge (you pay interest to use insurance cash value). In addition, using the money won't affect your ultimate death benefits.

However, would you really save that money, and would you like your insurance payments to rise steadily every five years or so?

You can, of course, start out with term insurance and later switch to whole-life. This, too, tends to cost less than a whole-life policy for the same period if you save diligently. But it includes the risk that ill health may have made you ineligible for whole-life by the time you decide to buy it.

Here are some basic rules for getting the best insurance you can for the money available:

Find an experienced agent, preferably a certified life underwriter (CLU) who has been in your community for several years. Don't use a relative or friend; you can't be sufficiently skeptical with them. If you don't feel comfortable with an agent, get another.

Shop around for a policy. Get quotes for both whole-life and term coverage from at least four companies. Do not sign with the first company you talk to.

Before you sign with an insurance company check its financial rating in *Best's Insurance Report*. If it's not A+ or A, skip it.

Look in the library for National Underwriters' comparative cost list for policies. See how those you are interested in stack up.

If you can comfortably afford to meet your protection goals with a cost-efficient whole-life policy from a highly respectable company, get it. Remember, though, that the dropout rate on whole-life policies is high; the policy will only be worth the extra price if you keep it in effect for many years. Should you have any doubts that you can afford it, don't buy it.

If you can't afford whole-life, get term insurance that meets your protection goals. Never, ever, no matter what any salesperson says, lower your protection requirements in order to afford cash value. The protection is the steak, cash value is the sauce. You don't give away the steak so you can afford the sauce.

Remember, if you can't afford whole-life today, the odds are that you'll still be healthy enough at the end of the term to qualify. And you might be better able to afford it then.

Ask where you work, at your church, school, fraternal group, or club if they offer group term coverage. If you are opting for lowest price, groups are the ultimate. The coverage is usually the same as for individuals but the payments are lower and, in most cases, you can convert the policy if you ever choose to leave the group.

Within the two basic kinds of insurance are myriad combinations with accompanying variations in coverage, price, and cost. To keep everyone from becoming totally confused, this overview has been somewhat simplified.

But remember that whatever the particular type of insurance you're looking at, what you want to achieve is the most coverage for the least cost at a price you can afford.

Partners

ALL OF OUR relationships—not just parental ones—are affected by the onslaught of adulthood. One friend of mine saw her old gang shift as the twenties moved in, "I remember feeling in college that my friendships were eternal. I had a group of close friends and it just seemed unimaginable that we wouldn't go on being close friends forever. There was an unwritten code in our friendship: We were there for each other twenty-four hours a day. Then, one of the people in this group got married and there was a sort of awkwardness about where her husband fit in. What if one of us were having a crisis and called at two in the morning and *he* answered the phone. The comfort and availability were somehow diminished.

"Little by little we all began moving ahead in our careers. Back in college we'd meet at lunch every day and fill each other in on the most miniscule details of our lives. Now, there was hardly time for a weekly phone call. Life started to intrude. For a while some of us would meet for brunch on Sundays. Then two of us had babies. Anyone with an infant knows that by brunchtime on Sunday you feel like you've already been up and working for a week. Brunchtime becomes nap time.

"As our lives changed, we each started making new friends with life-styles more like our own. And as the life-styles of the original group became more and more divergent, much of the closeness dissipated. There weren't really any fights or traumatic incidents. There just seemed to have been a process—call it life, I guess.

"In many respects when I think of those friends and how incredibly important they were, and what wonderful, intimate times we had together, I feel kind of sad. But it's not the kind of sadness that makes me want to invite them all over to my house and try to capture what we had. It's more of a wistfulness for a time in my life when that particular type of relationship was of paramount importance. Actually, when I see some of my single friends in their mid-thirties who are still involved in that sort of relationship, I feel kind of sad for them. It's almost as if they never took the next step."

Because our lives are in such states of flux and our circumstances in such upheaval, friendships and relationships in the early twenties seem to go almost out of control. We meet new friends when we move away from home or when we go to work somewhere new. Sometimes we're able to keep in touch with the old friends, sometimes the old friends vanish into the woodwork. A few of us will try to mate the old friends to the new, and find friction between them.

In addition, our psychological states change drastically during these early years. We move from teenage narcissism to a new realization of the people around us. We develop the beginning of a new capacity for loving and caring. Soon we will be more mature, more wise in our relationships. But for now, the major factor in our abilities to deal with friends and lovers is the enormous change occurring inside of us.

In our early twenties we often seek out people who can fill the gaps left by our shifting lives and changing self-images. Our experience in the outside world shifts from dependence to independence; inside we jump from feeling totally vulnerable to being utterly invincible.

When we are at our highs we look for someone who matches our strengths, who can keep up with us, and who won't point up or emphasize our weaknesses. We might even want a person who needs to be cared for in a way we are ready to attempt.

At our lows our vulnerability cries out for someone to care for us, to see our hurts and tend them, a nurturer who still won't overpower us or make us feel inadequate.

The person who seemed so perfect for us one month may be entirely wrong for us in another. Since we aren't formed and solid, our views toward important other people can't be consistent. What we need, what we want, is as changeable as we are. Our love is as unreliable as our confidence.

Carl Jung, the renowned psychiatrist, said that during this stage of life we are hunting longingly for the archetype that lurks back in our subconscious, an unreal compilation of our innate needs, childhood fantasies, family frustrations, and oedipal loose ends. When we find someone who rings the subconscious bell of recognition, we lunge at them with all of our emotions, with the intensity that only subconscious urges can generate. We want them for our own, we may marry them, all without giving the slightest consideration to the individual personality that may lie behind the facade our subconscious craves.

So many marriages that come out of the late teens and early twenties fail because the narcissism of both partners produces a marriage of self-images. A few years later they realize there's another person on the other side of the bed, independent and unhappy, and the marriage crumbles because it was built upon facile premises.

The key to developing stronger, more mature relationships as we enter our twenties is to confront and work through our residual teenage selfishness and narcissism. Only when we see ourselves with a certain amount of realism can we hope to look at others with some sense of equality. Psychologists say we have achieved the level of sharing affection, but not the pinnacle of intimacy.

FROM AFFECTION TO INTIMACY

Not too long ago a young friend of mine asked me if I ever saw my spouse almost as if from a distance, and thought to myself, God, she's acting like a beast. At first, the question seemed a bit strange, but he went on to explain.

"I've been dating this girl—Susan—for a while now, and we really like each other a lot. But last weekend we had dinner with an old friend of mine from home. He and his wife made this beautiful dinner. They were really gracious and intelligent and made an effort to have everything be just so. And Susan just mishandled everything. She seemed like such an idiot to me all night. She was giggly and hardly participated in the conversation. And she just sat around waiting to be served, when everyone else was sort of pitching in. I felt like everything she did was awful.

"When we got home I hated the idea of making love to her. I thought, How could I have ever been attracted to her? Then I didn't call her for a few weeks, which was very unusual for me. Finally she called me and I made a date reluctantly. And when we got together she seemed like her old self. And I really dug her."

After a while my friend and Susan talked about the evening. It turned out that she was incredibly nervous about meeting such old and important friends of his, and that she knew she was acting stupidly but just couldn't control it. What could have happened differently?

For starters, my friend probably could have sensed how uptight Susan was. He might have done some little things to let her know that he understood and that he was there for her. If he didn't pick up on her discomfort, she—in the context of an intimate relationship—might have been able to tell him. That sort of openness and acceptance and helpfulness mark the difference between intimacy and affection.

The difference is crucial. Affection denotes reciprocity, friendliness, mutual regard, tenderness, but still focuses on you. We *feel* affection for someone else, it's not a sensation we *share*. So, it represents merely a step forward from complete self-concentration but not the completion of the trip to adult interaction.

Intimacy, on the other hand, requires that we share. We don't feel intimacy, we achieve it. We can't have it without two-way participation. Intimacy also demands close up, unforgiving scrutiny of both partners; we want to see all the warts, all the scars, all the unpleasantness of another person. It is the exact opposite of the idealization we enter the twenties practicing.

True intimacy doesn't just spring up. It's like a hothouse plant: very delicate, finicky, fast to wilt. It must be cultivated, and learning how to nurture intimacy takes years of practice for most of us. That's what the twenties are for.

During this decade we can experiment with our feelings, test different personalities against our own. The links of intimacy are utterly different for each of us. We have to find out where we uniquely connect with other people. We have to move beyond idealization to affection and discover the many variations of affection to find what kind of relationship will draw us further along into the rich exploration of intimacy.

LOOKING FOR MR./MS. RIGHT

"When I was in college," Karen Lewis remembers, "the whole idea of relationships really seemed more like a contest than anything else. Who could I get? Would this guy ask me out? How could I make so-and-so notice me. The challenge really had to do with attracting someone. Once I had his attention, I don't think I really knew what to do with it. As soon as I had someone I basically started looking around elsewhere.

"It seems obvious to me now that I was just thinking about men—really they were boys—as some way of proving myself. Something like 'Look at me. I can have a great-looking boyfriend,' or 'Look at me, I can have a superintellectual boyfriend,' or an arty boyfriend. Whatever. I don't think I was evil or anything. I think I was just immature, which is no crime for a twenty-year-old. When I think back I feel bad because I know that I toyed with a lot of nice guys' emotions, but there was nothing I could do about it.

"Finally, the thing that turned me around had to do with a sort of growing loneliness. I always had boyfriends and guys to date, but at some point toward my mid-twenties I realized that I was lonely. Whatever it was that I was supposed to be getting just wasn't working. Ultimately, I was forced, by my own unhappiness, to take a really close look at myself and how I acted in relationships.

"The fact is that I couldn't take that close look by myself. I had to get help and I went to a therapist, who really sort of held my hand emotionally and helped me look at what *my* needs were. I began really thinking about what it was that I wanted from a man. Some of the men I went with during my early years might actually have been able to give me the things I needed—strong emotional support, openness, and such—but at that point I just wasn't able to let them give it to me.

"The whole thing is rather complicated. But when I did meet the man I was to marry, he was nothing like the man I thought I'd end up marrying when I was twenty years old. He wasn't like my father. He wasn't like my mother. But he was right for me."

Because of the intense psychological changes occurring in the early twenties, the pressure to marry—which comes from all sides, it seems, the minute we leave home—is felt very strongly. Again, the relationship we have with our friend or lover is often the product of our internal struggles, and only a small part of the relationship emanates from his/her needs, desires, and basic personality. In addition, the decision to marry in the early twenties is very often an acting-out of our adolescent images of marriage.

The image we have of marriage as we enter the twenties is comprised of equal parts media-fed syrup and false assumptions of our own. We don't know what marriage will be like, but we assume it begins in great gusts of romance and passion. We figure marriage begins wonderfully, even if it doesn't turn out so well later on.

Actually, marriages in the early twenties often begin more like winter storms than sunny summer days. At the decade's start we are all under enormous stress; marriage is one of life's biggest stress points, and the combination of the two means that most young marriages begin with more tension and testiness than splendor in the grass.

Each partner has personal living patterns developed over the course of a lifetime. Suddenly the two people find themselves alone, usually in cramped quarters, each working according to assumptions the other doesn't fully understand yet. Explosions are likely.

When Bill Adler began his senior year of college he began thinking about "the next step": What happens after being a student? How do I become an adult? What makes me stop being a kid? And he began exploring for answers.

"I never really thought much about anything except having fun while I was in school. It was all just going to bars, putting the make on girls, and feeling like a hotshot at Notre Dame. But when I was a senior things began changing. People began getting engaged and thinking about careers. And I sort of went along with all of that.

"I was dating a girl who was nice enough. She was pretty and fun to be with. And I'd known her for maybe six months or so and it just seemed like we should get engaged. It was what was happening all around us and it was easy enough to do. So I asked her to marry me and she said yes, and that was it. We were engaged.

"But as graduation approached and we began talking about what we'd do after school, reality began to set in. I wanted to go to the East Coast and she wanted to be in the Middle West, near her family. She was talking about having babies and I was panicking. It was like 'Hey, wait a minute, I'm just a kid myself.' It was all overwhelming. Finally, I broke it off.

"It seems funny because now when I think about marrying someone I think about all sorts of things. Is she someone I could go on respecting year after year? Does she want to share her life with me? All sorts of stuff. But then it was just like being caught up in what was happening all around me. I'm glad I broke it off. I'd rather be alone now than be part of the divorce statistics."

A couple in their twenties has to struggle, amid all the other challenges, to study and understand each other's long established pattern and construct a new mutual pattern with contributions from both and dominance by neither. For this reason, all the quarreling of a beginning marriage isn't necessarily bad. In fact, the misconception that fighting should be avoided is one of the biggest problems psychologists note in these unions.

The reality seems to be that young adults whose marriages end up surviving the twenties actually fight quite a bit. In effect, they fight their way from social love to married love. The quarreling serves to clear the air between them, and anger becomes a medium that allows them to blurt out true feelings they might repress when calmer. As a result, the couple finds out important facts about each other—fears, needs, habits, foibles—that end up making the relationship stronger and more equitable.

Psychologist George R. Bach says that "couples who fight together stay together." Without fighting, he claims, the best a couple can hope for is a kind of juvenile pseudointimacy. "A marriage that operates on the after-you-my-dear-Alphonse principle may last a lifetime—a lifetime of fake accommodations, monotony, self-deception and contempt."

The time to sweep these uncertainties away is at the beginning of marriage. The hearts and flowers can follow once the hard work is done.

ARE YOU READY FOR MARRIAGE?

"The only thing I would have done differently about my twenties is that I wouldn't have gotten married," recalls Patty Porris, a divorced mother and entrepreneur. "At twenty-one I was too young. I had all these responsibilities with my family, and marriage seemed a good way to get away from that. Deep down in my heart I knew I was making a mistake. My mother was against it. I stayed with it, in part at least, because I didn't want to prove her right. I suffered with a bad marriage through what should have been some of the happiest years of my life. But it taught me a valuable lesson: Never be ashamed to say that you've made a mistake. I would have avoided an incredible amount of ugliness if I had been able to admit that then."

For any author to assume that he/she can give *really* useful advice about the decision to marry is tricky, at best. The act of falling in love and deciding to get married is so personal, so deeply set in the heart, that there is nothing an outsider can say that can truly touch the basic questions involved.

But it might be useful to point out areas of concern, to ask if there are questions that have not been considered yet. It might be helpful to look at these nine areas before you take the plunge. Can you and your partner be of one mind about them, or at least agree to disagree?

Roles.   Roles in marriage can either be the basis of a couple's happiness or the undoing of a union. If your spouse is set on following a traditional role, your "script" is to take a complementary role. For example, your husband may want to be the *only* breadwinner; thus, your function in the marriage is to be the housewife. Such a relationship can work only if these roles are definitely fulfilling the needs that each of you have in your marriage and in your lives.

However, if she—let's say your wife this time—desires a career just as much as you do, the question is no longer who works and who keeps house, but rather can both of you share the household chores? Or does that remain exclusively her job? If your answer to the last question is yes, then you'd better find someone who wants to be a housewife and nothing more.

Money.   Thousands of young married couples are finding it increasingly difficult to bridge the gap between "what we have" and "what we want." Early marriage means doing without many of the things you may now be accustomed to—a new record album, meals out, a weekly movie. The only way to achieve a balance between having and wanting is to establish an agreed and shared philosophy of budgeting, paying bills, spending and saving, and pinpointing future financial goals.

Take into consideration, too, the fact that the country's present rate of inflation and high costs of living may demand that both of you work. This could mean that you each need to alter your ideas about roles in a marriage.

Religion.   Religious beliefs can affect attitudes about anything from birth control to marital fidelity. In particular, if one of you has strong religious convictions and the other doesn't, will it affect your relationship? Can your partner handle it if you don't want to attend church or if you don't want to raise your children to possess the religious beliefs of either of you?

Parental Influence.   Although you're marrying one person, not the whole family, you can't afford to dismiss your parents completely.

Suppose you're still "daddy's little girl" and daddy still wants you to have everything you desire? Or your mother can't stand her son's wardrobe and doesn't mind commenting on her daughter-in-law's housekeeping?

Moving away to avoid parental influence may relieve the tension, but a separation based on such a motive may also cause a rift between your spouse and his/her parents that could be blamed on you. If you can't resolve conflicts with parents, you have one of three choices: marry and hope that the parents resign themselves to the marriage; wait to marry until the parents are won over; or marry and be prepared to accept the consequences of their disapproval.

Sex. This is probably the most difficult aspect of marriage for young couples to discuss and yet the most important when you consider that sexual incompatibility usually leads to marital incompatibility. Psychologists and marriage counselors agree that the basis for sexual incompatibility is a lack of communication between partners combined with individual inhibitions.

The best way to overcome inhibitions and communication gaps is to remember that our need for sexual expression and fulfillment is as important and as natural as our need for food and shelter. Whether it's talking or doing, there is only one attitude one can have about sex: It is the deepest and most beautiful way in which two people can show their love for each other. Therefore, it should be approached in the most open-minded way possible, *without* hangups and *with* honest talking.

Children. The first year or so of a marriage is the most critical time for young couples—you're trying to make ends meet, to become adjusted to each other, to enjoy each other. Nothing can affect marital adjustment more than having a child during the critical period, especially since few people under twenty-two or twenty-three are emotionally ready to be parents. Unprepared for parenthood, at a time when you're becoming close to each other, you may see the new baby as an intruder, or an obstacle to your fun and freedom together. You're stuck at home, with less money for pleasures and few places to go for amusement with a baby.

The wisest time to have children is after you've decided that the marriage is going to work, when you're more financially secure and confident in your feelings about yourselves and each other. In addition, you should question why you want children—are your desires motivated by parental, social, or religious pressures, or by the idea that a baby will strengthen your marriage.

Individualism. Marriage means togetherness, sharing, companionship. It does not, however, mean losing your identity, giving up your interests or your privacy. Even if "doing your own thing" is going horseback riding (when the other is petrified of horses) or taking off on a fishing trip (when one of you is petrified of worms), both of you have the right to do the things you each enjoy. In addition, everyone requires some time alone to "sort themselves out." It's a basic need of every individual and a privilege that each of us should respect.

Habits. Does she interrupt you all the time you're talking? Does he laugh too loudly in the middle of a restaurant or theater? If little things like this bother you *before* marriage, they'll annoy you just as much after marriage. Telling yourself ten times over that you love him/her is not going to make annoying habits disappear, but by going back to honest communication again you can begin to deal with the things that bother you now.

Changing. The greatest amount of change in a person's life occurs between the high school years and middle twenties. This means that at the time you're newly married, both of you will be undergoing the most important changes in your lives—changes in values, standards, expectations, ambitions, desires, needs. And during this evolution change can either bring you together or force you apart.

Naturally problems that arise in the process of change can't be solved before they appear; some things you'll just have to handle as they occur. But the fact that you have discussed yourselves and as many aspects of marriage as possible *before* is already an advantage. Now you know at least that you can talk about problems and differences that will come up later, especially those created by changes in each of you.

When you discuss issues such as those in this checklist, you may discover some differences that can't be resolved. This possibility should not prevent you from exploring those areas, though. Ending an engagement or steady relationship may be a difficult thing to face, but it's much easier than the breakup and possible alienation of families and children or the legal and financial hassles of divorce.

CONSIDERING MARRIAGE

Here are ten questions you should consider before you decide to get married:

1. Are you really finished with "playing the field"? If you are not ready to have this one other person as your only date to all occasions, then you need to keep on dating.

2. Are you ready to put this special relationship with your spouse ahead of your own education, your career, or the accumulation of things (new car, television, house, motorcycle)? You don't have to give these up for good, but you will need to make some compromises.

3. If you marry right away, will you be forced to live with parents or in-laws? Such a situation often proves fatal to a young marriage. You need your own apartment or house where you two can work on problems without interference from anyone.

4. Have each of you established a new relationship with your parents in which you can listen to their advice without either rejecting it automatically or accepting it uncritically? If you still act like a child with your parents, you'll find it hard to act like a married adult.

5. Are you prepared to talk patiently through any issue that bothers your spouse—even if the issue doesn't seem vital to you? Your feelings and the feelings of your spouse are always important.

6. Are you ready to plan when to have children and conscientiously practice birth control within the limits of your religious beliefs? Unplanned children often delay or even destroy the long-range goals of couples.

7. Will you plan together, before you get married, what your educational and career goals will be for the next five years, and establish priorities that will give each of you the fairest treatment possible?

8. Are you ready to share all the work of keeping a house and raising children, even if it means learning skills usually considered the work of the other sex?

9. Would you be willing to go to a marriage counselor for help rather than just break up, if the going gets rough? Would you be willing to have a marriage counselor help you take a hard look at your relationship before you get married? Your willingness to seek outside help may be a measure of your maturity and readiness for marriage.

10. Do you want to marry because you love this person and

want to spend the rest of your life with him/her? You shouldn't marry for any other reason, including pregnancy, getting away from home, or even loneliness. A marriage has the best chance when both partners sincerely want to be with each other and are really willing to work at making it a success.

As I look back on the relationship with my wife that began at the beginning of our twenties, it sometimes seems incredible to me that we actually managed to get through those hysterical years in which we both changed personalities almost as often as our clothes. Yet we are still together and still close. I think if any single factor was most important in keeping us afloat it was openness. When the going got particularly rough we talked. When our lives seemed to be drifting we thought about what direction we wanted to go and felt our way forward until we found a path that felt comfortable to both of us.

Ultimately, in this early stage of the twenties, the best advice I could give is for you to remain patient—with yourselves, your lovers, and your friends. Remember, the inner life of the early twenties is in as much turmoil as the outer life, and try to appreciate the qualities of friendship for what they are—enduring aspects of one's personality and character that far surpass the ordinary, day-to-day struggles.

Stress and Your Health

OUR BODIES ARE our pride and joy as we enter the twenties. They have outgrown their teenage gawkiness and are looking the best they ever have. We feel stronger than ever, too, more agile, more physically competent. The positive sense we have about our bodies can lend a positive glow to the entire transition period into our first adult years.

"I never thought much about my body," a twenty-three-year-old medical student explained. "But I started becoming aware, a few years ago, about the fact that other people *did* notice my body. If I walked by a bunch of construction workers they made crude comments. Even very establishment sort of men would turn and look at me when I walked by. It's not that I look like Cheryl Tiegs or anything, but I've come to realize that I've got a damn nice body.

"Sometimes I stop and look at myself before I get into the shower and I think, Umm, not bad. It's a good feeling. I look good in clothes. I like wearing things that emphasize my good points . . . my breasts or my legs. Of course, it all gets focused around the sexual issue. I don't really hop in and out of bed with strangers. But when I do go to bed with a man I never feel uptight about taking off my clothes. I never have any doubt about the fact that he'll like what he sees. Feeling that way is a turn-on in and of itself."

As we enter the twenties we feel as if we are immortal. Nothing can hurt us. Sometimes this sense of complete protection from harm leads us into wild and excessive behavior. It seems as though we can sin and get away with it. We can rock all night and drink all day and still, somehow, function. We can toy with drugs and drive ourselves without respite and not show any signs of it in our face or form.

Happily, the early twenties are probably the best possible time to get all this craving for action out of our systems. Our bodies will never be better able to take it. And psychologically, the extreme paces we put our bodies through now are an important sign of our emerging personal power and independence. No one can determine our limits any longer but us.

The effect that accompanies this newfound power is stress, our reaction to circumstances that defy our attempts to control them. During our teens we all felt stress. Every time we took a test or went out on a date, every fight we had at home or car accident we suffered through on the interstate, stress paid a call. But none of what we have experienced is anything like what hits during the early twenties.

Teenage stress results from symbols. An F on a test is merely a symbol, a "no" on a date isn't earthshaking. But now we are playing the game of life with real money, for high stakes. If we get turned down for a job, we have no money to buy food. If we can't set up a workable social life for ourselves, we will be alone, perhaps friendless in a strange place.

At the same time, stress has an enormous positive potential for us during the early twenties. It is the rush of adrenalin that gets us through job interviews; the hidden strength that allows us to work late into the night; the push that prods us into new relationships and situations. Without positive stress we might never move ahead and grow.

REDUCING STRESS

But the pressure we put on our bodies to prove our freedom, combined with the wear and tear stemming from all the other changes we are going through as we enter the twenties, exacts a quiet but dangerous price on how we feel and how healthy we are.

There is no way to go through such situations without paying a high price in stress. And there is no way to face a siege of stress without suffering some bodily impact. It may be muscle fatigue or eye strain, headaches, irritability, memory lapses, any symptom that ties in with tension or preoccupation.

While we can't eliminate the problems life will bring or the stress that comes with them, we can do a few things to reduce the impact of stress on our minds and bodies.

First, we can ascertain how serious our stress situation is. A University of Kentucky team has produced a chart that allows us to figure just how much stress we are under. For each of the events on this list that has affected you in the past year, add the corresponding stress value to your total.

Event	Stress Value
Death of spouse	100
Divorce (of yourself or parents)	73
Pregnancy (or causing pregnancy)	68
Marital separation	65
Jail term	63
Death of a close family member	63
Broken engagement	60
Engagement	55
Personal injury or illness	53
Marriage	50
Entering college	50
Changing dating habits	39
Gain of new family member	39
Business readjustments	39
Change in financial state	38
Changing participation in courses, seminars	38
Death of a close friend	37
Change to different line of work	36
Change in number of arguments with mate	35
Trouble with in-laws	29
Outstanding personal achievement	28
Mate begins or stops work	26
Begin or end school	26
Change in living conditions	25
Revision of personal habits	24
Trouble with boss	23
Change in work hours or conditions	20
Change in recreation	19
Change in church activities	19
Change in social activities	18
Going into debt	17
Change in sleeping habits	16
Change in frequency of family gatherings	15
Change in eating habits	15
Vacation	13
Christmas	12
Minor violation of the law	11

If you scored less than 600 you have had a much easier than normal entrance into your twenties. Scores between 600 and 1,000 show a constant, chronic presence of stress in your life. Above 1,000 you can expect significant repercussions from the load of stress.

You *can* minimize the effects of stress on your life by giving yourself something comfortable and secure to fasten upon. This can be either real or symbolic. A sauna and massage is real; a favorite, relaxing meal in an old, familiar restaurant is symbolic, bringing to mind the good times of yore. Whatever the specifics, you are striving for a comfy return to known quantities, a recharging of your batteries.

Among the activities that can help are:

1. Seeking out friends or relatives to whom you can speak freely and unburden your problems. Loneliness is, in itself, a cause of stress. Facing stressful times on your own simply compounds your problem. Seek out *companionship,* nothing complicated, just warm, human contact.

2. Doing something simple and repetitive. Jogging. Whittling. Playing a piano. The repetitive routine takes your mind off your problems and the small-scale success of simple actions soothes jangled nerves.

3. Establishing a routine. One of the biggest causes of stress in the early twenties is the sudden loss of familiar routines. You should try to establish some kind of routine in your new life. Start each day with a brisk walk down the block to the newsstand for a paper. Or stop at a particularly soothing bar for a beer every night at a certain time. You can pick a special lunch spot and go there often, so you feel at home there. These "little things" will become the pegs on which you can hang your new life.

4. Meditation, hot baths, standing on your head, whatever can get your mind wrenched away from the daily routine and focus on yourself. Imagine yourself as the clay on a potter's wheel. The edges swirl, the outside swirls, but the center is absolutely calm. Center yourself on the strongest, calmest part of your personality. The pot does not fly off the wheel. You won't get spun away by life.

5. If nothing else, sleep provides physical respite from the rigors of stress. Extraordinary amounts of sleep can indicate real depression, but naps and other minor escapes into dreamland can help you weather a stress crisis without any detriment to your mental well-being.

The key to handling stress is in how we react to pressure-filled situations. Our primitive caveman component insists that we either fight the enemy or flee from it in terror. Both of these responses to stress are unhealthy. They waste our energy in basically battling against life, which all our angst can't alter. Fighting—rage, hysterics, worka-holism—leads to heart attacks and ulcers. Flight—booze, drugs, drop-ping out—eats away at our innards and self-esteem.

To master stress we must first accept its existence as given and concentrate our efforts on working at changing the elements of life that cause the stress to begin with. Remember always that stress is a reaction. Our effective action has to be aimed at the cause—the prob-lems in our lives—or the cause will never go away.

YOU ARE WHAT YOU EAT

In Chapter Five we discussed the issue of food shopping and men-tioned some monetary reasons for not buying candy, cake, soda, and other nonnutritious foods. But there are other, more profound reasons why we should avoid them and be aware, in general, of everything we eat or don't eat. However good we may feel about our bodies—how-ever strong our feelings of mortality—the fact is that a few years down the road we're going to be struck by reality.

Eating well is, unquestionably, one of the best antidotes to the fatigue that often controls us. I'd go so far as to say that the periods of my life during which I've made a concerted effort to eat well have been among my most productive. Eating well can mean including daily vitamin, mineral, protein, and fiber requirements in our daily diets. The most natural way to get what we need is from our food. There are lots of books published that list foods and their nutritional content, but most of us have a pretty good idea of what good eating means. Good eating does not mean, for example, eating two Clark bars at 11:45 and skipping lunch. The sugar from the candy may give our brains the message that we're no longer hungry, but the rest of our body isn't so easily satisfied. We need nutrients.

Lots of people, particularly in their early twenties, simply don't feel like they have the time to properly feed themselves. There are some nutritional shortcuts that can help our bodies maintain them-selves while we're on a low-maintenance life-style, but they require some research. Adele Davis swore by brewers' yeast, which, unpalatable as it is, gives us the energy we need from breakfast without the pan and plate to scrub.

Tricks like mixing bran into hamburger meat can provide us with necessary fiber without ruining the taste of America's favorite convenience food. And virtually every vitamin and mineral can be swallowed in tablet form with a tall glass of water. A calcium pill isn't quite as nutritious as steamed broccoli or a glass of milk—two natural sources of calcium—but it does the trick.

All of these supplements, however, are precisely what they're called—supplements. We can't walk around feeling healthy if we swallow a bag of pills everyday and continue to munch on junk food. And we can't feel the emotional satisfaction that comes from smelling, cutting, forking, chewing, and swallowing a good meal after we've downed our various pills.

EXERCISE

Have you ever noticed the enormous variety of physical types of people who are in their early thirties? Some look youthful, vibrant, and healthy. Others look like they are on the fast track to middle age. When these people entered their twenties, chances are they looked much more alike. But the twenties, between the stress of setting the basic issues of life and the natural process of aging, are a tough time on bodies. But we can battle the onset of aging through diet and exercise.

The early twenties are the time to develop good exercise habits. At this point we can fight back the beginning of sagging waistlines or streamline our cardiovascular systems. It's much easier to practice preventive medicine by exercising our bodies now than to overcome excess weight and the ravages of the sedentary life in our mid-thirties or later.

Besides the terrific physical benefits, there are significant mental benefits as well. Research has shown that people who exercise have a healthier metabolism and enjoy the "glow" of physical activity for up to twenty-four hours after a workout. They are mentally alert throughout the day, have an outlet for the stress of their lives, and are able to cope with ups and downs with a better perspective.

I won't even start to prescribe an exercise program—there are so many out today. I *do* recommend investigating aerobic programs, because of their combined muscular and cardiovascular benefits. I also recommend that you choose for your basic physical activities a mixture of your long-standing favorites (riding a bike or playing tennis, for example) and new experiences in new social settings (such as racquetball or squash). The more you enjoy the exercise and keep your enthusiasm up, the better your program will be in the long run.

MENTAL HEALTH CHALLENGES

The early twenties are also a time when we face new mental health challenges. Psychologists state that depression in the early adult years is actually a sign of good mental health because it is the only response to all the changes that makes sense.

But healthy depression is a fleeting feeling. It comes on like a wave and then passes over us. The sensation is intense but temporary. Depression that lasts and lasts may be a sign that something more profound is at work than simply confronting the adult world.

The National Association for Mental Health has put together a list of ten danger signs for serious depression:

1. A pervasive feeling of hopelessness and despair.
2. Trouble concentrating, which makes reading, writing, and talking difficult.
3. Changes in sex, sleep, eating, or other major life habits.
4. Constant questioning of your self-worth; a continuing lack of self-esteem.
5. Paranoid cycle. Withdrawal from others for fear of rejection and an increase in loneliness and sense of self-worthlessness.
6. Threats or attempts to commit suicide.
7. Unrelenting irritability; hypersensitivity to what other people say.
8. Out-of-control feelings; anger directed toward everyone and no one.
9. Unshakable conviction that you are to blame for others' unhappiness, that you are always in the wrong; constant guilt.
10. Dependency cycle. Becoming heavily dependent upon other people. Feeling helpless, then guilty and angry at this helplessness.

But very few of us will confront anything like that during our early twenties. For us the mental challenges we face will be well within our coping capabilities; they will help toughen us for the tests ahead and will pass off as quickly as summer storms.

Rob Ferguson, now twenty-six, remembers well the balance between mental and physical health during his early twenties.

"I remember being incredibly overwhelmed by everything that was happening around me . . . almost paralyzed. There was a girl I thought I loved, but I couldn't allow myself to let her know my true feelings. There was work I wanted to do, but I felt so pent-up that I couldn't function to my maximum potential. And I was absolutely freaked by authority. Every gray-haired man above me was my father, and I'd just sort of smile and shuffle around being a nice boy whenever I encountered them. And, of course, afterward I'd feel angry and start coming down really hard on myself.

"One day I bought a pair of running shoes and began running. I have no idea what motivated me to start running, but it was like a magic release for me. I'd run and feel like I was Rocky. And while I was running I'd keep telling myself how tough I was. 'You're strong . . . you're powerful . . . you're tough.' It may sound crazy, but by the time I ran a few miles I'd feel physically exhausted and fantastic at the same time. All my anger would be out. I still run a couple of miles every morning before I go to work and I'm sold on it. For me it's the best therapy. And as a side benefit my body is in great shape, which makes me feel real good about myself.

The Need for Networks

IN THE CHAOS of the early twenties, as our moods swing and our lives seem to dangle perilously close to the edge, it becomes supremely important that we prize and value the support systems that form our psychological net. As we hastily throw together the pieces of our lives, never certain how long or firmly everything will hold together, we must have some people and organizations around us that have stood the test of time and that we feel certain will be around even if everything we've erected recently comes crashing down about our ears.

Sometimes, people in their early twenties actually strive for chaos. Some may feel that until now their lives have been safe and orderly and that their first moves toward independence should involve living a bit closer to the edge. Significantly, many people who move to the edge this way make a point of doing it with other people. Liz Farrel was one such person.

"I moved to Nantucket just after my junior year in college. I didn't know if I'd go back to college. In fact, I got it into my head that I'd stay in Nantucket for a couple of years, which was very disagreeable to my parents. I smoked dope for the first time. And my friends that I went there with moved around every couple of weeks. We spent nights on people's floors. We took care of ourselves. If one of us had no money, someone would cover for her. We were really scrambling around surviving.

"And none of us knew anything about the most basic facts of living. We didn't know how to cook, for example, and we'd eat the strangest things. In the winter it was cold and we really had to hustle

121

just to get enough money to cover warm clothing and a tiny apartment. We took all sorts of odd jobs.

"The thing that impresses me most when I think back to those times is that I was never afraid. In fact, things were pretty scary, being on our own that way. But none of us were ever afraid. It was more of an exciting challenge . . . an adventure . . . than anything else. I know now that the reason we weren't afraid was that we had each other. We really felt like a family. There was something romantic—not in the sexual sense—about going through insecurity with a bunch of friends your own age. We were really there for each other, almost like combat buddies. We took care of each other. And we had this real sense of pride about ourselves as a group. On our own none of us would have made it. Together we felt invincible."

The heart of our support system at the beginning of the twenties grows from the solid ties we have built up through our lives. Our families, long-time friends, churches, schools all represent stability and certainty in our world of instability and change. We could turn to them at our worst moments, because they know us best and so can help us most.

Of course, not all of us come from equally stable backgrounds. For some, our adolescent years were wildly tumultuous and found us estranged from our families and communities. Even so, during those years we developed bonds that could help us in our twenties. We may not sense the network around us, though, until we actually reach the new stage the twenties represent.

For those of us who come from a background without many built-in supports, the early twenties represent an intensification of what went before. I was this kind of person. Even though I had put myself through school and had lived with a woman and had been fired and had been bored while going to school thousands of miles from my family, my entrance into the twenties hit me with an even greater sense of being on my own. Not only the familial but also the legal supports that might have bailed me out of a total disaster evaporated. I had lost the luxury to loaf. I had the choice of buckling down to adult work or being a penniless bum. My girlfriend was friendly but she really couldn't assuage the feeling I had that the entire world was pressing down upon me.

People from more supportive backgrounds face a different experience. For them the release from their parents' dominion means a cutting loose from long-established and trusted modes of conduct and protection. They have to redefine their relationships with all the institutions that once made their lives stable. While some people might feel burdened, they are more likely to feel lost.

For both types, the vital task is to figure out a way to get the most from existing support networks around us and to begin to establish networks of our own.

What is a network? It is any group of people that provides us with a place to talk with those having problems similar to our own and a matrix for trading vital information, contacts, even money. It is, in short, a safety net for the worst drops in our newly embarked upon swing through adulthood.

In many ways, people who have had a harder time getting through adolescence actually enter the twenties with an advantage. We had no choice during our teens but to scrape together some kind of support system. It may not have been much; it may not even have been conscious, but we created some arrangement that kept us from going over the edge. For some it might have been a rock band, for others a school team or cheerleading squad or street gang or church missionary society. Or we found boyfriends or girlfriends as alone as we were and made mock adult lives for ourselves in small apartments near campus. We became for one another a pseudofamily, providing the support our real families couldn't provide.

None of these attempts merited adult attention; they were sophisticated playacting, but they did at least give us some practice in finding other people who could help us.

Twenty-year-olds from happier backgrounds have more adjustments to make to the cold world outside of their comfortable upbringings. Certainly growing up in the bosom of a supportive family and community is no drawback; rather it is a situation anyone would hope for. But it does mean that the shocks of adulthood may sting more, because they've never been felt before.

The best course for a person who has enjoyed support while growing up is to turn to the same sources he/she has always felt comfortable with. A churchgoer will feel comfortable confiding in the local priest; a person close to his/her family can always call them up or fly home in a serious crisis for consultation. An intensely social person can become involved with local organizations that keep him/her active with people like himself/herself.

In reality networks don't define themselves until we face a crisis.

Then the people we rely on step forward, the circumstantial friendships we have made separate into true supportive friendships and mere social acquaintances, almost of their own accord. We may even be surprised by who comes through in a pinch and who doesn't. To some extent, at least, our networks choose us as much as we choose them.

At first, though, for someone who has never faced it before, going out and soliciting support can be a terribly uncomfortable sensation. Before, everything came naturally, an outgrowth of childhood, as unrequiring of thought as taking a shower. Now, though, the request for help must be personal and overt, something many people find hard to accept.

Sometimes it takes a crisis to get us off dead center and into contact with our neighbors. Tim Berman recalls moving to New York from a small town in the Middle West, prepared for the cold unfriendliness he'd always heard about the city. He didn't make any effort to talk to his neighbors and they, in return, didn't do much more than smile when they saw him.

"One night I came home from work and found that my apartment had been broken into. It was just awful. The drawers were all overturned on the floor . . . my closets were stripped . . . the TV and stereo were gone. I don't know how it happened in broad daylight. But I freaked. I think I must have felt as close to a woman who's been raped as any man can. I ran into my hallway yelling, 'Help, help' and every door on my floor opened. The people were incredible. One took me into his apartment and made me some tea. Another called the police. They were as kind and attentive as anyone from my hometown could have been.

"Once I got over the shock, a few weeks later, I made dinner for all of them. And now there's a really warm feeling of neighborliness. It really makes a difference in my overall feeling of security, knowing that I have friends on either side of me."

It's best, though, if we can sketch out a network before crisis strikes. One friend of mine recalls consciously making a decision to be the pursuer in regard to friendships.

"Usually, I come out of almost every experience with a pretty close friend or two. I have my close high school friends, my close college friends, and close friends from both of my jobs, and a good friend from my apartment building. When I first began working I really felt the need for some kind of community at my office. I sat around waiting for people to ask me to join them at lunchtime, and it just didn't happen. After a few weeks of waiting and feeling lonely, I decided 'what the hell,' and went over to a woman who I'd noticed all along—she just seemed like someone I could relate to—and asked her if she were free for lunch. She was pleased that I'd asked her and it broke the ice.

"The thing I found was that most people are uncomfortable making a first approach. As long as I didn't let my ego get involved— like saying, 'People don't like me'—I was perfectly capable of making the first move. In fact, over the years I've come to admire that quality in myself, and I think other people like it too."

AT WORK

For just about all of us, as we start our twenties, the most reliable networks we can find center around institutions. We haven't had enough time yet to search out individuals who link together well around us, forming a personal chain of protection. Instead, we have to use ready-made supports for our beginning adult lives.

The most common, of course, is work. Downtrodden employees troop off to lunch or an after-work hangout to complain about how bad they have it. That's a support network. The office bowling league that let's you meet members of the opposite sex in unthreatening groups is a support network too.

As we establish ourselves on the job we also create a web of people who are going through virtually the same experience. They can help make the trip much more comprehensible and less terrifying; at least we know we are not alone in our confusion.

In the course of moving up in our professions, an awareness of networking can be especially important. Ben Good, a journalist who began his career in a summer internship after his sophomore year in college, is particularly impressed with the importance of the people he's met and formed relationships with over the years.

"I always made it a point to be associated with a newspaper whenever I could. At one point in college I had no classes on Tuesdays and two other half days free during the week. I went to work at the local newspaper. First they started me on obits, and then rewrites. We wrote all kinds of things. Then, little by little, I covered a story or did an occasional feature. I loved doing it and wanted to soak up as much as I could. I always felt that way on a newspaper. I wanted to get to know people and just absorb whatever I could from them. I watched everyone and what they did and tried to make connections so that I could learn. I tried to do it in a way that didn't make them think I was a wise guy hoping to steal their jobs or something.

"Years later, when I applied to teach journalism at Mesa College, I was asked to provide verification of having worked as a journalist. I sent a request for verification to every newspaper I'd ever been associated with and they sent letters back to me. One editor at a place where I had worked when I was twenty years old filled in the verification form and wrote in under his signature, 'He was a nice boy.' When I think that he remembered me there—after years and years—I feel very moved. Those connections mean a lot to me on every level."

School groups can remain as support networks in big cities where many grads may have migrated or in the campus community itself. These are people with whom we have long-standing relationships, whose foibles we know and whose trust we take for granted. In many instances, college buddies can help us greatly in the transition to post-college life and we can help them. However, the caveat here concerns change. Our lives and theirs may begin to diverge after school, even if we live close by. The cohesiveness of our college days may wear away and we may find ourselves looking for support to people who no longer understand us or our problems. That's simply a necessity of growth.

Personal relationships can sometimes help buffer the knocks of starting out the twenties. That is one reason why so many of us settle down into a steady relationship of some kind soon after we head into the real world. It is nice to know after a rough day in the salt mines that there will be at least one other person on earth we know will be willing to listen to us and try to understand. So much else is uncertain during this time that having one certain person can seem enormously important.

We should keep in mind, with all this explanation about networks and crises, that what we are really talking about here is friendship, in all of its many forms. We are seeking new people we can be comfortable with and trust. The process of establishing a network isn't some cold and callous spinning of a personal web. We can't accumulate supporters as if they were building blocks. Life doesn't operate that neatly.

Friendship comes in its own time and of its own accord. We should keep our eyes open for potential friends and encourage new relationships that seem strong and promising. But they won't appear on demand and we can't summon them. Genuine friendships spring up, often in the least likely places, and we have to be ready to embrace them and enjoy them when they come along.

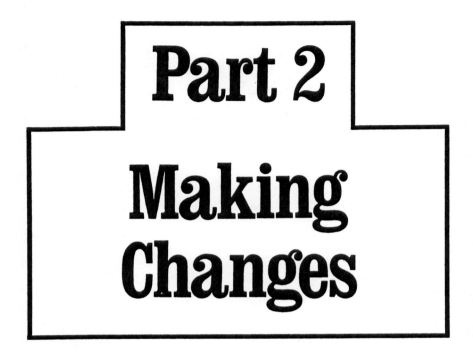

Part 2

Making Changes

A Sense of Limits

THE SECOND STAGE of the twenties begins with our first adult identity crisis. We are surrounded by a world we have created and suddenly find ourselves wondering: Is this me? Did I do this? Not only do we question the world around us, but we question ourselves for having fashioned that world.

Sometimes the impetus for this identity crisis comes from outside, in the form of our first failures. It might be job shock—the sense that all of our expectations for our first professional experience won't pan out. It might be the collapse of our first new friendship, or a failed love affair. We might glance around the apartment and suddenly realize we wouldn't bring a dog into it, let alone a new acquaintance.

In response to this crisis, we begin to tinker. We feel that if we could just fix one or two things in our lives, everything will fall into place. We look for a new apartment. We look for new friends. The second stage is a period of coming apart and rebuilding.

Just as we had to fight the urge to rush into everything during our first stage, we have to resist the compulsion to take things apart in the second stage. We need to proceed cautiously, because every choice we make eliminates dozens of other potential choices. We begin to sense the limits in our lives, as well as the enormous potential in them.

TRAPS

In the mid-twenties we can begin to help ourselves through the rough periods in our growth by thinking about and picking out destructive attitudes that are known as psychological traps. Surprisingly often, social scientists have found, we allow life to drag us into corners and pound on us. We stand there like palookas, seemingly unable to realize that all we have to do is walk out of the corner and the beating will stop. This is a trap, a point where we blind ourselves to legitimate alternatives and let a bad situation prey upon us.

Because, in our mid-twenties, we have just completed our first adult structure, the concept that we can change whenever it is absolutely necessary, the fact that life is malleable to our wills doesn't come to us naturally. It is easy to assume that the structure we have made is either good or bad, and we must stand or fall by it. So traps become common during this time and are a significant source of our disquiet in the mid-twenties. Recognizing them and ducking them before they get set in place can make this period much easier for us.

We can fall into traps in every sphere of our lives. Businesses, friendships, marriages—they all have trap potential. Consider the situation Alex found himself in fifteen years after marriage. He married Maureen when he was twenty-four and she twenty-one.

"I was just a year into medical school when I got married. If you know anything about med students you know that they don't have time for meeting people and dating. That's probably why so many of them get married early on. I met Maureen at a school mixer and thought she was good-looking. I guess I was pretty insecure about myself socially, and she made me feel like Mr. Right. She thought I was sophisticated and successful, and I liked hearing it. In lots of ways she wasn't a companion—her education was way below mine and she came from a very different kind of family—but I figured I'd be a sort of Henry Higgins.

"So, despite a lot of family opposition we got married, and I didn't have to worry about sexual outlets or anything like that while I was in school. I really thought I loved Maureen at the time and she seemed to love me. Right after school I began an internship and we had a baby. We moved to another city and things started going kind of sour. She complained that I wasn't around enough and that I didn't make enough money. So I began moonlighting to make more money and I was around less. I was twenty-six at the time, and I pretty much hated coming home. I'd somehow fallen from the pedestal, and without it there wasn't much the relationship gave me. But I do have very strong feelings about being responsible for a kid—and I didn't want to be a divorce statistic. I felt like I just couldn't admit publicly that I'd made a mistake, especially since so many people kept trying to tell me the marriage was a mistake even before it actually happened.

"When our son was sixteen months old our daughter was born. At that point Maureen went nuts. I think maybe she actually had a breakdown. She just couldn't cope with two kids so close in age. We hadn't planned on the second pregnancy, but we didn't want to terminate it—at least she didn't and I didn't feel I could make her. I worked incredibly long hours. Whenever I was home Maureen was complaining about one thing or another, so I found myself really avoiding being home. At about that point I met a woman who was a nurse. She was someone I could talk to about everything. She was smart and very sympathetic to the pressures I was under. We began to have an affair that went on for a very long time. I still see her a couple of times a year and it's more than ten years since I met her. I think she's really the great love of my life.

"But even though things were so bitter between Maureen and myself I felt like I had to stay with it. I'd invested so much time in the relationship and, even though I didn't see all that much of them, I still had two kids. If I couldn't leave one kid, I surely couldn't leave two. And what would people think if I left my wife a few months after she had a kid? I couldn't be cast in such a villainous role. So we stayed together.

"Basically, I guess I've got to admit that I'm a pretty lonely guy, even though I've got this big family around me. I keep remembering something my mother said not too long after my oldest son was born. We asked my parents to come visit us because we were really unhappy and figured they might have some advice. My mother, who believes with all her heart in the sanctity of marriage, sat in my living room and said that we were both very young. I was twenty-six and Maureen was twenty-three. 'If you don't love each other you still have a chance to find people you do love and make a life for yourselves. Now you have one child. If it's wrong, admit it and make it right, before you've lost too much of your youth. The baby will be better as a part of two happy marriages than as a part of one miserable one.' "

How can we fall into traps? How can we avoid them? Essentially, we fall into traps by being so eager and needy that we lose our rational, thinking ability. Alex didn't want to have to think about women. He wanted to get married, and he bit the bait that was easiest to get. He wanted to avoid the difficult work of self-searching that's a prerequisite to finding a mate, and he did.

Avoiding traps requires both self-awareness and an awareness that the field is lined with mines. First, you need to know what your weak spots are. What issues are so vital to you that they stop you from thinking clearly? What do you want so badly that you can't maintain any distance between it and yourself?

Second, you've got to set real limits for yourself. Alex might have said to himself, "I won't hook up with a woman until I can feel really good about myself without her." Someone entering a business venture might say, "I'm going to give myself three years. If I'm not turning a profit by the end of that time I'll chuck it and count my losses." If you don't set limits you'll continue to invest just to save face. Alex stopped investing only after his third child had been born.

Third, you've got to rely on yourself to see what you're doing. Don't look to others in your peer group for advice. If you're relying on others you'll probably keep looking until you find someone who agrees with whatever you're doing.

Finally, you've got to remain persistent. Keep reminding yourself what the trap has already cost you, and work hard at dismantling it.

In the mid-twenties it is vital that we begin to realize that down times are part of life and not a deadly reflection on us and our progress toward maturity. We have to accept the fact that every day isn't a good one, that we can't always be doing what we want to do, that even the best boxer slips a few punches. In the early twenties we experienced these sensations for the first time and had to ride through them. Now, we must learn to live through them. We don't have the luxury now to slow down under the weight of bad tidings. We must keep in mind that today's bad news will be followed by tomorrow's good news. We want more of the good than the bad, and to achieve that we have to face up to the black periods and keep our eyes forward.

If we do that, if we keep moving slowly ahead during good moments and bad, we will be ready for the challenges of the crucial third stage, the construction of our long-term adult life structures.

Work: Center of Growth

IN THE MID-TWENTIES, work often seems to be the most important aspect of our lives. Psychologist Roger Gould, in his book *Transformations,* quotes a young man named Richard, discussing a scene from Ingmar Bergman's movie *Scene from a Marriage.*

The movie shows the growth of a man from a rather self-centered and arrogant character into a more gentle, much more at-ease person. As Richard relates in Gould's book, "Well, in the last sequence he's older, softer, and for the first time in the film really he's sympathetic.

"He never got to Cleveland, he never published anything that made him famous. I mean, he had a solid career, but he never did anything to distinguish himself. And this is what tore me up. I thought, well, this guy has finally made peace with himself. He's warm, calm, attentive . . . that's what I thought.

"Here's what I felt. He's a broken man. He gave up his dreams of greatness, he's a pitiful shell of what he was and what he wanted to be. He's so mediocre—he's just given up, surrendered, let life beat him down. If I were him, I'd rather die. I just couldn't shake the fear that I would wind up a sniveling forty-year-old, living in a rented room, feeling mediocre and unimportant."

As we enter our mid-twenties, our dreams for the future clash head-on with the reality we have created in the early years of the decade. For many of us, our jobs are at such variance from what we expect from ourselves and demand of life, that our need for stability is overmatched by our craving for getting out of our rut. Many of us become serious risk takers. In our initial job search, most of us weren't anymore the risk taker than a foot soldier in a war; he was at risk to the same extent as all his unfortunate colleagues. Now, driven by desperation, some of us may hurtle from the trenches and make a valiant personal attempt to beat the odds and capture our career objective unscathed.

The practical form this daring takes can be anything from simply taking your job and shoving it, to marching into the president's office to denounce the way your boss operates the department, to dropping out of your field entirely and starting over again in a different region or a totally new way of life.

The basic question behind such actions and behind the unease with our jobs most of us feel in the mid-twenties is: Am I on the right path? Did I make a good choice?

We begin our careers working with secondhand information from books, counselors, parents. After a few years on the job we have our own store of experience to guide us. We can see inklings of the good and bad in our situations, and we have to begin to evaluate for ourselves whether the reality we find ourselves is what we expected, whether it offers us what we hoped it would, or whether our lack of information led us to make a terrible mistake that we must rectify quickly before it is too late to start again elsewhere.

Many of the people I interviewed for this book termed this initial conflict "job shock." For some, it occurred when they were fired from their first job. Others found their career expectations being trashed by the ways of the working world—they either went back for more education, switched careers, or modified their visions of the future.

There is also, in the mid-twenties, a very important adjustment that occurs between our personal lives and our careers. (Later on in this chapter we'll discuss the married versus the single employee.) We begin to sense the sacrifices our careers ask of our personal lives. Perhaps nowhere in the middle stage of the twenties is the sense of limits stronger than in this conflict between career and personal life. We must assess the expectations we have for success in our work and in our families and friendships. Crucial decisions will be made. It is a time of unique challenge and, ultimately, growth.

EXPERIENCING SKILLS FAILURE

Skills failure—being told, overtly or symbolically, that we haven't got what it takes to remain at our jobs—is one of the most shocking, upsetting, devastating experiences of the twenties. After all the toil we underwent to get into the job market and then to land a job, the thought that we might be rejected, tossed out, not good enough makes everything that went before seem like a cruel joke.

It will take months for the truth to sink in, that a skills failure in the mid-twenties is not so much a judgment of us as individuals but of how well we worked through the job hunting process the first time through. Whatever might have been said to us or about us on the first job, the fact is that any unhappiness was derived from a unique clash between us and that one job. Another job certainly would not have created the same tensions or resulted in the same conclusion. So, the vital situation to study is how and why we chose that job, why the employer chose us, and what was it about our mutual decisions that was dead wrong, so that we can avoid this conundrum in the future.

Of course, saying that is easy. Getting past the horror of being tossed out the door, which is imperative before we can evaluate what the experience means, is something else again. Like coping with death, the process takes time and can't be rushed. We must pass through the stages of coping to get the poison cleared out of our systems.

After tasting failure it's only natural to suffer emotional pain and recurring attacks of self-doubt. The bad experience has driven through our egos like a nail, and our feelings of incompetence well up from the deep corners that have been broken open by the wound. We have to try and staunch that wound and force those feelings back down where they belong. Here are some techniques that might help you face up to failing.

1. Separate I, the person, from I, the worker. On the job we all are basically performers. We are judged by how well we fill the particular role we have. And, just as Al Jolson might not have succeeded at Shakespeare, we can't succeed in all roles. The key is not to change the performer, but to change the role he/she plays.

2. When a performer fails, much of the blame rests with the director who cast him/her in the part. The boss who decided you were right for his/her job shares all blame for any failure you suffered. You couldn't know as well as he/she whether or not you were right for the

job. He/she took a chance on you and you took a chance on him/her. He/she failed, too.

3.   There is a tangible reason for what happened, separate from personalities. It might have been lack of experience, improper education for the tasks at hand, unhappiness in living or working conditions, reality shock, simple physical exhaustion after a grueling job hunt, or hundreds of other reasons. Pinpoint the specific causes of the problem. It's not you, it's your situation that is at fault in the vast majority of cases.

4.   Don't avoid thinking about the problem. Sweeping trouble under the rug won't help. In fact, it will allow fears to fester and swell. Instead you should face them four-square. Take nobody's word for what happened other than your own; your gut reaction to the experience is far more valuable than anyone else's report of the events. You should look upon the shocking encounter as a learning experience. You might even want to make a list of "Things I know now, I didn't know then."

5.   You should jump back in the career swim immediately, but not precipitously. Following a skills failure is probably the worst time to abandon a career. Just because one boss didn't like you doesn't mean you should bail out and give up on the training and aspirations you have held dear. Stick to your guns. Think long and hard before letting your feelings fall before an employer's opinion of you.

6.   You should turn to your personal support network in the crisis, particularly the long-standing buttresses of family and long-term friends. Co-workers will sympathize but they are of limited help because they are usually haunted by the thought that it might have been them. What happened to you makes them a little squeamish.

7.   You might be glad it happened now, when the stakes are smaller, rather than twenty years from now, when it could represent a wasted working life and bring on truly depressing hardships. The twenties is the decade to learn about yourself and adulthood; this is simply one of the less pleasant parts of the process.

CHANGING YOUR JOB, CHANGING YOURSELF

Even for those of us fortunate enough to be spared the rigors of being bounced from a first job, the question often arises in the mid-twenties: Am I happy with the job I have? Should I change jobs? Or should I change myself so that I am more comfortable with what I have?

The decision to stay with or change jobs, obviously, doesn't merely rest with employers but with each of us as well. This second stage of the twenties is the time when we step back after the smoke of the battle to get a job has cleared and look over ourselves and our work. The reactions we come up with are as varied as our personalities. But the pattern, the balancing of our satisfaction with ourselves and our happiness with our work, runs through each of our lives during this stage.

A good example of the kind of self-evaluation we go through and the change it can bring is Fran Lewin's decision to leave not only her job but the familiar region of the country that came with it.

"By my middle twenties I had grown up somewhat," Fran Lewin recalls. "I remember thinking one day when I decided to make the move from being a reporter to being an editor, I'm so tired of going to these boring school board meetings and staying at them until eleven o'clock, coming to the office, writing my story, getting home at one o'clock, getting back to the office at eight o'clock the next morning. When am I supposed to sleep? And for what? It just wasn't worth it.

"And I got bored with the town I was living in. I'm a big-city person, it was a small town and I knew it was time to move on. I'd been there three years. So I started writing to different papers. And the job that worked out was in Jackson, Mississippi. Why Jackson, Mississippi? I really can't tell you.

"We had three bad winters in a row and I thought, Well, maybe I should try the South. This paper flew me down there. I was not accustomed to being flown down for an interview, and I was impressed that they'd want me that much. And all of a sudden it was like, Well, why not take it? They're offering you more money; you've never lived anywhere but Illinois. Just go for it.

"It was definitely the right move. I loved every minute of it. Southerners are wonderful and I learned so much working on that paper. I moved down to Mississippi. I knew no one, and every day there was like an adventure. I met new people every day, saw new things every day, and had a great time finding out about myself.

"I was given a lot more responsibility and had to learn how to handle it. It was the best of my early working years."

While some of us move during the mid-twenties and change jobs out of a sense of expansion and a demand for new experiences, others must cope with the realization that their present job is a mistake. With all the best intentions they have walked into a snake pit. They are forced to change as the lesser evil to enduring an uncomfortable nowhere situation.

Eric Rosen found his dream job turn into a nightmare before his astonished eyes:

"I felt as though I wasn't going to go any further and that I couldn't continue where I was. I loved my job, but I was psychologically worn down by a personality clash I was having with one of my superiors there. I felt that because of that I was never in the pool of people considered ready for promotion. And, if that's the case, then it seemed to me that I had to take the initiative and go looking for something that will advance me. So, I took the leap and looked hard for a new job.

"I did the normal things, I went to a couple of employment agencies and I went out for a few interviews, but none of the jobs really intrigued me. I was turned down for one job that I would have very, very much liked to have had, which was a disappointment, but I figured sometimes you get them, and sometimes you don't.

"And then I read the Sunday *Times* classifieds and saw something that sounded just like me. I wrote a cover letter and enclosed a résumé. And, all of a sudden, found myself with a job offer. And I said to myself, Well, this is a really good job offer. Is it worth it to turn it down? And the answer really was no. So I took it.

"It's not the course I would have taken if I didn't feel pressured at my job. But considering how badly things seemed to be getting the offer looked better than what I had. At the least, it got me out from under a situation I didn't entirely understand and didn't seem able to control."

What can you do after deciding your first job was a mistake? How can you gracefully extricate yourself without harming your career, your personal relationships any more than necessary?

First, you must answer the critical question: Why did I make a mistake? You have to answer this question with specifics. There must be some reason underlying your problem, and you can't eliminate it without identifying it first. Here are some tricks for doing it.

1. List the reasons why you originally took the job.

2. List the factors you now feel you need to be happy and productive.
3. List under each heading the pros and cons of the job.

Once you know you're unhappy and why, you face a second question: Should I quit?
In making this decision, you face three crucial considerations.
  1.   Finances. You must assume when you quit that you will be without income for a long time. You can't count on anything. Even if your state offers unemployment compensation when you quit a job (as opposed to being fired or laid off), the benefits may take weeks or months to arrive and may run out before you find a new job. Vacations or holidays may slow the pace of your job hunt. Before you jump ship, you should have twice as much money in the bank as your worst scenario says you need to survive for a couple of months. Don't forget to keep your insurance coverage functioning, as well.
  2.   Job hunting circumstances. If your present job makes it relatively easy for you to job hunt surreptitiously, why quit? If, on the other hand, your search for a new job will ruin your performance and reference at your current one, perhaps a clean break would be best.
  3.   Stress. If your present job has made you so upset that you are physically ill or mentally distraught and unable to present a positive image of yourself to prospective employers, quit before you do yourself and your career severe damage.

Whatever you decide, remember that it should be your choice and not that of friends, family, or co-workers. You are the only person who truly knows how you feel. If you do quit, don't bad-mouth your former colleagues or supervisors. It's a small world, and you don't know when you may run into these people again. Keep your bitter feelings to yourself. It's better for everyone.

USING YOUR NETWORK

In the early twenties we had to rely upon the existing networks left over in our lives from the teens and childhood. Now, with a few years of work and postschool life under our belts, we have begun to establish support networks of our own.
The most valuable place for most of us to have our own support network in the mid-twenties will be at work. The incomprehensible

pattern of allegiances, the interests and personalities that flow through our working environment, should have begun to make some sense to us by now. We can pick out the people we work with who seem to have similar interests and backgrounds to our own or who are stuck in similar situations. As often as not, these associations grow up as naturally as mushrooms, through daily meetings, encounters in the lunchroom, conventions, and the other ordinary pastimes in business.

However, there is an important difference between having a passing acquaintance with a fellow worker and being part of a support network. It is the difference between a pile of unrelated strings and a cat's cradle, where every string is bound in some way to every other. A network can only come into being when people are willing to offer and ask for assistance.

If you have a situation where you genuinely need some advice or support from other workers, pick out the few you have become acquainted with whom you think may have the desire or ability to help you. Ask them to lunch one at a time. Explain to them what you need, why you have turned to them, what you were impressed by in their personalities or performance, and that you think it would be a good idea for young strivers in the firm to get together and help one another out as best as they could. If they have anything you could help with, you'd be more than happy to. Some may think you're crazy, some may resent your suggestion, but some may respond and help and then your network is on its way.

By the same token, if you see someone at work who looks like he/she could use a helping hand or a shoulder to cry on—offer one. Your colleague may be no more comfortable asking for help than you would be. Make it easy on him/her. You'll do a good deed and chalk up a favor owed.

I faced such a situation shortly after going to work for a small energy conglomerate in the South. The only female member of our department had always struck me as being aloof and virtually unaware of what was going on around her. When she was out of the office the salesmen would talk about her in the most insulting and chest-thumping fashion. I began to slide into the expected mode of behavior, but then I thought, How can I make these assumptions without even getting to know this person?

So one day I sat down at her table in the cafeteria and started talking. I made sure she knew I was married and not interested in anything but getting to know a colleague better. When she relaxed, it turned out she was quite a delightful person whose resentments of the men in the department had caused her to build up a thick shell of defenses. She was overjoyed to have someone there who didn't lear at her.

Once we got to know one another we could work together more smoothly and our projects were some of the best the company had ever seen. Later, when I began to wonder about whether I made a mistake taking my job, she was the only sympathetic ear I could find. My earlier frankness wound up bringing a benefit back to me.

Use whatever institutional networks your employer offers as well. This could be anything from a company health club to a softball team to formal corporate retreats to the country. Many companies are savvy enough to realize that workers support networks are good for morale and performance. The company's structured setup is probably too big and disparate to be a true help to you, but it's a great place to find the kind of people who will help you establish a network of your own.

You shouldn't forget your friends from school and home either. Even though you've gone off to different jobs, possibly even different states, you still have a lot in common and abiding affection for one another. Turn to those old friends when you need help or advice. Visit them if you can or at least talk to them by phone. Never assume that you are totally alone. Even if your old friends have no clout in your existing situation, their sympathetic ear can help and their outside perspective may see possibilities you have missed.

Apart from work-oriented networks, you should think about networks in your personal life. No man is an island, the cliché says, and it's quite true, as clichés tend to be. All work and no play . . . says another, and it's true too. In our mid-twenties we become so obsessed with work and careers that in many cases we sadly neglect our personal lives where networks and kindred spirits are at least as important, if not more, than they are on the job.

COMPETING WITH PEERS

When we're hunting for jobs, we are competing alongside our peers, more against the job market than against one another.

But once we're into the world of work that situation changes. Now we are genuinely competing against one another—for raises, promotions, new offices, trips, accounts, and so on. Even if we don't want to compete actively, the situation creates a competitive atmosphere, whether we like it or not, as Loretta Wolesley, a psychiatric social worker, discovered:

"When I was twenty-eight I got a promotion. It wasn't the first promotion I'd ever gotten, but it was a very significant promotion because it altered my status from a regular employee to management status. Actually, I was terribly nervous about the whole thing. I'd always thought of my co-workers as friends. There's not really a competitive atmosphere at the agency. It's not like private enterprise, where everyone is trying to outdo the person sitting next to him. We're dedicated to helping disturbed people, and we really rely on a sense of camaraderie to pull us through some disturbing work.

"But when I was offered the management position I felt tense. I didn't know how it would affect my relationship with my friends. There's a real difference between social workers and management— not just in income, but in terms of the union. I was the head representative with our union. We'd been on a long strike not too long ago. And as management I wouldn't be able to go on strike. In fact, I'd have had to cross the picket line.

"On the other hand, as management I'd be able to put into effect a lot of programs I'd been fantasizing about. I knew that I'd be able to be more effective if I were in a management position. And I was getting kind of bored with what I was doing. I needed to expand professionally.

"In the beginning things were just as uncomfortable as I had been afraid they might be. My co-workers sort of joked about it at first but I felt a real difference in their tone. I felt excluded from their activities. I felt lonely. And I also had a hard time directing them. But little by little I just did what I had to do, and they pretty much accepted me. When they *didn't* accept me as a director, I had to make them accept me, and there was some tension around that.

"I've been part of management for seven years now and, obviously, I've made the adjustment. My primary concern to this day is the quality of work and how effective I am in helping the patients. Over the years I've come to see myself as someone that can direct other professionals, and that slow realization has been very good for me. But it took time. I think it all had to do with seeing myself as an adult who could have responsibility for other adults. The more comfortable

I was with my new role, the more comfortable my people were with my new role."

Loretta's handling of her situation points up some of the cardinal rules for handling the touchy situation of competing with your peers. Here are some suggestions that might help ease the strain:

1. Keep a mental distinction between yourself and what you do. Improving your performance at work doesn't necessarily mean that you are better than those around you. It just says you have done your job well and caught a wave of luck. As your responsibilities change your personality remains the same.

2. Aggressiveness in pursuing your objectives may lead to short-term resentment at crisis points, but that will fade. You should shun hostility, which goes beyond aggression in the meanness and single-mindedness of its method. If you are hostile to those around you as you struggle to achieve, they will certainly return the favor.

3. Don't overemphasize winning and losing in your work and in your relationships with co-workers. Life is more complex than that. If you react in a limited way to your circumstances you shouldn't be surprised if the response to you is flat.

4. Praise the achievements of others, if you want them to praise yours.

5. Remember, there's room on this earth for many, many successes. Your success is entirely relevant to you, it doesn't preclude anyone else's ultimate achievement. By the same token, someone else's success is no bar to you. You may miss out on a specific job but not necessarily on the greater goals you have set for yourself.

ASKING FOR A RAISE

Lisa Marcus, twenty-six, was an associate editor in a major paperback house. Her duties, which she fulfilled admirably, involved acquiring and editing paperback originals, covering hardcover houses to pick up books for reprint, and developing packaging and publicity strategies for her books. Lisa was on her way up—in every respect except her salary benefits.

"I come from a family in which everyone works and to relax everyone works some more. We were always out doing yard work, washing the car, baking cakes for charity drives, sewing our own dresses. . . . It makes us sound like the Waltons, but that's just the way it was. When I got out of work and into publishing, I realized that my real strength was that I wasn't afraid of working hard. I may not have been brilliant, inspired, or innovative, but if there was work to be done, I was there to do it. My best friend at work, another editor, named Sally, told me to watch out, that I was going to become known as the 'clean-up woman.' Sally was right about that—I suppose that did become my reputation—but then Sally was fired along the way and I was promoted . . . although my salary only went up a wink, less than a cost-of-living increase. But who was I to complain? I was being recognized and commended—crass money concerns weren't for me to worry about.

"Then my firm launched a line of romances. The romance craze was on. Harlequin Books seemed to be, at some point, the only people moving books off the stands, and so we started a similar line of cheap, simple romances called Contessa Books. And who do you think was picked to be the countess of Contessa? Yours truly. I became editor-in-chief of the line. Because the books followed a formula—girl meets boy, girl's heart flutters, problems intervene, problems are solved—the work was mostly organizational and administrative. Geniuses need not apply was the message, and so I got the nod.

"I worked my pants off. Every day I was at the office till nine at least, dealing with free-lance writers, artists, art directors, sales staff, publicists, and so on. I was like the generalissima of the Contessa campaign. After six months of this, with the line launched and doing about as well as was expected, I asked for a raise. My employer, a smooth-as-silk patronizer who still thought of me as 'the girl,' told me I'd have to wait for the usual review period. And I had never even gotten the raise when I was given the promotion! I hate to admit it, but I backed down. Basically the problem, I later figured out, was that I didn't realize that my talents were exactly the talents that were needed to make this new line a success. I thought of myself—and let others think of me—as a drudge, when I should of presented myself as an organizational mastermind. Fortunately, another publishing firm began to 'romance' me, and when I was hired away I managed to get a sizable wage increase. But I was stupid—I should have known my worth and demanded it all along."

Knowing what you're worth is the key to securing raises. In an ideal world, an employer would come to his/her employees with increased wages and benefits to demonstrate his/her satisfaction with their performance. In the real world, this is about as likely to happen as a visit from old-time TV's "The Millionaire." People have to fight for their raises, and the way you can win this fight is with training, strategy, and determination.

The training involves thinking of yourself as a successful and marketable employee. You are special—otherwise you wouldn't be on hand. When we fully realize the difficulty that personnel people encounter filling jobs, we can begin to sense the particular worth of those of us who perform a job well. Brilliance is not the proof that must be presented when asking for a raise. In many cases, the people you are asking for a raise have no more claims to brilliance than you do. Responsibility, dedication to good performance, and professionalism are invaluable qualities to be found in employees, and if you feel you've demonstrated these, don't be afraid to remind your employer.

Strategy is the next step. Find out when the company's budget plans are being drawn up. Never go knocking on doors for a raise and allow yourself to be told that the books are closed for this year. If your employer knows that your salary will take up another $3,000 of his money in the next fiscal year, he may well opt to satisfy you instead of buying the latest Pitney-Bowes office gadget. Also, when planning strategy, remember to tell yourself that you are going to be making a pitch, a performance. You can't go into the boss's office and play with the hole in your sock while you, uh, wonder if, uh, you might, uh, possibly, if it could be managed, uh, make a little more, uh, money next year. You've got to present the boss with the facts of your accomplishments. In Lisa Marcus's case, her accomplishments were simple enough to present and strikingly impressive. She started something from scratch and she had success with it—enough said.

Determination is the third key to successful raise requests. You *are* worth that money. If you don't get it here, you'll get it somewhere else. That is not to say that you must throw the gauntlet on the boss's desk, but if you know your worth and are determined to be remunerated for it, this will be conveyed to the person controlling the purse strings.

Remember that in our society the amount we are valued is directly related to the amount we are paid. Your employers are well aware of this ratio; we, as employees, must never forget it nor must we ever be afraid of it.

MARRIED VERSUS SINGLE EMPLOYEES

The mid-twenties are a time of great career push. For most people career concerns dominate the days and nights. Young lawyers work all hours. In industries like publishing and film, business and social activities overlap and both are very important. Although a husband/wife and even a family might provide a sense of purpose and bolstering companionship during this period, they also create some conflicts. When others are working with blinders on, people in their mid-twenties with families feel the pull of outside responsibilities. Consider the case of Richard Bond:

"I was in a really difficult position. My son was born three months before I began my job as director of creative affairs for a small film production company. On the one hand, I was ecstatic about the job because it paid incredibly well and I needed the money. I felt a great need to be a breadwinner. On the other hand, I was the only person in this entire company who was married. To complicate matters, I was the only person—except for my direct boss—who wasn't gay.

"Here I was in this really high-powered situation, with people who worked until all hours and then went out drinking. Not only didn't these people have families, but they never *would* have families. They never had to think about supporting a kid through college, and I'm hustling as hard as I can, thinking about this three-month old kid and college.

"In lots of ways it was very frustrating. I knew that if I worked until ten or eleven every night and went out with agents and editors for dinner every night (I had a huge expense account) this job could be a very important career step for me. But by seven o'clock my kid was asleep. Sometimes I'd leave the house before he woke up and come home and find him sleeping and feel as though I had this hollow ache inside me. I mean, my career really was important, but my baby was only going to be a baby once. And my wife was really understanding, but I needed time with her.

"It's one thing to say, 'Well, I just have other things in my life that they don't have and I'm smart and I'll work as best as I can whenever I can'; but the fact is that they were really smart too. And if a smart person is working and making contacts eighteen hours a day, and another is working and making contacts nine hours a day, there's no question about who's going to come out ahead. They were sky-rocketing ahead, and I was running.

"Ultimately, I chose to get out of the whole race and work as a free-lance writer. I don't make as much money, but I can work late hours at home. I'm with my family, seeing to another aspect of my needs. There are plenty of times when I feel ambivalent about my choice. It's not an easy choice. But it's the choice I made. I just don't believe a marriage can work when there isn't a lot of shared time. We need intimacy. And there's no question that kids who grow up with absent fathers have problems."

Married and single workers during the mid-twenties face different sets of problems. Oddly, the problems may even vary by sex: Married men and single women make the most money as they get their careers going, while their wives and boyfriends suffer by comparison.

While he may often make more, the married man, as Richard's story attests, gets tugged in two directions. He can't be as dedicated to work as a single employee without neglecting his family. The same holds, of course, for a married woman—with added complications. If she chooses to favor work over family, the resentment she engenders could actually harm her career; whereas a man who loses himself in his work is looked on favorably.

I faced this dilemma when I worked at a major corporation in Richmond, Virginia. The job took me out of town frequently and unexpectedly. When my second daughter was born I was shipped out to Atlanta the day after her birth for a meeting. If I'd been single I might have loved all that travel, but as a father I loathed it. I had no choice but to quit and go to work for myself until I found a job that fit in with the life I wanted to lead.

Being single is not without its career problems either. Some employers steer away from hiring singles because they regard them as more "temporary," therefore less stable, therefore less desirable. As there is no law prohibiting discrimination on the basis of marital status, employers have in the past been quite blatant in telling employment agencies to look for "marrieds only."

Even when hired, singles often get shortchanged when it comes to pay and raises. One young woman in her middle thirties told me of a former boss who paid her $11,000 a year less than the three male department heads with whom she shared equal status on the organizational charts. "He said I didn't need as much money as the men, since

I didn't have a family to support," she recalled. "My reply was that my economic needs were as great as theirs, and it wasn't my fault that I didn't have a husband to supplement the family income, as those men's wives supplemented their family incomes."

These attitudes are slowly changing. According to the *Wall Street Journal,* some employers now think being single is an asset. A female middle manager on the West Coast found that being single "frees you to spend the time a woman is expected to spend to get ahead." A woman in a San Francisco securities firm said, "The company seems to think you're a lot more serious about your job if you aren't attached." The single state also allows for more travel, a prerequisite for some positions and promotions.

As attitudes shift, "behavior away from work seems of little concern to employers," the *Journal* adds. "As long as your work gets done, they don't care what you do outside the office," a single woman told the newspaper. One corporation official "attributes the easing of corporate attitudes to 'a phenomenal increase among working women who are also breadwinners.' "

The constant interplay of our personal agendas and the working world can leave many of us feeling vulnerable and afraid. But there is another sense of things, one that approaches the maturity that will mark the final stage of the first decade in the real world, which begins to develop now.

"One day at my office," Chris Pauling recalls, "I started thinking about my peers—the people who had entered my particular industry at about the same time I did. We were all at about the same level of employment in our various departments. Then I began to look at middle and upper management. I realized that these levels were occupied by a large variety of age groups. I knew then that somewhere along the line my own peer group would "shake out." Some would become successful, some would drop their expectations for success, and some would go god-knows-where.

"It was, in a way, terrifying. There really is no 'ladder of success' that you can rely on to take you up to the top. There is just a long chain of decisions, large and small, with which you make your way through. The working world is so arbitrary, so chancy, that the best you can do for yourself is define your own goals, your own standards, and achieve them for yourself, using your job as a tool—not allowing your job to use you.

"Although that was a terrifying moment, it was also exciting— I guess because I'm an optimistic person. I felt that I could achieve some kind of control over my own goals and my own inner security. Whenever things get crazy and desperate now, I try to return to that sense of myself."

Mastering Intimacy

SOMEWHERE ALONG THE line, our eyes raise from the difficult tasks of the first stage and we begin to look ahead, toward a life that promises something more than jerry-built, temporary compromises.

As we discussed in Part One, our first years in the twenties bring a transition from self-absorption to a sense of intimacy in personal relationships. As our security about the outside world increases in the second stage, our capacity to share intimacy with another also increases. We may find ourselves thinking about establishing stronger relationships with friends and lovers. We may begin to seriously think about marriage, or at least about making our present relationships more steady, more able to survive the buffeting of the world's forces.

At the same time, we are still largely unprepared for the demands and challenges of a serious relationship. Although we might have plenty of helpful friends and relatives offering advice, experience teaches us most wisely about our hearts, and we have to live through this stage.

The urge to tinker—to take apart and rebuild—comes into play now. Our dissatisfactions with the way a relationship is going will no doubt give way to the urge to drop the other person altogether. We often see, at this stage, people who break apart just because "there wasn't any other way to handle it." In many cases, this drastic solution is inevitable because we haven't mastered the subtleties of making a relationship work. But we also have to realize that we can't go through life tossing away relationships that don't work as if they were batteries that had run out of power.

152

As with our careers, the first failures in relationships in the mid-twenties give rise to several questions: Is the cause of failure me, or is it the other person? What am I looking for in a relationship? Can I find it, given the kind of person I am? We have to learn to go back and forth in our own minds, to handle seemingly conflicting questions and solutions in the hope of coming to know the truth about our goals, our ideals, and our desires. We have to come to terms with our own limitations as individuals and with the limitations of our friends and lovers. We have to learn when to give and when to take. In asking the crucial questions of the mid-twenties, we begin to define the style and substance of our personal relationships throughout adulthood.

MAKING A STRONG RELATIONSHIP

David Mace, a counselor who specializes in the problems of young adults, has developed what he calls the three essentials of creating a strong relationship. These points deal with the early days of what one hopes will become something lasting.

First Essential. "The couple must reach a mutually acceptable decision to make a commitment to grow together," Mace says. "A lasting relationship is like life; you must keep growing and changing. If you think you're going to settle down, you're going to settle down to dullness and disillusionment."

It is very important in the first year of the relationship, Mace believes, for the couple to work to adapt to each other. "People bring in to a marriage or other lasting arrangement a heap of raw materials and rake them together, and then set out to make a life for themselves."

No longer are relationships governed by the notion of suitability, as they were in the first stage. People shouldn't seek a mate who will complete them, like fitting two pieces of a jigsaw puzzle together; they must find someone who wants to grow in the same direction.

Second Essential. "In our society we are taught not to communicate," Mace says, "or to reveal ourselves. If you wear the right suit, you can get by. But in a lasting relationship you can't conceal your real self. You may be able to hide the source of your real self, but not what you really are."

The typical example is the wife who keeps the house spotless, with a husband who doesn't give a damn about dustballs but instead wants more affection or more intellectual stimulation; or the husband who works late to make more money, while his wife would rather have his company.

Third Essential. "The most crucial and difficult essential," Mace states, "is to use conflict and anger as the raw material for growth. Conflict is constructive, conflict is creative. Like the squeak under the hood of a car, conflict is a warning signal."

In our twenties we may learn about practical affairs in school, and about jobs from mentors, but we rarely learn about relationships from other couples.

"There's a marriage taboo in our society," Mace says. "You can talk about sex, but you must never talk about what's going on in a relationship. Couples associate with each other, but they won't talk to each other about their problems. That's why it may come as such a shock to find out that John and Mary are splitting up. In any other activity people get together. Tennis players watch each other play. Rose growers ask, 'How'd you get that?' "

But commitment to a permanent relationship in the mid-twenties is a dangerous undertaking. The pace of change still moves extremely quickly for us. We haven't really anchored anywhere in life yet. At any time, for any number of reasons, we could suddenly change, or our partner could, and the basis for our relationship could vanish as quickly as it arose. This isn't always the case, certainly, but it happens often during this period. And it is a possibility that should never be denied in making choices.

We constantly find ourselves testing our relationships throughout the mid-twenties. Is this arrangement more important than career opportunities or new partners? Are we building up toward commitment or are we trading-off into a relationship that doesn't have the potential for commitment.

CHANGES THROUGH GROWTH

Not only careers but internal changes can batter a mid-twenties relationship. Sometimes we grow at different rates through our twenties, our spurts and quiet periods come at different times. A couple may have been much alike when they began to get serious, but a few years later the process of growth has vastly changed one of the members of the team. The other can't keep up—or doesn't want to. Sometimes, as in the case of Melanie West, the realization that personal change has left the relationship in pieces can be deeply upsetting yet still seem valuable for growth:

"Martin and I got married while I was still in college and he was in his first year of medical school. In retrospect I'd say that one of my prime motivations for marriage was getting out of my parents' grasp. It seemed like the only way I could get autonomy was by getting married. Of course, I didn't really plan it out that way. But that was the underlying reason.

"For several years, while Martin was in school and I was working, everything was pretty much all right. I was pretty immature. He sort of was a daddy to me . . . protected me from my mean boss and that sort of thing. I think our big problems began after he was out of his residency and going into practice. He became very ambitious. He wanted to have a very status sort of practice—office on Fifth Avenue and stuff. And he wanted me to join all these doctors' wives organizations, start having kids, and settling into his idea of the good life.

"The problem was that he'd reached some place he'd been aiming for, but I felt restless. I'd been teaching elementary school to help put Martin through medical school, but it wasn't something I really loved doing. I wanted to find myself . . . as clichéd as that may sound. The more he began climbing his social ladder, the more problems we had. He didn't think I kept our house nice enough for people to come over. I didn't prepare an elegant enough dinner party. I didn't dress well enough. All that sort of thing.

"In many regards he was right. But the point is that I didn't aspire to looking and being the way he wanted me to be. By the time we split up he was twenty-eight and I was twenty-seven. Within a year he was living with the person he wanted me to be, and I was in law school. It's terribly painful for a marriage to split up after eight years. We were kids together. We really grew up in each other's family. Both of our parents were shocked, and I got the worst of their rage. What more could I want than a husband who wanted to give me beautiful things and a comfortable life?

"But in many other ways the end of our marriage was very liberating for me. It gave me independence. I didn't go right from Martin to another man. I'm seeing someone now and he feels very right, but I'm not in any hurry to marry. First, I want to feel comfortable with myself. Then I'll know who it is I want to share myself with."

We can see clearly what a breakup or shift in our relationships means for us, but it is shamefully easy to lose sight of the other person in our focus on ourselves. What should we expect of the other person in such a situation? Well, what if it were you? Would you be hurt, perhaps shocked if the shake-up came suddenly? Would you need to be reassured that you were a desirable, likable person? You'd certainly like to feel your options hadn't been closed off.

I think the best we can offer our partners when we get pulled apart in the currents of the mid-twenties is this kind of reassurance. We should try to explain carefully and gently what has happened, to praise our partner for what he/she has brought us, and to suggest new paths we think would be happy ones for that person. We shouldn't expect the situation to always be friendly, even with our best attempts, but the bitterness fades, and if we have been fair and kind the residual affection the two of us have will rise to the surface in the future. A bitter, thoughtless break, though, can leave scars that last forever.

In the happy circumstance that a relationship really clicks it can offer tremendous support against the uncertainties that the twenties bring. Steve Black found that his marriage to Susan made some of the change he went through much easier:

"Right after I got out of school I got married. We were out of school in May and I think we became engaged in June and married the following April. And Susan, my wife, has a unique ability to understand things that get me down. I would come home and talk to her about my problems, and she would make judgments that I was too emotionally wound up to make. She had an opportunity to point out things that were not necessarily wrong but where she saw room for improvement. For example, when I left the insurance business we had a family meeting and decided this wasn't really what I wanted to do. She helped me. She helped me align myself and goal-orient myself, sitting me down and going through the checklist of what I really wanted and what I didn't want; what I was confused about, and what I was certain of. She was crucial to my development. I never would have gotten to know myself so well without her."

In the first stage our personal relationships were characterized by individual questing—each of us was searching for self-perception—and we chose people who fit neatly with our quest. In the second stage our relationships became much more symbiotic, each partner taking from and giving to the other. The individuals become a team, encountering together the parameters of the partnership and its prospects for success. We haven't quite achieved the full commitment of life-long ties, but we're getting closer.

We're beginning to see limits in our relationships too. Our lives were so chaotic during the first stage that it was impossible to separate intrusions by outside factors and our own inner uncertainties. Now we can. The pressures of career decisions, parental attitudes, the desire for children all impact on our relationships, change them, perhaps even tear them apart. But still we react as a team to these pressures, whereas during the first stage they most likely would have sent a relationship reeling into oblivion. We are beginning to see that good relationships have to withstand the inevitable and recurrent buffeting of life

Real Money

THOSE WHO HAVE worked through the problems of setting up a basic financial structure in the first stage should have little trouble proceeding to the fine tuning that comes now. Those who haven't, should go back and keep at it until they get it right. It is impossible to build any kind of coherent financial setup without first establishing a simple but strong foundation. In the early twenties, the challenge we face is getting our hands on enough money to survive and finding some way to keep it from disappearing before we pay for essentials. Now the question of degree comes up—what is the *best* way to handle the money we have.

Where once it was enough to get money into the bank, now we have to decide if the bank we have is the best for us. Whereas getting some kind of credit was the question a few years back; the question now is whether we have the right kind of credit and are using it well.

THE JOYS OF BANKING

At the bank we should now look over the many options available for saving money. The typical passbook savings account, while still available, has been joined by a plethora of new vehicles for saving money. Since life, hopefully, has stabilized since our early twenties, we may now be in a good position to use one of these new alternatives. Here are some of the more common possibilities:

Term Accounts. A term is a specific period of time the bank gets to hang onto our money. In exchange for agreeing to leave it in the bank for that period, we can receive a much higher interest rate than with any passbook account, often two or three times as much interest. The variety of term accounts today is staggering. If you have a large chunk of money you can get a six-month term certificate that pays interest based on the rate paid for U.S. Treasury securities, now about 13.5 percent a year. For less money you can set up a two-year term that brings in 12 percent, or so, annually. Many banks also have ninety-day term accounts for any amounts, and the variations know no end. Comparison shop among your local banks for the term that suits your plans, at the best interest rate.

Consumer service accounts. Some financial institutions, particularly savings and loans, are trying to make their accounts more attractive by making up in service what they lack in interest. For instance, in most cities savings and loans now have available bill-paying services for savers. In this setup we can have an account at the bank which allows us to call a special number to give instruction on having our bills paid. The bank will deduct the amounts we specify and send payments where we have directed. We don't have to write any checks or keep any record. The bank does it for us. Another kind of consumer service is the electronic transfer account. In some communities the bank is actually tied into major local stores. We can give the merchant our bank card and our purchases will be automatically deducted from our account. "Look, Ma, no cash." Again the new wrinkles here are innumerable, so shop around.

NOW account. The NOW account is a new kind of bank vehicle that combines savings and checking into one. The arrangement is a little complicated, so we should approach it carefully. Basically in a NOW we agree to keep a certain minimum balance on deposit with the bank. The bank will pay us interest. We can then write checks against any additional money we want to put into the NOW account. Most banks will charge a fee for the checks, and a penalty if we cut into our minimum deposit. If everything works out right, the NOW account will allow us to write checks while every last penny of our money bears interest. If it doesn't, we can end up getting less interest for our savings than we might, and having less flexibility with our checking. Whether a NOW is for you is something you should work out in detail with a local bank.

IRA. An Individual Retirement Account allows us to stash up to $1500 per working member of the family away for our retirement. The money we put in the account comes off the top of our income taxes. But we suffer substantial penalities if we try to use any of it before retirement. You should probably begin thinking about an IRA in the mid-twenties, familiarizing yourself with it, but unless you have plenty of discretionary cash, actually setting one up will probably have to wait.

PROBLEMS WITH CREDIT

As our lives become more complicated and demanding in the mid-twenties, we may begin to run into problems with credit. It is exceedingly tempting in today's recession-ridden consumer society to turn to foolish use of credit to fill in the gaps in our economic lives. Especially in the twenties, when we are not yet hardened veterans of the fiscal wars, the lure of easy credit leads thousands of us into hot water.

How can you tell if you have credit problems looming ahead? Finance columnist Sylvia Porter gives the following warning signs for a deteriorating credit picture:

1. You are continually lengthening the repayment periods on your installment purchases and putting down smaller and smaller initial payments. At the same time, your interest-charge load is mounting just because you are sinking deeper and deeper into debt for longer periods.

2. What you owe on your revolving charge accounts also is climbing steadily. You're never out of debt to the local stores at which you have revolving charge accounts.

3. Before you have finished paying last month's bills this month's are piling in. You're always behind these days in your payments and you're now regularly receiving notices that you're delinquent. You might even get an occasional notice threatening repossession or legal action against you—something that has never happened to you before.

4. Slowly but unquestionably, an ever-increasing share of your net income is going to pay your debts.

5. You are so bedeviled by so many separate bills coming from so many sources each month that you turn to a lending institution or lending agency for a loan to 'consolidate" and pay off all your debts and leave yourself with just this one big consolidation loan to meet.

But you continue to buy on credit—thereby adding more new bills on top of your one big debt you must pay each month.

6. You are taking cash advances on your credit card to pay such routine, regular monthly bills as utilities, rent, even food.

What is a proper amount of credit to have? Generally you should never owe more than 20 percent of your annual after-tax income. An even more specific guide is to determine your discretionary earmarked for rent and other essentials—and set one-third of that amount as your credit limit. This means you will always have your basic expenses covered and an emergency fund available on top of whatever you owe.

Realistically, though, meeting such guidelines is extremely difficult for young adults today. Still, using credit too freely can suck all the joy from life and leave us thinking of little else than wiggling out from underneath the weight of responsibility. It is imperative to keep in mind that credit is not money. When we use credit, we are giving up a tiny slice of our future. We are taking home a product today by promising to give up some of our future income to pay for it, as well as the interest we are charged for the privilege. When we use too much credit we sell away our entire future for months or, in extreme cases, years. All the money we get isn't really ours. It belongs to the finance companies and credit card backers to pay for items purchased that may already have broken, been stolen, or lost their allure. When we buy with money, we buy today using what we made today. It is a far more satisfactory form of commerce for our twenties than credit.

Credit does have its place, though. It works wonders for traveling, and renting a car is virtually impossible without a major credit card. It lets us centralize our bills, which makes watching our budget easier. But it never allows us to spend more than we would if we had cash. Credit offers convenience but never, despite what the TV ads say, clout.

CONSUMER STYLE

As we begin to earn a little more, we can afford to become more selective in our purchases. We begin to think that the old rock-star posters on our wall might look nicer in the trash, replaced by a handsomely framed print. We might want our clothing to reflect our new affluence, and we begin to look for clothing that expresses the way we feel about ourselves and our work.

In the course of things, our personal preferences and dislikes begin to develop into a pattern. We are setting our own style, and it feels great! Certainly, we can't afford everything we want. But we can afford to avoid buying things we dislike. We no longer have to "make do," and so we go for what makes us happy.

Later, as we make important decisions about our careers, our friendships, and our long-term relationships, our "consumer style" will adapt as well. One acquaintance of mine recalls how he went from being a spender to a saver:

"When I first began earning some money I went nuts, I got a Visa card and I don't think there was a single electronic or consumer good I didn't want. I just started buying. I had strobe lights that blinked in time with my stereo, cameras and all sorts of lenses, colored TV . . . the works. After about a year my Visa debt was really getting up there and I began to slow down. But still I was buying a lot and really feeling like a big shot because I would see something I wanted, just whip out a piece of plastic, and take it home with me.

"When I was about twenty-five I met a woman I really cared for. She was different from a lot of the other women I went out with. For one thing, she did the same kind of work I did—she was a CPA—and she was really an equal. I didn't have to impress her, anymore than she had to impress me. I started losing interest in all my gadgets and began to think about money differently. I come from a family where having money in the bank is almost a religion. And the more I thought about my own future, the more I realized that it was important to me too.

"I don't know what tomorrow is going to mean for me. Maybe I'll be sick. Maybe Carla and I will get married and have a kid and she'll leave work for a while. If I take the money I used to spend on stereo equipment—which adds up to thousands—I'll have some sort of rainy-day shelter. I still get myself a treat from time to time—I just bought an encyclopedia set that cost $300 bucks. But I give a lot of consideration to the things that cost a good deal. I'm not what advertisers call an 'emotional buyer' anymore. I don't go shopping for the sake of shopping. If I know I need a shirt, I go, look for a sale, and buy a shirt.

"There are a lot of big things I see coming up in the next five years or so. A house, a car, a family. I want the money for those things when they happen. I don't want to spend it on junk."

BUYING FOR IMAGE

As consumers in our mid-twenties, we are prone to a conservatism as extreme as our impulsiveness as when we entered the decade. Having seen the dangers of excessive consumption and having suffered through our first round of commercial encounters, we are now ready to be choosy. We know we can be burned by a bad purchase, and our tendency is to pass unless we can be fully convinced we need the item.

However, there is one area where our impulsiveness actually increases during the mid-twenties—buying to shore up our adult self-image. Our jobs may not be what we'd dreamed of, our salaries may not be as high as they should, our apartments aren't as snazzy as we might wish. Everything in our economic lives has become a compromise and a disappointment. The pressure becomes tremendous for us to go out and splurge on something—anything—that can be just the way we want it to be. It's not so much that we really want the object, or even that we really want to spend the money. What we want to do is exert some control over our overwhelming circumstances; we want to prove that in at least one case we can get what we want.

Budgets fall and sensible plans crumble before the onslaught of intense feelings like these. And the situation is rather common among us in the mid-twenties. What can we do?

First of all, fighting the feeling off isn't always the best idea. Our egos are at stake here, the crux of the personal power we need to push our way ahead in our work and lives. Self-denial and puritanism are marvelous concepts in theory, but in practice total righteousness can leave us feeling drained and depressed.

Rather than denying the need for gratification through buying we should try to channel it into some reasonable area. For example, if you must buy something splendid, make it a suit you can use to improve your image at work, rather than a leather jacket with rhinestones on it. If you absolutely have to get out of town, why not go to some exciting place you have always dreamed about working, instead of just hopping off to the Bahamas. Perhaps you could buy a painting that could increase in value, instead of a color TV that won't.

All this is said, of course, with the assumption that your purchase, while not entirely prudent in purely financial terms, isn't downright stupid. Only you know how much money and credit you have available, and how much you can afford to spend without courting disaster. By all means, stretch your budget to the limit if it improves your battered self-image, but don't blow it up. The ramifications of ruining your finances will end up slamming your ego far more than present circumstances are.

The key to avoid destroying your fragile financial framework in your search for a gratifying purchase is to remember that what you need is something you've picked—any something you've picked. The first thing that comes to mind may be ruinously expensive, but somewhere out there must be something that will soothe your ego without blasting your bankbook. Spend a couple of weekends searching for it. You'll get the double benefit of buying something for your ego and patting yourself on the back for being a smart shopper.

Your Health:
Combating Excess

ALAN GREER, A journalist, has worked in one capacity or another on newspapers since his teenage years. He somehow always knew he wanted to be a newsman. The profession provided him with romance and challenge and he never had a second thought about it. Along with this commitment went an extraordinarily high level of energy. He worked, on the whole, sixteen hour days, sometimes as much as seven days a week.

"It's very hard for me to let up and relax. It seems like stories are breaking all the time, so I should be working all the time. A lot of people started coming down on me about being a workaholic around the time my first kid was born. My wife complained that she barely saw me. I'd get home to sleep for about five hours and then be off again. It really was taking its toll on me, on my marriage, and on my life. But I didn't know how to get out of the cycle. Finally, I didn't have to find a way. The way found me.

"I guess you could say I had a collapse. I'd had a cold for weeks and weeks that I ignored. My cough turned into constant hacking. My head felt like it weighed fifty pounds. And finally, one morning, I couldn't get out of bed. It was as simple as that. I just couldn't do it. Every time I tried I felt a pain in my chest and I'd fall back against the pillows. My wife freaked. She called a doctor who actually came to the house and told me I had, among other things, pneumonia and would have to stay in bed for a while. Of course, my impulse was to say that I just couldn't stay in bed, but there was the simple fact of my being physically incapable of getting out. So, I did what he said.

165

"After a month of real rest, normal hours, and time with my family I was pretty much better. But I was somewhat changed. I didn't feel the sort of invulnerability that I had before I got sick. I was twenty-six and had to begin making some pretty serious choices. First off, I chose to live, and that meant a real change in the way I worked. It meant that work was a part of my life—an important part, but *just* a part. I began jogging, a little bit at first and then more and more, and pretty soon began to feel good. The better I felt, the more I realized how lousy I felt before my collapse. I guess what I discovered was that I need sleep, food, and exercise. I used to be cynical about people who took care of themselves. I'm not so cynical anymore."

Health problems in the mid-twenties are not marked by any general maladies, but by specific problems, many of them related to the stress of overwork, poor diet, or general tension. Our bodies, having made the leap into adult life, are beginning to show both their weak and strong points—where they've been able to adapt and where they need to be bolstered.

Besides the exercise programs we discussed in Part One, there are two areas that should be watched carefully at this time in our lives: sleeping and drinking. In our urge to tinker with our life-styles, many people in their mid-twenties try to cut back on sleep, often with disastrous results. Drinking, as one enters the adult environment, becomes a fact of life, and now is the time to decide how we are going to handle it.

In addition, because every illness or medical problem now represents lost wages or lost time, we are growing more conscious about good health and decent living habits. As a result, during this stage many of us will think seriously about finding a good doctor for ourselves.

FINDING GOOD MEDICAL CARE

Here are some of the attributes widely cited for selecting the best possible medical practitioner:

Doctors with ties to university hospitals may keep more up to date on the latest treatments and diagnosis techniques in their fields than less well situated colleagues. If you have any specific complaint that seriously worries you, you should take them to a specialist affiliated with the nearest teaching hospital for the most authoritative opinion. There are specialists for every nook and cranny of the body, and if one spot bothers you badly, go to the expert on it.

Any doctor can practice any medical technique. A doctor whose residency was in pediatrics can claim to be a plastic surgeon, for example. So check to make sure your doctor is board certified in that field of practice. Each medical area has its own board, with standards far beyond medical school and residency for its members. Look at the diplomas on the wall or just ask before making an appointment.

You might also want to check out the diplomas in the doctor's office to see where the doctor was trained. Did the doctor attend good schools? Was the doctor trained in the United States or overseas? Does the overseas connection bother you? Is the doctor a board-certified specialist in the area that concerns you?

Don't forget that medical care is a consumer item. You are purchasing it and should be happy about your purchase. So don't neglect the mundane commercial questions: Do you feel comfortable in the office? Do you like the staff? Are they courteous and reliable? Do you feel comfortable talking with the doctor? Does the doctor give you as much time as you need? Does this professional really listen to you? Are billing and fees reasonable and flexible? Does the doctor return your phone calls? Don't be any less aggressive about doctoring than you would be for any other service.

SLEEP

Because we grow so involved with work in our mid-twenties, we may forget to sleep as much as we should. It is important both for our success on the job and for our health that we establish decent sleep habits during the mid-twenties and know something about how our bodies restore their energy and clear thinking.

We sleep in three stages, scientists say: light sleep, delta sleep, and REM sleep. REM stands for rapid eye movement, which is what happens during that phase.

Light sleep is merely a transition from being physically awake to being utterly asleep. We soon drift into deep, all-encompassing delta sleep, named for the unique type of brain waves we demonstrate while in that phase.

Delta sleep is considered to be the time of actual physical rest. During delta sleep the mind takes a break and the body straightens up the physical mess of the day before.

After a period of delta, the length of which varies from person to person and night to night, comes REM. We move more, maybe even talk in our sleep. Our dreams become symbolic and dramatic. During REM sleep the mind is thought to be going over the events of the day, ordering them, coming up with our reflective feelings toward them, smoothing our psyches by letting us dream that they happened in a way we would have liked better. We also are thought to anticipate what is coming the next day, mentally preparing ourselves for what is ahead.

We can have some influence on how much of each kind of sleep we get in a night. To increase delta sleep take a medium physical workout no later than three hours before bedtime. Don't exercise so much that it hurts and don't exercise less than three hours before sleeping.

To increase REM drink a glass of milk before going to bed. Milk contains proteins that create enzymes in the body that help sleep, and it actually increases REM sleep, although no one knows exactly how.

On days when you are dog-tired you might want to increase delta. On days that have been mentally wearing you might want to up your REM level.

DRINKING

During our mid-twenties we may also begin the characteristic American flirtation with booze in a serious way. We have drunk at school for fun and on vacations or special occasions. But now we face the challenge of drinking alongside work. Booze is the lubricant of American business. Where all other drugs, even cigarettes, are frowned on during business events, booze is tolerated, even encouraged. And the after-hours drink has become something of an American ritual.

Liquor has carved a role for itself in virtually every major event in American life. It is our tonic and our social crutch. Abusing it is far and away the worst drug problem in America.

Americans love their booze. What's a baseball game without cold beer? What's a fancy dinner without wine? What's a party without cocktails? What's good for the common cold, sex, depression, headaches, thirst, indigestion, and just about everything else, according to inaccurate but widely held beliefs? Booze.

Alcohol taken in moderation—usually less than two average-sized cocktails, beers, or glasses of wine per day—does not seem to have serious long-range effects upon behavior. Some studies even indicate that light beer and wine drinking is beneficial to health because it relaxes us.

The dangers of booze escalate quickly with amount and circumstances. Any amount taken away from home is dangerous because it will affect driving. Any amount taken in conjunction with certain other chemical substances could cause serious trouble.

You should know some basic facts about America's favorite drug:

When we take alcohol, 20 percent of it is absorbed directly through the stomach walls into the bloodstream and reaches all organs and tissues of the body within moments. The other 80 percent isn't far behind, although it is processed through the gastrointestinal system. When alcohol reaches the head, higher and higher levels of alcohol in the blood anesthetize deeper and deeper layers of the brain. The upper, or "newer," parts that store learned behavior patterns, such as self-control and judgment, are the first affected. Thus with a little alcohol in the system, some of us shed some inhibitions and become the life of the party, while others of us become depressed or aggressive. We think we're driving better, when in fact we're driving much worse. And sexually, as Shakespeare has written (in *Macbeth*), "Drink . . . provokes the desire, but it takes away the performance."

It is important to note that the rapidity with which alcohol enters the bloodstream and exerts its effect on brain and body depends on several things.

1. How fast we drink. The half ounce of alcohol in an average highball, can of beer, or glass of wine can be burned up (oxidized) in the body in about one hour. If we sip a drink slowly and do not have more than one drink an hour, the alcohol will not "jolt" the brain and will not have a chance to build up in the blood, and we will feel little unpleasant effects. Gulping drinks, on the other hand, will produce immediate intoxicating effects and depression of deeper brain centers.

2. Whether the stomach is empty or full. Eating, especially before drinking or while drinking, will slow down the absorption rate

of alcohol into the bloodstream and the body will have a more even response to the alcohol.

3.   What we drink. Wine and beer are absorbed less rapidly than hard liquors because they contain small amounts of nonalcoholic substances that slow down the absorption process. These substances have been removed from hard liquor in the distillation process. Diluting an alcoholic beverage with water also helps to slow down absorption, but mixing it with carbonated beverages can increase the rate of absorption.

4.   How much we weigh. The same amount of alcohol can have a greater effect on a 120-pound person than on a 180-pound person. Alcohol is quickly distributed uniformly within the circulatory system. Therefore the heavier person will have smaller concentrations of alcohol throughout his/her bloodstream and body than will the lighter individual.

5.   Where we drink. The setting and circumstances play a part in our reaction to alcohol. For instance, if we are comfortably sitting down and relaxed, having a drink with a friend, alcohol will not have as much effect as it would if we were standing and drinking at a cocktail party. On the other hand, if we are emotionally upset, under stress, or tired alcohol may have a stronger impact than normal. Our expectations will also have an influence. If we think we are going to become drunk, the ease and speed with which we will feel intoxicated will indeed be increased.

Another fact about alcohol usage is that chronic consumption of large amounts of alcohol over long periods of time seems to alter the sensitivity of the central nervous system to the effects of alcohol. As a result, larger amounts of alcohol are required to produce the same effect. The pharmacological term for this central nervous system sensitivity is "tolerance." Tolerance is the phenomenon common to chronic use of addictive drugs and allows the alcohol-dependent person to consume large quantities of alcohol without the impairment the nonaddicted person experiences. Another way the alcohol-dependent person differs from other drinkers is that the abrupt removal of alcohol causes dramatic behavior and perception changes known as the alcohol withdrawal syndrome.

What all this means for us in our mid-twenties is that when liquor is mixed with a volatile situation such as we face, dependence upon it can arise distressingly easy. So keep aware of your drinking habits and pull back at the first sign that your hands instinctively reach for the bottle when a crisis strikes.

Parents As Friends

"I FOUND THAT as I approached my twenty-fifth birthday my dad and I really began to get close," Bob Geffen recalls. "We'd had our problems during adolescence about haircuts and drinking and stuff like that . . . nothing really major. But we'd never really confided in each other or shown much affection. But around the time I was twenty-five my dad had a terrible heart attack and I remember thinking, I'm not ready for my father to die. It seemed like there was so much I wanted to tell him and do with him.

"During the year after his heart attack I really grew a lot. My work was going very well and I was feeling like an adult. I took care of myself, and I felt like I wanted to take care of my dad too. Once I went out to visit him on a Saturday. He was sitting in the living room in his pajamas and we watched a game together on TV. It was World Series time, and he's a great Yankee's fan. When the game was over I went over to hug him good-bye and I felt like he really hugged me a tiny bit longer than usual . . . like he didn't want to let go. I think he was saying, 'I love you' or something.

"I stood up and said, 'Now you take it easy and don't give Mom any trouble. I'll see you next week.'" And then I got in the car to drive home. Suddenly on the road I started to cry. It struck me that all during my childhood my father had said exactly those words to me when he'd leave on a business trip. I felt so moved . . . as though we'd switched positions or something. I wonder if he noticed it too?"

In the first stage of the twenties our parents faced a difficult conflict concerning our adulthood: they wanted us to get out on our own, but then again they didn't. By the second stage they have reconciled themselves to our independence, but there is still a note of their resentment of the continuing change that marks our lives. We're free now, they think, why don't we calm down? Why are we still questioning so much? Why can't we accept things as they are?

On our side of the fence we've found that we can't simply accept a mode of life our parents prepared for us. We have to test everything. We aren't in rebellion against them but, rather, are demonstrating our adult need to control our own lives.

Often our parents' response to what they see as our inability to stop rebelling is an attempt to exert renewed control over us. They cling, we pull, and sometimes the tear that results can be most severe.

We have to break cleanly, but we don't want to hurt them. What do we do?

Sandy Nelson recalls her unique solution to the problem: "I grew up in a family where everyone got married in their late teens or early twenties. And I was a real freak. I didn't want to get married. I had all these ideas about going through college, getting my own place, and having a career. Maybe I'd seen *My Gal Friday* too many times. I don't know. But I felt like there was a whole big world out there with lots of experiences and somehow marriage meant missing out.

"By the time I was twenty-four my parents were getting worried. They never gave me any encouragement for anything I did. I had an important job selling advertising space for a big magazine, I made more money than my father had, I always gave them beautiful gifts— I guess I wanted them to approve of me. But they didn't. Once they came to my apartment, looked around at all the beautiful things I had and started shaking their heads and sighing. My mother said, 'What good is it all when you're alone. At night you come home, you're alone, you sleep alone . . . what's it for?' I felt like assuring her that I didn't sleep alone *all* the time but I stopped myself. It would have been too hostile.

"When I was twenty-seven my parents celebrated their thirty-fifth wedding anniversary, and I decided that I wanted to make a party for them. I invited all their close friends and family and my apartment looked fantastic. The party was fantastic. After it was over and everyone had left, the three of us sat around with our shoes off, talking about the party. Suddenly my father said, 'You know, Sandy, we're very proud of you. You're different than any girl I ever knew, and it had me thrown for a while, but I'm proud of you.'

"Maybe some shrink would say it was screwed up for me to want that from my parents, but the truth is I wanted it very much. I began to cry and my mother came over and held me and suddenly I was laughing. I was so happy. And they started laughing and it was as though six years of tension had lifted.

"Until that point I felt very good about myself professionally, and I also felt clear that marriage and kids wasn't something I wanted, but my parents' disappointment was like a side issue that weighed heavily on me. After their thirty-fifth anniversary it changed, and I don't think it was just because I made a great party. I think they felt like they were getting older, and it suddenly struck them that at twenty-seven I was getting older too, and that I was able to take care of myself and take care of them a little bit as well. Really what bothered them all the years was that they were worried about me being taken care of. Once they let themselves see that I was very well taken care of, they relaxed."

To be free from the clinging parent, marriage expert Howard Halpern says, we have to be able to recognize the child in *them*. In doing that we can recognize some of their anxieties, see how their emotions are tied to ours, and begin to deal with them on a real level of needs—both theirs and ours.

This necessity is most clearly seen in the process of working out a relationship with a guilt-provoking parent. "It's really just a little girl or boy desperately trying to hold on to you," Halpern explains. "To see the parent in that way removes some of the power from them, and allows you to see them in more human terms."

Once you recognize the very childlike, fearful element in a parent's personality—the last thing that keeps them from letting you go completely—you can begin to talk to them as a mature adult, addressing them as another adult and aware of their ability to slip out of one identity into another. Basically, parents at this stage need to be reassured that they are still loved and still needed.

Often, Halpern states, there are parents who find it difficult to address their children on an equal footing. Among the several types he has categorized are:

The little man who isn't there. This is the very weak father. The role of the father is to help the child and the mother separate, to help the child become independent, navigate the world, and develop ethics and values. Boys may grow up seeking authority figures or be unable to assert themselves; girls may seek out weak men and try to prop them up; both boys and girls may try to make the weak father seem strong by themselves failing.

Solution: Try to react to the father's strong moments. Try to find a male figure who can act as mentor, lover, or friend, in a fatherly sense.

The despotic father. Fighting him is another way of being tied to him, Halpern believes. Daughters may end up seeking as mates either junior despots or weak men, and being unhappy with both. Or the child may surrender, such as a lot of hippies who rebelled against the system, wound up without any skills (besides rolling a joint, etc.) and so had to come home and work for daddy. Then there are the children who decide to imitate daddy.

Solution: Try to treat the despot with compassion and adult behavior, insisting on being independent without flying into tantrums or destroying yourself.

The saintly parent. This parent is not necessarily religious; he/she simply believes he/she has the absolute truth, whether in politics or just how to live one's life.

Solution: To break free, the child must find different values and act on them rationally, explaining this in a compassionate manner to the parent.

The remote, unloving parent. The danger to the offspring of a parent who withholds love is in trying to symbolically win the parent's affection by trying to win the affection of similarly remote mates. Also, the offspring may end up imitating the remote parent, or may be left with feelings of being unloved and unloving.

Solution: Realize that your parents are unloving, that it has left you with feelings of worthlessness and impaired your ability to love. Next, abandon the futile job of getting them to express that love, but seek it where it can be found. Halpern also suggests playing "videotapes in your head" of positive experiences: Those times parents were loving, or of loving experiences with friends, teachers, spouses, etc.

"I have never known anyone," Halpern states, "even those who have made much progress toward real independence, who did not regress to the old ways many times before attaining a mature relationship. It is important that you do not berate yourself for not achieving your individual identity right away."

A different problem is faced by children of divorced parents, Halpern feels. "Becoming autonomously separate from one family system is difficult enough, and now the task is suddenly much more complex," because the "offspring is confronted with . . . not simply one family system . . . but three!" That is, the mother and her new family (if any), the father and his new family (if any), and the original family formed by the now-divorced parents.

The goal of parental relations during the mid-twenties is friendship, although we don't always attain it. We enter this stage as erstwhile, rebellious underlings in our families' structure. After the smoke has cleared, our parents will hopefully be able to view us as adults. No longer their dependents, we can begin to become their friends. After all, with whom do we have more in common than our parents?

The mid-twenties should let us see our parents unvarnished by the layers of experience we shared with them as children. The fights and discomforts of this stage should scrub them away. Our parents are people. They can't control us, they have made mistakes with us, they have many faults. But they remain uniquely special for us, deserving of our adult regard and affection.

At the same time, we must assert that our relationship with them is now by mutual consent. The number of times we get together, the way we spend holidays, the form of our friendship cannot be determined by fiat. We have to listen to each other and compromise between our developing lives and their developed ones. Friendship is a two-way street, and that sensation will be new to our dealings with our parents.

By the end of the mid-twenties that street should be opening. In the final years of the decade we face the challenge of getting used to walking on it.

Part 3

Arriving in One Piece

The Rise of the Inner Self

BY THE LAST year or two of the twenties, many rules and patterns of beliefs we established during the second stage begin to break down. The conspiracies become stale. We are gripped by a need to make things right. We want more from life than we have become used to up to this part. In work simply doing our jobs and getting a paycheck no longer seems enough; we want to get somewhere important, fast. We want to have some impact. In marriage compromises that might have seemed reasonable at twenty-four now grate at twenty-eight. We don't want to waste our lives in empty relationships.

The strength of these feelings lies in our realization that we may have been straining to capture a brass ring that does not exist. It would be grand if the final emotion of the twenties were elation at our conquest of life, but it's not; instead we are filled with angst at what we see around us. The landscape remains strange, life seems beyond our total control.

Suddenly, the truth of the old verities of life begins to rise before us: Life is not fair; we are going to die; we are not always going to be happy. As psychologist Roger Gould says, "Our perception of our inner needs grows, until we must either listen to it and change our lives, or else suppress it ruthlessly. We either change careers, develop a richer personal life, or we throw ourselves into other hedonistic pursuits. In this case, either work or pleasure may be a way of escaping reality rather than obtaining it."

But, as Gould notes, "We never make enough money or have enough power to free us from our childhood traumas. We can only achieve happiness and success by facing the reality of the world, the reality of our inner beings, the reality of our spouses and loved ones, and coping with them in a realistic and adult manner."

The harsh light of life in all its unfairness etches in stark relief those unresolved conflicts of our first adult decade. We can see and feel every inadequacy, every spot where we haven't coped well, haven't paid attention, haven't grown as we should have. The more unresolved problems we have, the harder the transition into the thirties will be.

Still, it's perfectly natural to have unresolved issues at the end of the decade. No one can develop his/her life perfectly and neatly; there are always loose ends. The self-appraisal that comes with the end of the twenties, while it may be gloomy or startling, should never convince any of us that we have failed. There is no failure in self-growth.

Instead, we should see this experience as a marker thrown in our path, a point at which we stop and take stock before moving ahead. A symbolic challenge before we ascend. We have to see and accept our shortcomings and then force ourselves to find the inner strength, the inner security to say, "That's all right, I have faults. I can work on them and exist with them as I move forward."

To do this we must first get back in touch with the person we were at the beginning of the twenties. Who were we then? What did we think of ourselves? What do we aspire toward? What made us tick?

Then, we must introduce that person to the individual who now inhabits the same mental space—the person we are today. The odds are that these two people will have some serious disagreements with each other. We have to let them fight it out, argue back and forth, resolve their varying views of life and attitudes toward their accomplishments and failures. It is an uncomfortable, but necessary process because only with a unified personal vision of ourselves can we face the realizations of the thirties, the big truth that nothing life offers is permanent—not the good parts nor the bad parts, not the things we want to hang onto nor the experiences we fear we will have to endure forever. Everything shifts, everything changes, everything grows and becomes transformed—even us.

At the same time, we may be experiencing another powerful force in our lives—the loss of control. We come to know that while we might have partial command over our course, the chaotic elements of the world are strong and can intrude at any moment. So, having commandeered this great period of change in our twenties, when we have been building toward what we thought was the permanence of adulthood, we come to find that adulthood means only more changes—in many instances more difficult and more painful than those we have already endured. But we have the first journey at our backs, and we are ready to move forward.

As we look about the surprising landscape of the approaching years, we must take heart in the knowledge that adversities fade, and have courage against the certainty that good things vanish also. To do that we have to turn inward, to find deep inside ourselves the sense that we can endure through whatever kind of change lies ahead.

If we find ourselves becoming more tolerant, more "mellow," it may be because the fears and anxieties that loomed large in the ego-centered world of our twenties now seem less earth-shaking. We let them go. We know now that each and every one of our desires is not crucial to the universe, or even crucial for us. We begin to husband our personal resources and concentrate on keeping the best parts of our lives with us for as long as possible—and letting the less important parts follow their natural course. The experience of leaving the twenties is the experience of letting go, of prying our fingers from beliefs and associations we built up during the twenties, of forcing ourselves to move on.

In the mid-twenties we thought that building our lives in an orderly fashion would bring us, fully protected, to adulthood. If we were careful and prudent in choosing friends, establishing finances, shepherding our careers, everything would link together smoothly into a strong and lovely work of living art. Now, by contrast, we can see that the structure we are building floats along in a raging flood. We can grab twigs and bricks to build with, but we can't stop the flood. We are being drawn along by life totally apart from our own actions. Luck, fate, chance can scatter our rickety framework at any time. But—and here is the major difference from the mid-twenties—we now have much greater faith in ourselves, in our personal power to persevere. We see that our control of life is a chimera, but our control of our inner selves is within our grasp. We can do it. We will survive. We dragged ourselves through the twenties, we know ourselves better than we ever have before. We know the world far better too. In an almost mystic way, we know we're ready.

These internal changes manifest themselves in new attitudes toward the major components of our lives. In work, for instance, the catch-thirty transition is a time of both security and insecurity. On the one hand, we feel more competent. We have acquired some skills and we have shown we can do some jobs. On the other hand, we increasingly gain the sense that we have limits to our abilities that must be considered—wer'e not kidding around with life anymore. We must move carefully ahead in the best way for us, not according to some arbitrary preset plan.

There's a sense for the first time of vulnerability, of the potential for suffering. It is also a time when we have learned the difference between a compromise or an evasion of reality and the sense of truly dealing with the facts. We become determined to deal straight with reality.

We realize that our lives are often a mixture of contrasts and complex interdependencies, and this impacts in every corner of our existence.

If marriage suited our needs for independence and support at twenty-four, but doesn't contain the seed for genuine mutual regard of two individual adults, it may break up at this time. The career paths we chose and followed so carefully may now appear as dead-end runs to oblivion; sudden career shifts occur more often now than at any other time. We may change our appearances, move or redecorate our apartments. We may take up, or bring out in the open, long-suppressed hobbies or pastimes that ratify our adult self-images.

Our sense of finances also has changed. Money isn't any longer the adolescent toy or the tool for immediate gratification of our middle twenties. Now it becomes a barrier from life's difficulties, an insulation from inconvenience and distress. Our desire to accumulate and to make our finances stable grows precipitously during this period.

This feeling is abetted by the increased responsibilities of job and family. They demand planning, so we simply must be more aware and astute in dealing with money. Now is the period when many of us turn to professional help for our finances for the first time.

We may also be considering major life purchases during these years: a house, condominium, or investments. They too require increased attention and care to be obtained successfully.

Our social relationships, as we move out of the twenties, grow much more varied and personally idiosyncratic than ever before. We don't just have friends, we have many different kinds of friends—tennis buddies, confidantes, business allies, neighbors, lovers, out-of-town acquaintances, friends from the past, in-laws, partner-friends—an infinite variety. We are more willing to make limited bargains with others than ever before; each relationship doesn't have to be richly textured and soulfully meaningful. Having come to terms with our own personalities, we can accept others as they are.

Finally, the thirty transition brings us to an understanding of our parents. We comprehend that we necessarily are like our parents in many ways. This doesn't mean that we *are* our parents, nor does it mean that we are controlled by our parents. It means that we have inherited certain attitudes and outlooks from them, and that as adults we are capable of using them for our own purposes and ends, in our own fashion.

During this period we also must come to terms with the increasing realization that our parents will, in the future, become increasingly dependent upon us. The baton has been passed; they are gasping and falling back while we are fresh and picking up speed. Now we are no longer their equals; we dominate. For many, this is the strangest feeling of all.

Often during this period, the family undergoes a true emotional renaissance, a flowering of good feeling, or at least a catharsis that burns out lingering animosities.

Because of the depth of reevaluation and change, depression is a stepchild of the transition into the late twenties. Part of this is a healthy reaction to the fact that the compromises, the deals we made with ourselves and others earlier in the decade are breaking up. The simple wearing of time has eroded them until they can no longer function. We feel depressed in losing them, and aren't sure what will come.

STARTING OVER AT THE FINISH LINE

Other roots for the depression of the late twenties lie in pondering all we have failed to do: the money we wasted; the relationships we botched or never got started; the career opportunities we didn't take or couldn't generate; the chance to grow closer to our families we let slip by. For a time it seems as if all we did was fail, that anything worthwhile that occurred was happenstance amid the welter of negative events.

One of the crucial goals of this period is learning to forget about what we haven't done or can't do. These things are in the past and irretrievable. And brooding over them represents an unnecessary wallowing in self-pity, a misdirected ego-trip. We must face the implacability of limits. No one can live all lives, we each get just one. We need to concentrate on the one we have, not bemoan all the others that lay beyond our grasp.

INTIMATIONS OF MORTALITY

The other dark emotion that lurks around the edges of the transition into the late twenties is the gloomy shade of mortality. By this time some of our relatives and friends will probably have died. We enter the decade of the twenties convinced we are omnipotent and immortal, and leave it feeling constrained and mortal. Particularly if our parents or partner has been seriously ill or has died, we experience a sudden wrenching in our guts that one day—maybe soon—that will be us on the hospital table, in that mortuary, in the newspaper story. We now know we don't have forever.

For all of us, the sense of passing time becomes immediate, almost palpable, during this period. And that, psychologists say, is vitally important, because it is from our uneasy sense of lost time that we derive the power to achieve our adult goals.

So we buckle down and get to work: on our careers, ourselves, our lives. The urgency of impermanence propels us into adulthood. This is the ultimate positive outgrowth of the end of the twenties, a period that is, for most of us, a scary experience.

The Enduring Relationship

As Chris Clarke moved into his late twenties, it seemed that he had everything going for him. His job, as special assistant to the president of a large corporation, was one of particularly unique responsibility for a man so young. He had a good marriage, two small children, and lived in a very pleasant suburb. Certainly, there were doubts that came up now and then; he often tried to analyze his success, find out what had worked for him and why, and often he wondered if something that had come together so well and so quickly would endure.

One day his boss called him into his office and told Chris that he had resigned. The boss felt that Chris was in an excellent position to remain in his job, and that the staff was an excellent one with which to grow and become successful in the industry. Well, it wasn't that simple. A few days after the new president arrived, he fired Chris. "I don't need a special assistant," Chris was told, and then he was on the street.

All of his doubts about his career enduring came true with shocking clarity. In the first few weeks that it took Chris to rebound from his dismissal, he found that he began to rely more and more on his family for a sense of stability.

"To begin with," he says, "the insulation of the office was removed. If I was going out to make copies of my résumé, if I had a phone call about a job, my wife knew about it. She never knew when I was working what the very basic elements of my job were; now she was finding out. And she was incredibly smart about these things, although she had never worked in my business. We began to talk about a lot of things I never had talked with her about before.

"And as my insecurity about opening up my own life began to

die down, I began to become far more interested in my family, in their day-to-day workings. I remember one day, in the grocery store with my son, I thought to myself, Okay, so you're out of work, your career is uncertain . . . that can happen again and again and again, who knows? But this will endure, this will remain. And here is where you can plant the seeds of your most valuable flowers, where they can blossom and grow and where you can always turn to find real beauty.' "

We have discussed the way support networks form around us in the first stage of our twenties, and how we very often don't discover them until we are in the midst of crisis. Often it isn't until we have a crisis that we discover the inner meaning of our intimate relationships as well. And when we do begin to discover the hidden, surprising resources of our intimate relationships, we also discover the enormous power that they hold in our lives. Unlike our support networks, there is a genuine give-and-take going on here. Like Chris, we find that it isn't enough to have our lovers or spouses find out about *our* day-to-day lives—we must learn about their orbits as well. We have to begin to care about them, to nurture them, to take responsibility of our lives with them.

The process of establishing friendship involves asking for and receiving help, support, and comfort. These demands are a kind of test of the other person's character and loyalty. We do a lot of this kind of testing during our twenties, seeking out those people who offer their hand to us and to whom we can do the same.

By the decade's end we have usually found the folks who count for us and our need to test them has faded. Now we are glad simply to be with them. They are our friends because of who they are, not because of what they do for us. We are comfortable together. We know and appreciate what we offer one another.

With our friends, our spouses, and our lovers, we discover in the late twenties that we can find real security in the midst of an intimate relationship. With a person we love, trust, and care for we can find a place to be ourselves, to express our real feelings about the world, to support us in our times of need, and to bring out our own ability to be human, caring, and loving. But this two-way street is sometimes too much for some people.

By their late twenties, Carol Houseman and her husband, Bob, had bought a condo. His business was flourishing and they were on solid ground socially and financially, but their marriage was going down the tubes. "It was right when things were going so well," Carol says, "that I began to chafe in the relationship. I was submissive, my husband was protective, dominant. I had liked that at twenty, but now it bothered me."

Bob, for his part, had grown weary of working as a team with Carol in a graphics business they ran from home. "He wanted to be out on his own and get an office," Carol remembers. "I said, 'Gee, that'll be great for your business, but it'll ruin our marriage.' And he said, 'Yeah, I think it will.' "

Bob got the office and became involved with one of the women he worked with there. Carol stayed home and grew more and more sullen and angry. She was twenty-nine.

One night at home she began to cry spontaneously and said to Bob, "There's something really wrong here." He responded, "I'm leaving." Actually he didn't leave until after a year of counseling, in a last ditch effort to save things. But at thirty, Carol found her marriage in pieces.

She was stunned. "I was wearing rose-colored glasses when I got married," she says. "I thought everything would turn out well for me. Now I say, well, things may or may not turn out for me. There's no magic formula; nobody's going to insure my happiness. That's a hard wall to hit up against."

OUTSIDE PRESSURES

As we move from the twenties into the thirties the outside forces pressing in on our relationships grow stronger than ever. We are evaluating all parts of our lives, the sense of impermanence and change is everywhere. Our personal relationships are in the center of this turmoil, buffeted by each shift, shaken by each uncertainty. As this turmoil increases, guilt, anger, resentment, and unhappiness can be thrown to the surface. All the hidden surfaces are exposed. We have to find the flaws deep inside ourselves and be willing to fix them, or the relationship will crack and crumble.

Perhaps the most volatile surface issue at this stage is money. In fact, money is at the root of 50 percent of the marital problems in our country. We are confronted by the realities of working and living. We have to pay bills, make financial decisions, plan for the future. If one partner is a spendthrift and the other is an inveterate saver the reality of their differing attitudes will pull them apart.

Even when money isn't always in short supply it causes problems in relationships. What is the personal cost of getting it? Is financial success gained at too great a personal price? How will the money be used—for a home? to support children? for pleasure?

Money has become a medium for forming a life-style. Each partner wants to control the funds to those areas of life that he/she considers most important. Money becomes a heated battleground because it comes to represent the realization of our dreams.

And yet this conflict between our dreams and the means of realizing them cuts right to the heart of the intimate relationship. There is only one way to defuse this problem: being able to share our dreams, to want to nurture and care for each other's lives. We have to be able to say, "This is how we are going to make each of us happy." Although money problems have a tendency to make each partner point a finger at the other and accuse them of being selfish and greedy, in fact most of us are neither. We want to be able to love the other person, to show them how much they mean to us. And we don't expect them to give up everything to satisfy our desires.

The challenge, then, in this stage of the twenties, when we are trying to discover and work with the essential inner power of our relationships, is to have faith in each other, to trust that the other person will be true to us and true to the promises we have made to each other. As we'll see in other areas of life, money has a way of overpowering our own best instincts. But this is a time for discovering those things that endure, that have the power to keep us together.

Our careers also contribute to the volatility of the late-twenties trials. We may decide to jettison our careers and start over, forcing our partners to accompany us through sudden adjustments and deep uncertainty. We may be transferred. One partner sees the move as an advancement, a promotion. The other sees it as a forced march, an exile, a sign of utter subservience. The intrusion of our careers into our personal lives is making itself felt now: the late nights at the office, long hours of work and travel, which are so vital to success may prove a strain on our lives together.

Elizabeth Woods recalls a career decision she had to make that ended a relationship. When they met, Richard had helped her get over the shock of a business failure. He made her laugh. He wanted to get married and have children with her and she wasn't entirely adverse to the idea.

The relationship progressed, Richard and Elizabeth becoming steadily more involved and committed. But Elizabeth always held back a tiny bit. Her career as an art director in Richmond, Virginia, was extremely important to her, and her career goals were as yet unfulfilled.

"I loved him. I knew he loved me. There was no problem in the relationship itself," she recalls. "But I knew if my career took me away from Richmond his pride wouldn't let him come with me. And, in truth, I wasn't sure if I would want him to come. But I kept all that to myself. It never intruded on our life together until the very end."

As the catch-thirty transition approached, Elizabeth felt an overwhelming need to head for New York. She traveled to the city with her portfolio and made a stab at fulfilling her dream of art directing a major magazine. She kept her job hunting trips a secret from her boyfriend—if it didn't work out she wanted to be able to go home and fall back on the reliable relationship.

After a great deal of searching and string pulling, Elizabeth got her call from New York. She could be associate art director of one of the country's largest magazines. She had three weeks to get to New York and start work.

That night, when Richard came over to talk about plans for a vacation, Elizabeth couldn't bring herself to stop him from going on about all the great sailing they would do at the shore. Finally she said, "I won't be there, I'll be in New York." Richard, stunned, could hardly believe it. He stormed, cried, kicked furniture, and swore.

"I felt horrible," Elizabeth recalls. "I really cared for him. I had only avoided telling him about it because I never thought it would actually happen and I didn't want to make him sad for nothing. I should have told him, I suppose. It would have hurt less."

Although one can't really say if the relationship between Richard and Elizabeth would have lasted, their story does point out one of the biggest mistakes people make when trying to juggle careers and close relationships: They don't tell their partners what they are going through. While it may seem to us that the world of work and the world of love and friendship are two completely different realms, they meet within us—we can't break off one from the other.

It's important, then, when going through the fundamental shifts in career that often occur in the third stage of the twenties, to remain open with our partners. Share the ups and downs with them. Allow them to give support to us, and be flexible enough to listen and work with their suggestions and ideas. Again, only by bolstering the fundamental structure of our relationships can we avoid the more serious cracks and holes in them later.

THE DECISION TO HAVE CHILDREN

Unlike in our parent's generation, children do not "happen" to us as couples. We decide to have them—and more often than not decide to postpone having them. Especially in today's difficult economy, the decision to have children seems to weigh heavily on all of our resources: on our career plans, our living arrangements, and our personal relationships.

The decision to have or not have children is an extremely personal one: We often are dealing with our own childhood images, our feelings about our parents and other parents we know, and our expectations for the future. We have to examine our spouses—how do they feel about the decision. In some cases, couples who have been married for a number of years find that the decision about whether or not their marriage would produce children has never come up until one day one or the other just seems to be obsessed with the idea.

If the last stage of the twenties produces some joy and also some anxiety over the enduring quality of our intimate relationships, that same joy and anxiety is magnified many times in the decision to have children. Spouses and lovers are temporary fixtures compared to the undeniably irrevocable nature of children. I don't have any hard and fast quiz for the decision to have children—other books have been written about this subject alone. But I do want to discuss them in terms of this last stage of the twenties—the stage in which we discover our inner selves and assimilate this quality into the lives we built in the early twenties.

In this light, what will the decision not to have children mean for you? Many people have had fulfilled, meaningful lives without having children—some of them have been terrific mentors to their professional protégés. Others "adopt" the children of their brothers and sisters. Others feel no desire to have children at all, and are happy to have been true to themselves in this way. What seems to unite all these people is knowing that deep within themselves they have made a wise decision about not having children and that decision was made in a *positive* way. They have affirmed the best nature of their own lives by not having children.

And then we have the many millions who *do* have children, who have reaffirmed their lives by creating new ones. Their decision is often made on the basis of an intense desire that overcomes all rational argument; despite the fact that they aren't as financially established as they'd like to be, despite the fact that their careers are shaky, they still decide to have a child. It is perhaps one of the most self-assertive, life-affirming decisions one can make, and brings with it a hundred and one lessons about being true to yourself, your inner needs, in the midst of change, chaos, and uncertainty.

On the practical level the decision to have children has to be weighed in terms of a couple's dreams for the future. If they are a two-career couple, as is most often the case, they have to decide if it would be best for the child to have one parent stay at home during the infancy or to hire someone to care for the child. Where will the child sleep? If someone is hired to care for the child, who will be responsible for the times when childcare falls through—for example, when the "nanny" is sick or when the child needs special attention, such as being brought to the pediatrician. Later on, how will the child be educated? What are the schools like in the area where you are now living? Will you have to move?

The list is endless, and in many ways begs questions that are so far in the future as to be unanswerable. Perhaps it is wiser to focus on the more immediate concern: the pregnancy.

As a couple approaches the conception and pregnancy, they most of all have to ask questions of each other: How do you feel about this new life? Will you take care of me through these nine months (this applies to *both* father and mother)? Do we want to use a form of childbirth that involves both of us as parents?

The pregnancy also brings about subtle but powerful shifts in the relationship. As couples, we begin to sense a kind of permanence settle between us. Most of us delight in this—here at last is the refuge, the harbor for our lives. We sense changes in ourselves as well, which again revolve around the sense of permanence, and also the sense of "immortality" that begins with our own child.

Finally, then, the decision to have children is in many ways tied up in the decision to affirm or negate our own lives. Do we want to bring a new life into the one we've created for ourselves, or do we feel the need to change before having a child? It is typical of many of the decisions we make in our late twenties, but perhaps the most meaningful, and promising of them all.

GROWING TOGETHER AT DECADE'S END

Even where there aren't overt pressures pushing on a relationship, it can founder during the turbulence at the end of the twenties because we build up our own internal pressures, which can be even more destructive than those of life. Faced with uncertainty about our lives and awe at the thought of lifetime commitments, we are filled with growing doubts about our personal relationships. We begin to question: Did I do the right thing? Did I commit to the right person? Has he/she changed since we teamed up? Have I changed in ways that make the relationship anachronistic?

Many of us are also smitten during the third stage of the twenties with an acute attacks of the greener-grass syndrome. We feel as though we are surrounded by potential partners more interesting or exciting or compatible than our own. The more insecure among us turn toward younger partners to hold back the passage of time; they haven't worked out the problem of their twenties yet and don't want to leave the decade behind for whatever adult potentials may lie ahead.

Divorces and breakups are high at this time because so many of us brood on these questions. Often it seems that if we can't answer resoundingly yes to every possible doubt we feel as though we must throw the relationship aside in hopes of something better.

The questions we ask ourselves at the end of the twenties are natural and inevitable. Sometimes the answers make it clear that a relationship has run its course or never should have started in the first place. But overwhelmingly, these questions about relationships are unanswerable. How can we compare a present relationship with some potential one? How can we realistically compare today's relationship with past ones, since we and everyone we were involved with were different people then? We also seem to have lost sight of the fact that a relationship is a process; it flows, ebbs, swells. It isn't static. Neither are we nor our partners. We should attempt to pick up the rhythm of the relationship, get a sense of how it has flowed in the past to ascertain how it might flow in the future. If the flow is agreeable, not chaotic or utterly distasteful to us, the relationship can succeed.

Couples at the end of their twenties seem to separate into those who are growing apart and those who are growing together. Growing apart was a component of relationships in the mid-twenties, and I think many of us get stuck there and never leave. We are impatient with relationships, too quick to say that they aren't right for our new circumstances. When we change, we want new partners, new patterns of life.

Far preferable, it seems to me, is the idea of growing together. We always keep growing, as do our partners. But now, as our sense of commitment grows, we are willing, as we weren't earlier in life, to lash ourselves to the mast and say, "I'm going to go through this with this person." Now we can see that the storms that strain the relationships will eventually subside into a sunny period when we won't have to restrain ourselves, when we will be overjoyed to have that special person with us. In fact, the shared experience of the crisis will make every aspect of the relationship richer later on.

In today's high-stress society this attitude is particularly important for relationships to survive. Couples need to make trade-offs. We need to take the long view and realize that a woman's years of mothering infants don't preclude her return to work, while a man's time of house-keeping while she goes to school doesn't mean he has squandered his career for an apron. His time comes, her time comes; she is up, he is up; again, the sense of flow and steady change as part of a continuum comes out. A relationship is not an object, it is a process, it is always becoming.

In the shocking but brilliant movie *Shoot the Moon,* Bo Goldman has one of the characters, a bitter child of parents who are approaching a brutal divorce, ask why people break up. Her mother answers that it is like going through doors. At first the couple goes through each door together, then they begin to fall away, one going through first, the other later, until they get farther apart, lose touch. Why, asks the child, can't one wait for the other to catch up? The mother says she doesn't know.

We do pass through doors in our relationships, and we do become separated by circumstances and personal needs as time goes by. But we really should wait patiently at the door while our partners catch up. Otherwise we lose both our partners and the value of the lives we deserve to share together.

Beyond Career Survival

IN OUR EARLY twenties, when we were out looking for our first jobs, we encountered many people in their late twenties and early thirties who seemed successful, and perhaps some of us wondered: How did *they* get where they are? Will I ever make it to the point where I won't be constantly wondering if I'll have work, if my career will prosper? What is it that separates them from where I am? Now, in our late twenties, we *are* in that position, and we've discovered that it's nothing more than experience that separates the novices from the pros.

And it's quite a wide variety of experiences too. We've passed through our first jobs, job shock, skills failure, promotions, raises, perhaps a switch in careers, the numerous changes in fate and fortune that carry the average wage-earner through year after year. And we've learned that we have the stuff to survive, that we can ride the waves of change and arrive on shore in one piece.

Somewhere along the line in the late twenties, the question occurs: Now that you know you can *survive*, don't you think it's time to *really* do something with your life? At this point we begin to project ourselves well into the future. We might start making new plans, setting real goals, determining our standards of achievement for the years ahead.

The late twenties are, for the most part, a time of exhilaration— and perhaps that is why the early thirties can seem like such a comedown. We have to *use* the energy of our late twenties, build on this positive affirmation of our career goals. In the midst of realizing that we are survivors, that we are strong, we have to take full responsibility for our lives and say, "No matter what, I can make it."

If this reminds you of the invincible nature of the early twenties, you're not very far from the truth. But there is an added degree of wisdom in the late twenties that brings patience, persistence, and knowledge to the fore. The problems this chapter covers are completely new, and are based on the fact that once we've had experience with the world, we now have the chance to come to terms with it, to decide how we will handle the future, and what the future will bring.

RENEWING YOUR CAREER GOALS

Having been through the dismantling and reassembling of careers that occurs in the middle stage of the twenties, most of us are satisfied with our professions, although there may be aspects with which we are unhappy. We discover within ourselves the urge to make improvements, to succeed within the world around us. We might take on new responsibilities at work, making a bold step out in front of our peers. We might create new opportunities at our jobs, taking on tasks that broaden the range of our companies' goals. This is the age of the "young turks," those who feel their strength and want to go out and test it. What distinguishes young turks from rebels or entrepreneurs is that they remain at their places of employment, channeling their energy into corporate goals, but rewriting some of the rules in the process.

How do you know if your sense of career restlessness in the late twenties is that of a young turk? Simply, if your dreams and visions, your greatest excitement in your career, is directed toward the goals you perceive at your workplace. Do you think about advancing a new product line for your company? Do you see ways to reorganize the sales department? Are you ready to challenge your superiors with the kind of plans that say to them, "I'm terrific, and you better listen to me"?

Andi Geralds remembers the day she took her bold move: "I had been working for my company for seven years, and over that period of time had moved up the ladder, evenly but slowly. I had gathered up my own little list of complaints and grievances about our operations and policies, but they didn't really amount to anything until one day when I just—well, I just had one of those days, and I was ready to walk out the door. But I didn't, because I still liked the company I was working for.

"What I *did* do was sit down and figure out where all of my frustrations were coming from, analyze them, try to see if they had some kind of pattern. Sure enough, I was looking at a plan to remake a large segment of my own department. I deal with warehousing and deliveries, and could see that if a few things were changed, and one person placed in charge of the new operations, the company could save money and satisfy a lot of customers.

"What I had to get over was the sense that I had devised this plan purely out of my own career ambitions. I *knew* this would be good for the company, but I didn't want to hand it to them as an ultimatum. So I wrote up the plan and presented it to the head of the sales department, who had worked with me before but actually had little idea of who I was or what I was capable of.

"I wish that I could say that everything happened overnight. But it didn't. The whole plan took close to eight months to implement. But working it through the channels, making sure that the right people saw it, and finally seeing it come true carried me along. I got what I wanted, and I've also established a new pattern of working in the company. People know who I am, and I've developed a reputation as an idea person. I feel like I'm on my way."

SWITCHING JOBS

Leaving an established career path today is far more difficult than it was ten years ago. The sagging economy holds no promise of automatic acceptance in a new field. The person who decides to change may face months or even years of joblessness or underemployment before getting re-established. And this is no longer the postadolescent beginning of the decade; most of us have responsibilities now—possessions, partners, perhaps even children.

Yet, in the face of all that, the prospect of enduring a life centered around a job that simply doesn't fulfill us anymore is bleak enough that quite a few of us will brave the hardships and try to start our careers anew with the benefit of our hard-fought twenties' experience to guide us.

How can we tell if we are ripe for jumping from our career nests at the end of the twenties? I believe the key sensation is restlessness. Those of us whose career tracks have traveled smoothly alongside the development of our personal lives feel a paced calm as the twenties close, something like a long-distance runner feels when settling into his/her stride; everything seems in tune and without undue strain. But those of us whose careers have developed at a divergence from the desires of our personal lives feel intensely restless. Success at work doesn't stem the feeling; changing jobs within our career fields doesn't either. The joys we may accrue in our personal lives have a muted impact. We see the real chance of entering our thirties at nearly the same state we entered the twenties looking for work. Does this make us failures? Doesn't this mean we have wasted an entire decade?

Absolutely not. Now we know what we want. The twenties have been an invaluable time of career and personal discovery. Now we can set about the rigors of finding the right career with experience under our belts and a much deeper and more precise focus on what we're looking for than ever would have been possible at the decade's beginning.

And, sure, making the leap is risky, especially now. But staying put is false security. We know we are unhappy where we are. What kind of stability is that? We should keep in mind that each of us will ultimately fare best in the career that suits us best. If this change brings a temporary drop-off in our earnings or prestige, we will make it up in the decades ahead, when we are working in careers that suit our adult lives and bring us joy.

John Rich fled the madhouse of a major metropolitan newspaper staff as his twenties neared their close. He had entered the decade with no other hope than to reach that precise spot in his career. But life hadn't developed as he had expected it would. He was a father now, and extremely happy to be one. He began to resent the intrusions of his job on his family life. He saw that the more successful he became as a newsman the less he'd see of his children. If he ever achieved his ultimate goal of becoming a foreign correspondent, he'd see them hardly at all.

So with great reluctance he jumped off the fast track and headed to a small college in a small town, where he teaches and advises the student paper. The job was not what he had once set out to do, but it well suits the life-style he has chosen from experience. While he has his moments of wistfulness, John is basically satisfied that he made the right choice:

"Once in a while," he states, "I get into discussions with people my age, talking about here we're thirty years old and making enough money to pay the bills and not much more besides that—where have we gone wrong? Have we failed? No! Wealth is not the only measure of success. There's a lot of other things that denote far more important values. But on a day-to-day basis—buying a new pair of shoes or your kid wants to go to the movies, all that kind of thing—money is the measuring stick that just keeps jumping out at you all the time, especially when you get into the economy's problems. But that pops up in everybody's head once in a while, I suppose, and I really argue against that feeling of 'Ney, I'm thirty years old, I'm not rich yet, I must have failed.' I don't need to be a university president—I'll be very comfortable with what I've got. I made the right decision for my life."

One of the most difficult tasks in changing careers at this stage is maintaining your self-esteem in the face of a job hunt—a process that was humiliating at twenty and could be far worse at thirty.

My advice to those of us facing this bleak prospect is to get Richard Bolles's books *What Color Is Your Parachute* and *The Three Boxes of Life*. Bolles's personality-related method for paring down a job hunt and increasing its chance of success will work better with an experienced adult than with a fresh-faced graduate. We are in a better position to choose an employer than ever before. We shouldn't look for an employer to choose us. We just got rid of a career we obtained through that method. Now we are looking to bring into our lives a career that suits us. We aren't searching, we're shopping. We should act like discriminating consumers, choosing the best environment for our talents.

Cathy Arnow found the shifting times slowly erasing her career as an American archaeologist. She loved digging through the telltale leftovers of American Indian civilization. But funding vanished, and so did her job. At the end of her twenties she was forced by circumstances to start over, to hit the streets and job hunt in a totally new field.

"When I moved back to the Midwest, I was handling a number of free-lance archaeology jobs. But the funding kept getting pulled from them and I thought it's only going to get worse. Sure enough, federal funding for archaeology was cut back drastically.

"I had no work, so I thought, Okay, let me mainstream myself. . . . How do I go about that? I thought, I'm twenty-seven years old and I'm going to job interviews. What's job interviewing all about? I never really had done it. I'd gotten into the one college I applied to, I got into the grad school I applied to. I could always direct myself, hang on feet first, and jump. So I thought, Job interviewing, what a great opportunity to get into every office building in the Loop to explore new possibilities.

"I called anyone and everyone initially on a complete fact-finding search. What does one do, how many fluorescent lights are there? Any kind of information I could get.

"I networked, went to friends of friends of friends. I didn't ever look in a phone book or a newspaper, because when you look in the newspaper help-wanted ads, they want keypunch operators and I'm not even sure what one is. So I used any personal connection I could. I was pretty gutsy. I wanted to talk to one ad agency where I didn't have any connections so I just called up their president and said, 'Listen, I'm going to send you a résumé and I want you to consider me,' and he said, 'Well, I'm not the right person to be talking to,' which I knew, of course. 'But,' he said, 'talk to . . .' what's-his-name, so I called him up and I said, '*The president* said I should call you.' Of course he had to interview me.

"I loved job interviewing. I know a lot of people hate it because they take it personally—Oh my God, someone's judging me—but I was doing some of the judging. I was saying, 'Well, do I want to wake up some hypothetical December morning in yukky weather when I feel lousy, maybe I'm hung over or something, and I don't want to go to work, but I have to go to work? So where would I like to work most? Given all those adverse circumstances, what would be the place about which I'd find myself saying, 'Oh boy, I'm going to go there!' And it turned out to be the ad agency where I am now.

"I found to my surprise that in advertising I was an anthropologist. I was still doing what I'd always loved doing—I was getting to be a major snoop, I was studying people's reactions to things, I was working with people, getting them to articulate what they liked and didn't like about the product, about advertising. I just felt at home . . . and it was fun. The first time I went to a two-hour marketing meeting, I thought, Oh my God, these people can't be serious! And then I realized these people were talking about making future culture; they were talking about tangible dollars and cents with the meticulous care we used for potsherds. In that way, the meeting made sense to me.

"I had grown past my misconceptions. I'd never thought of advertising as a career because it was one of those horrible fields where people were just in it to make money—those nasty people, of which I am now one. No, I was supposed to just sort of wander around and be ethereal and artistic, and live with nice, pretty people who go to the galleries—all the things I do now still. But never in advertising. Yet now that I'm here, I love it."

GOING BACK TO SCHOOL

Some of us find, as we approach the finish line of the twenties, that we are satisfied with the careers we are in but not with ourselves. The experiences of the first adult decade have shown weaknesses in our characters or training that we could gloss over while getting started, but which we feel must be corrected for our careers to advance through the years ahead.

Barry Posen saw his career skyrocket during his twenties. As the end of the decade neared, he found himself as senior editor for a major New York book publisher. But his pleasure was laced with a cold fear—that he'd achieved his peak too early, that he had already gone as far as his training would allow him. If he wanted to continue moving, he would have to temporarily suspend his career and go back for the extra background he required.

"I was recently accepted to an M.B.A. program at Columbia University, which I'm very happy to have been accepted to and right now I'm toying with the idea of going to. It's a full-time program, which would mean quitting this job, and going back to being a 'poor' student. What I think I'm trying to avoid is plateauing at this level at this age and for the next thirty years until retirement."

In considering whether or not to go back for more training, there are several factors we must consider. By far the most important is whether or not we are committed to the career we have. In a case like Eric's, where we know we are in the career for the long haul and we can point to specific knowledge we feel will make us more productive or happy in our chosen field, then I think getting the training can pay off.

However, many times people go back for training simply to slap another badge on the boy scout banner. Others are responding to realities that don't exist anymore. The two most abused programs here are law degrees and M.B.A.'s. There still seems to be an active school of thought that holds, "When in doubt go back to law school." Others counsel that the M.B.A. is the cornerstone of any career touching upon business. On the other hand, the streets are full of M.B.A.'s who are wildly unemployed, and law graduates below the top 10 percent have to hike around looking for satisfying jobs like everybody else.

Forget the hype. View the situation as an individual. Each of us is unique and the training or retraining we need is entirely dependent upon us and our situation. If we are unhappy with our careers, we shouldn't get new training simply to open up new, unspecified opportunities. We are investing too much time and effort in a scatter-shot operation. If we are still moving forward in our careers, we should wait before jumping into new training, because we may find that our experience will make it unnecessary.

THE SPECIAL PROBLEMS
OF WORKING WOMEN

For working women the end of the twenties brings particular compelling questions. The peak of their fertility is passing, which means the decision to have children should be made soon, if ever. It is an irony of nature that the pressure for establishing a family reaches its peak at the same moment working women, like working men, are eager to build on the career base they've established and get on with the adult work of life.

Women who have maintained both families and careers during the twenties, reach this point dog tired. "For the dual career woman," says psychologist Gene Bocknek, "management of home and paid employment will often impede progress in one or the other area. But there is no evidence that psychological development is impaired. Nevertheless, personal stress may well be increased by the extensive demands on her energies."

Strangely enough, the best career decision for women to make at this point may be to slow down. Margaret Hennig, in a 1970 thesis study, followed women executives who had moved to become presidents of corporations or businesses. She found out that those women who, in their early thirties, decided to attend more to their personal lives were the ones who finally became presidents. In opting to let their careers plateau for a while so that they could devote more time to their personal lives, these women opened themselves up to human experience and became stronger. These women executives felt that that new openness was the key to bringing them into top management.

The women executives who opted to keep their noses to the grindstone never became top executives. They were too rigid, too inflexible, finally too weak to become top executives.

Of course, the problems of balancing family and career don't assail women alone at the end of the twenties. We all face the question of making time for loved ones and finding the space for everything we want to get from life.

For women who, in the past, have often had their decisions made for them by others, this is a new sensation. For men it is an old one. But for all of us it is crucial. And I wouldn't be surprised to find, if someone did a companion study, that men who managed to successfully concentrate some of their years on personal growth and sinking roots also wound up with greater career success than full-time hard drivers.

BURNOUT

The worst thing that can attack our work lives at the end of the twenties is career burnout, a condition in which we become so wound up in our work, so dedicated and intent, that we begin to fry mentally. After several years of pushing too hard and demanding too much of ourselves, we burn out. Our enthusiasm vanishes. Our good ideas no longer appear. Our overwrought enthusiasm for our careers often turns to silent loathing. We become useless to ourselves and our employers.

Burnout is becoming much more common as corporate life becomes more cutthroat and competitive. We all work under incredible pressure today because of the stringencies of the economy. It is fairly easy to feel impelled to work too hard, to try for too many fancy plans and complex business solutions. We use up our store of ability much too fast.

And success is no barrier to burnout. In fact, it is usually the ultra-successful go-getter who is the strongest candidate for burning out. This person's lack of balance and patience has sent him/her into a smoking spiral that will leave him/her gutted by exhaustion.

Burnout usually starts with stress. It is especially common in jobs where our performance is not allowed peaks and valleys; where it must be sustained at the same high level over a fairly long period of time. This unnatural pressure eats away at our confidence and our strength. We fight it until we have used up our emotional reserves and are no longer able to do the job properly. Then flight seems the only possibility. We refuse to function any longer. We burn out.

Not everybody in high-pressure jobs suffers burnout. Some people seem to understand instinctively how to pace themselves; they give just so much of themselves and no more. The key problem seems to be commitment. The more committed we are, the more we believe in what we are doing, the more likely we are to have at least some of the symptoms of burnout. It's not necessary to be disenchanted to burnout; we can love the work we do and still develop the symptoms; even love affairs suffer emotional overloads.

What's the difference between incipient burnout and a bad case of Monday morning blahs? The most common signs of true burnout include:

> Emotional withdrawal. We don't seem to have any contact with our work; everything feels as though it is at a great distance.
>
> Need for crutches. Food, booze, drugs; whatever helps us through the day or night.
>
> Personal withdrawal. Even family and friends are spurned. No one, we think, can fathom our troubles.
>
> Fantasy. We dwell on intricate plans to escape the burden: starting our own business, fleeing to Tahiti, and such.
>
> Amenities disappear. We don't even bother to make the attempt to let people think work is fun. It stinks and we let everyone know it.
>
> Exhaustion. We go to sleep exhausted and wake exhausted. Our lethargy has no relation to physical exertion.

Burnout is becoming more and more common as job pressures rise and more of us are forced to accept career compromises in the face of the economy's malaise. Once the symptoms occur there are quite a number of things we can do besides quit. Here are a few:

1. Vary work routines as much as possible. We should try to break up the established habits that got us into the rut to start with.

2. Talk even if it hurts. We should get the problem off our chests to our family and our support groups. We shouldn't be ashamed to let them know how unhappy we are. It's no sin. They will understand and can help. Being bottled up is one of the biggest problems in burnout.

3. Cultivate new friendships. All that fresh, positive reinforcement may help reconvince us that we're not bad folks.

4. Strive for perspective. Burnout arises when we feel the weight of our decisions and responsibilities too heavily. Put them in perspective: Will the universe crumble if we make a mistake? Will the sun stop spinning or the galaxies snuff out? How important is our job in the cosmic scheme of things after all?

5. Be patient. Burnout arises slowly and dissipates slowly. We wouldn't expect to play ball the day after breaking an arm. Our psyches need time to heal just like the arm does; we need to give ourselves that time by taking vacation or keeping our work loads at a reasonable level for several months. If we jumped back into high gear too quickly, we will just burn out again. And the second bout will probably hit harder than the first.

STARTING YOUR OWN BUSINESS

For those of us with the entrepreneurial spirit, the mid-twenties is often the time when we begin the long, painful financial crusade to establish our own businesses. Always a difficult, gritty process, getting together a stake for a business in the face of indescribable interest rates and an economy that is flatter than Kansas is harder than at any time since the early 1950s.

Dan Baughman went through all this and has the scars to prove it: "I wanted to start my own belt business. I had to sell everything of value I owned. I got nowhere with any banks and was forced to start on a shoestring. Even with the $1,800 I was able to scrape together I couldn't afford the buckles I needed for belts, so I started making ornamental brass barrettes, instead. I used my out-of-work friends as salespeople. Everything was C.O.D., and sometimes I had to jump in my truck and drop off orders I had just received, in person, to get enough money to cover my payroll.

"I was driven. It would have been so easy to throw in the towel back at the beginning, but I couldn't do it. I knew that businesses that start on a shoestring have moments like this and I was determined to weather them. I knew I could succeed."

There is a special turn of mind that marks the entrepreneurs among us. They have no doubts about their destiny for success, despite all logic and the most insurmountable odds. They are willing to accept the most severe privations, to humble themselves in pursuit of their goals. They simply refuse to be stopped.

The third stage of the twenties is the time when the entrepreneurs among us will most often take flight. The first adult decade provides an excellent interlude between school and self-employment for the budding entrepreneur. It allows him/her to gather experience in basic business or in a particular field of endeavor. It also provides time to make commercial and financial contacts that can be invaluable in setting up a business.

Mounting an entrepreneurial enterprise is harder today than it has been for a long time. The economy is sluggish, rents are high, and so is interest. But that won't stop entrepreneurs. The dream of owning one's own business still maintains a strong hold on the American psyche. Here are some tips for the emerging entrepreneurs in our generation:

Starting a business of our own is never, ever a reasonable solution to burnout or other stress problems. If anything self-employment is more stressful than a salaried job.

Bankers are not the young businessperson's best friend. They prefer proven money-makers for customers. Unless we have family money, the search for financial backers should be the first priority of getting started. No young business ever had too much early backing.

A marginal business plan should not be pursued. First of all, every small business should have a complete, detailed business plan finished before the first dime is spent. This should include every possible expense and only the most certain income. If that report doesn't cry out for development forget it and think of a better idea. What is marginal on paper is often disaster in practice.

Never discount the possibility of buying out an existing business. It has a proven record, it has all its equipment in place, it has an established clientele. A brand-new business has none of that.

Remember: We should never just want to go into business for ourselves. We should want to go into one specific business with good reasons to support the decisions and personal talents and training that make us competent to handle the problems that business engenders. Specifics are the difference between success and failure in self-employment.

Planning a
Financial Future

THE LAST STAGE of the twenties is a time to make plans for our money. Our scrounging days are, for the most part, over. We have the talents and connections to keep money coming in, and now we are going to really do something with it.

Even in today's turbulent economy we can still make strong, sound plans for our financial lives. It is, of course, impossible to establish the entire financial framework for the next thirty or forty years in the few years remaining in our twenties. But we *can* lay the cornerstone—in fact, we must.

"Young adults have to make plans," counsels Gale E. Hurley, professor of business administration at Canada College in California. "And the first big investment they should make is buying a house. Even today with high mortgage rates, it's still the way to go. It still beats just about everything."

Of course, today when we speak of "a house" we could mean any number of alternatives—a condominium, a co-op, etc. But overall, we are still speaking of the stability, roots, permanence, and solid foundation that a house represents. In many ways, this investment is a perfect reflection of the inner stages of growth in the late twenties— we are willing to sink our resources into *ourselves,* to have faith in the ambitions, dreams, and aspirations we hold for the future.

In the late twenties we also begin to think seriously about having our money *make* money for us. We start to consider financial planning, investing, and other strategies. Later on in this chapter, we'll discuss that bewildering financial supermarket.

WHAT IS A HOUSE?

In the old days—twenty years ago—a house was pretty easy to define. A couple of bedrooms, a yard, a driveway. Now, though, it is possible to own any number of different kinds of abodes, with the traditional house being just one of them. With house prices being far out of the range of many of us, we may want to consider one of the alternatives to get the benefits of ownership without breaking our financial backs.

A *condominium* is a building in which each tenant owns the space his/her apartment occupies, while the builder owns the lobby, land, and other public spaces around the building. A condo allows us to gain a financial stake in our living space; this financial interest is called equity. It means that when we move out we can sell our apartment and keep whatever profit we make. In a rental you get nothing, no matter how long you have lived there.

A *co-op, or cooperative,* is a building that is owned by the tenants. Each tenant owns shares in the private company that owns and operates the building. He/she pays "rent" to the company and fees for maintenance. Each tenant own his/her apartment in the sense that he/she can sell his/her share of the company to someone else and pocket the profit.

Time-sharing has become a fairly popular way for people to own a vacation home and enjoy the financial benefits of ownership. In this plan you pay a fee for time and maintenance and have the use of the house for a specified period each year.

FINDING A HOUSE

Finding a place to buy today can be incredibly difficult. There are plenty of places for sale just about everywhere in the country. However, many are put on the market at inflated prices. And, with the difficulty in getting reasonable mortgages (see below for grim details) they can't find buyers. Still, the owners and their agents don't want to undersell the house so they keep the advertised price high. This means that a house hunter today will have to do a lot of hard looking and hard bargaining to find a good place. My advice is:

- Figure out how much you can afford to spend for a house (the experts estimate about two times your annual salary). Look at places priced at that amount. Try to talk the owner down.
- Begin the search with real estate agents. They can show what is typical at the price and can direct you around various neighborhoods.
- Check the local newspapers and see if there are any ads that seem to offer more than the agents said to expect. Follow them up.
- Ask everyone you know to keep an eye out.
- Don't limit your search to one neighborhood; don't carry preconceptions; judge the whole package—locations, layout, security, etc. —for each dwelling.
- Remember, if one deal falls through or suddenly turns unappealing, there is *always* another good place out there.

BUYING A HOUSE

"I'd like nothing more than to have a place I own," says Elizabeth Woods, "but with rents in New York as high as they are I can barely cover my apartment, let alone put money aside for buying a house or a co-op. It's as frustrating as can be. Here I am, a respected professional in my field. I make what sounds like a good salary, and I can't buy a place of my own. It's ridiculous."

Finding a house today is tricky. Buying one is becoming almost impossible. Money is tight, which means that banks and savings institutions demand high down payments, often as much as 30 percent. At the same time, interest rates are astronomical, making payments for any house breathtakingly high, even with the large down payment.

What can you do? Plan ahead through the twenties for that day. We have suggested a number of financial ideas for the twenties; following them makes it much more likely that you will have enough money around at the end of the decade to make house buying at least conceivable. By the end of the decade you should:

Have had a savings account for at least seven years, increasing by at least 10 percent each year.
Have kept a budget each year and checked it for accuracy.
Have purchased whatever basic insurance coverage you need.
Have paid rent on several different apartments.

Have established credit of some kind and, if you have had credit problems, resolved them.

Have bought and paid off an automobile.

Have had several different positions at steadily increasing salaries.

Have become familiar with your bank's operation and know at least one officer.

Have joined a credit union at work, if there is one.

All these experiences and habits contribute to your ability to get together the money to buy a house. Those who have skipped some of them should rectify the situation as soon as possible.

Even with these factors, though, buying a house is no snap these days. Just as a home used to be a home, a mortgage used to be a mortgage. Now, mortgages come in a bewildering variety, as financial institutions try to squirm around high interest rates without completely closing off the possibility for most of us to buy. Some of the current wrinkles include:

Fixed rate mortgage. The old standard. The bank tells you how much interest you'll pay and for how long. Your monthly payment stays the same for the length of the loan. Fixed rate mortgages are very hard to get now.

Variable rate mortgage. The interest rate on the loan goes up (or, theoretically at least, down) as the prime rate (which is what the big banks charge their corporate customers) varies. Monthly payments go up (or down) accordingly. This is the kind of mortgage most banks offer now.

Short-term mortgage. The payments are figured as if the mortgage will last the normal thirty years, but the loan is actually for five years. At that time, you must refinance the loan (at, presumably a higher interest rate) or pay it off. A pretty spooky way to buy.

Shared equity. In the place of some interest or a part of the down payment the bank agrees to share with you any profit you get from sale of the property. They become your partner in owning the house.

If it sounds confusing, it is. David Stoneman characterizes his search for a compatible house and mortgage as "the most bewildering experience of my life.

"We wandered around for months, from one suburb to another. We must have met ten thousand real estate men. Nothing worked out. Whenever we saw a house we liked, either the price was ridiculous or the commute was horrendous, or something.

"Finally, we found one we liked and went to the bank. The bank in the city where we have always saved told us to get lost. They weren't offering any mortgages anymore. The real estate agent suggested a suburban bank that quoted us an interest rate so high we felt like we were doing business with loan sharks.

"So, instead of wandering to real estate agents, we now wandered among banks. Finally we found a bank that would give us a variable rate mortgage if we could come up with a 35 percent down payment. We went back to the owner and got him to pick up that extra 10 percent on the down payment as a second mortgage.

"We are now flat broke and have enormous payments every month, but we have a nice house, a good place for our children to grow up and play, and we figure we invested in our future.

"Anyway it will probably get worse before it gets better. If we had waited we might not have been able to afford it at all."

NEW FACTORS IN YOUR BUDGET

After you have purchased your dream house, you should go back and rebudget your financial life. Houses bring with them many more expenses, particularly unexpected ones, than apartments. Your budget will need greater flexibility and a deeper reserve fund to get you by. Among the new factors your budget should include are:

Taxes and the related paperwork expenses of ownership.
Maintenance and repair fund for all major appliances and equipment. Figure about 10 percent of the original cost per year. This seems to provide enough money to get fixed whatever broke.
Painting every couple of years.
Payments for decorating and furniture purchased when you moved in.
Lawn or any other service work on the house: exterminator, cleaning, etc.

Keep in mind that everything having to do with a house generally comes a la carte. Anticipate your likely expenses and save for them. It's a terrible feeling to have a broken furnace in mid-winter and no money for the repairman.

MONEY MAKING MONEY

Conceptually, money shifts again in the third stage of the twenties. In the first stage it was a means of survival; in the second it was a tool for becoming established. Beginning in the third stage and continuing on through life, money takes on its own character. It has substance and life; when placed together in great enough amounts it reproduces itself in the form of profits and interest. In the late twenties we begin to think more about the ways in which our money can be used to make money.

As a result now is the time to look into investments. Once the first choice for investment would have been the stock market, but today the safer, if less exciting, money market accounts at banks have taken the lead. These accounts require large initial deposits placed in the bank for fixed periods. They pay very high interest rates, about 12.5 percent in June 1982.

Investing in stocks or bonds requires a great deal of information. We must keep abreast of business and the performance of the many different financial media. It takes time and savvy. The potential return is great, but so are the risks. It is much more entertaining than a bank account, but it's not insured by the federal government.

Some young professionals are turning to collectibles as a median kind of investment. They are buying paintings or rugs or dozens of other goods as investments, hoping that prudent selection will result in rising prices, and eventual profit.

Richard J. Roll and G. Douglas Young, investment advisers for young professionals, are avid supporters of collectible investments. The essence of their advice is to invest in durable goods whose value will increase along with inflation. An important corollary is "the pleasure principle" of buying only things that we will enjoy, and things we know about. For example, you shouldn't buy paintings if they all look like finger painting to you; only buy paintings you genuinely like to see hanging on the wall, and only if you know what's good and bad about art.

They point to a study showing that people who bought homes because those were the kind of houses they were going to live in actually made more money through appreciation than speculators, who bought houses strictly as investments.

USING A FINANCIAL PLANNER

Because the problems we face at the end of the twenties are more complicated and the stakes are so much higher than they have been we shouldn't automatically assume that we are our own best planners. We may need an expert to help us pick out the best path through the financial thicket.

But what does a financial planner do? Obvious from the title is that he/she plans finances for clients—but that's nothing that any reasonably bright person couldn't do by himself/herself. The advantage of a good financial planner is that he/she *doesn't* work alone: He/she assembles a team of experts in business and money matters and uses that pool of wisdom in analyzing each client's financial position, helping to define his/her goals, and designing the most reasonable and cunning plan of attack to realize those goals in light of the client's finances.

What do we get for our investment in a financial planner? Most of the major firms offer service packages that are similar in size and scope. They usually include analyses of our present finances, our lifetime goals, retirement planning, and estate planning. Like independent financial planners, the firms utilize banks of lawyers, accountants, and consultants to hammer out a client's financial strategy. Naturally, the higher the price, the more comprehensive the service. For $5,000 or $6,000 we get a bound report of 100-plus pages, monthly statements, personal interviews, and telephone advice. The no-frills economy package offered by some investment firms, on the other hand, is almost entirely computer-generated.

Judging whether the financial planner we find is going to be able to provide the cost-effective service we are looking for has to remain an individual decision. There are plenty of planners out there who don't know the difference between participating insurance and par-value stocks, but there are many others who can tell exactly what we need to know—for a price, of course. The only way to be sure is to conduct our own investigation before we decide to trust our new financial planner. But, as with any dividend-paying investment, there's always some risk involved.

Keep It Simple

As CONSUMERS, WE have most of the basics of life in hand by the end of the decade. Now our interests turn toward tools and symbols. We buy in two distinctly different fashions. To begin with, we want tools that will make our lives easier or more enjoyable. Tools that can save us time and money. The other kind of item that appeals to us now is the small, but often expensive, expression of our self-regard, a tangible extension of our adult attitudes and interests. It could be a fancy coffee maker or a snazzy European bicycle, jewelry, or any other item of the highest quality and glitter.

Why would we want such items now? First, we can finally afford them and want to prove to the world and to ourselves that our sweat and tears in the career arena have not been for naught. These small "gifts" remind us that, whatever our failings, we *still* like ourselves.

In both tools and symbols another buying pattern emerges at the end of the twenties—the quest for value. We have accumulated enough consumer experience in the first adult decade to become true critics of what we are offered. When we go shopping now, we examine wares with a *Consumer Reports* mentality. Point by point we rate each item: Will it do what I want it to do? Is it the best there is? Does it include features I will pay for and don't need? Do I really need it now or could it wait? How does it compare with all the other products of a similar nature? How do I like the store, am I confident of what they tell me?

We are thinking, in all areas, of the long term as we move out of our twenties. And we don't want to buy things that won't last. We are also rigorously appraising all parts of our lives and discarding whatever seems deficient or failed. By the same token, we don't want to add any physical goods that don't measure up to our more stringent standards.

"I don't simply go out to buy something anymore," says Eric Raven. "I used to, but now when I need a shirt, I'll go to the store specifically for a shirt and I'll shop until I find the best shirt for the money. I don't want to throw my money away on things I don't need or things that won't last. Sometimes it seems to me as if everything I did during my twenties was in haste and everything I bought was shoddy. I want to break away from that."

AROUND THE HOUSE

The end of the twenties is often a time for major redecoration around the house. First of all, it frequently marks the time when we move into our first long-term adult abode. In the process of moving from one place to another, an incredible amount of the junk we collected through the twenties will disappear.

When my wife and I made the big late-twenties move from our long-standing base of operations in the South to New York City, we found ourselves throwing as much into the trash as we did into the boxes. We couldn't fathom where some of the oddball items we found had come from. As often as not, we couldn't even recall who had bought them or why.

And even with the serious goods, a change in attitude came about during the move. The rocking chair that had always seemed so quaint now seemed merely shabby. The big scratched government-issue desk that had represented so much to me when I'd first started using it, now seemed like a dinosaur. Bookshelves, of which we'd once been so proud, now appeared rickety and tasteless.

We moved to New York with just hard-core personal possessions. And once there, we looked over the situation and got rid of still more stuff. We sold or gave to relatives possessions that previously we would have rescued from a burning building. Now, in the context of a settled adult life, they didn't seem so important. In fact, they cluttered up life.

CLOTHES

In clothing, by the end of the twenties, less is more. We have defined, during the swings of the previous years, a limited arc of personal style that works for us. Whereas we first swung widely from jeans to *Dress for Success* pinstripes or from Yves St. Laurent to preppie coordinates in our ventures to find an image that made us feel good and seemed to foster our goals in life, we now know the kind of clothes we like.

Since we aren't testing the fashion waters so much anymore, we buy fewer clothes at the end of the decade than we did at the beginning, but we get more mileage from them because we can plan our wardrobes far more carefully.

Generally, the bulk of our wardrobes during the third stage is dictated by the style of our professions and where we live. If we have settled into the banking business, we buy many more suits than a musician would. If we work in the Southwest, its informal style means that most of our wardrobe, even for working, is composed of leisure wear.

In any case, we have gotten past the point where we and our clothes are synonymous. Clothing is nothing more than what we use to cover our backs. We realize that everyone in our profession dresses basically the same and that it is the person in the clothes that will make a difference in our careers. We have become comfortable enough with our friends and partners so we can be confident that they like us for ourselves and not for what we're wearing.

As a result, our clothing purchases become more relaxed. We are more likely to hunt for bargains and shop at discount or outlet stores, because the symbolism of being in the right place has diminished. On the other hand, we know what we can rely on, so we are willing to pay a little more to get it. We may have one store that knows us well enough now to be an actual aid in selecting the right clothes.

Over all, clothes have diminished in importance. At parties, people in their twenties talk about clothes with personal passion. People in their thirties don't.

LESS IS MORE

In keeping with the sense that less is more at this time, we are willing to have fewer things, as long as what we have do their jobs well. At the opening of the twenties, we might have stretched our finances to the breaking point to get a fancy stereo with everything on it. Now, perhaps, we know we don't listen to the radio very much. All we want is a simple turntable, but it had better be the best turntable our money can manage.

We simplify a great deal now in what we buy. My wife and I bought an enormous and incredibly doodad-strewn refrigerator in our mid-twenties. Its very complexity was a sign to us that we could afford grown-up goods. A few years later, we gave it to a relative. We no longer wanted a complicated appliance; all we needed was something to keep food cold. We wanted our machines simple, so they wouldn't intrude on our lives beyond the limited sphere of their operation.

The same goes for cars. A twenty-year-old wants an automobile with prestige. A thirty-year-old wants a car that is effortless. An Austin-Healy, with its fancy lines, speed, and sleekness is a twenty-year-old's fantasy car. For a thirty-year-old the fantasy is the utterly dependable, quiet, long-lasting Mercedes-Benz. The Austin seems like a ridiculous and impractical extravagance. .

We want fewer items overall. When I was twenty-five my kitchen was filled with so-called labor-saving devices. I had gotten one of everything, figuring I'd use it at some point. By the end of the twenties I knew I never would and fully 80 percent of that junk in the kitchen disappeared. Now there is a coffee maker, a blender, and a can opener. Period. My life requires no more, so why clutter things up?

In the end one rule can sum up purchasing during the third stage of the twenties: If life doesn't demand its presence, who needs it? And if we need it, let's keep it simple.

Guarding Your Health

DESPITE ALL OUR best efforts, as we move across the adult decades, our bodies will gradually lose their punch. But our personalities, our minds, our spirits face no such limitation. The more we work on them, the stronger they become, decade by decade. Our attitude toward health as the thirties nears becomes one in which we want to make sure our bodies stay well enough so that they don't interfere with the more important program of developing our inner selves.

We aren't over the hill, but we are atop it. We can see our bodies entering the curve of change that heads toward middle age, becoming more susceptible to the slings and arrows of life. Our bodies begin playing little tricks on us, even though we remain fit and feel wonderful—small twinges, a touch of fatigue, a hint of soreness, intimations of the changes that lie ahead.

LIMITS

One of the realizations that comes at the end of the twenties, is that there are physical goals we have that will never be attained. If we always held hope for "getting into shape" at some point in the future, we now realize that the shape we have is what we're going to have for a long time; we'll never be Mr. or Miss Universe. We'll never play Wimbledon or climb Mount Everest. Each of us sees physical limits that will form the outline of his/her body's adult life. The degree of physicality will differ with each individual, but the fact of limits is universal.

None of this is to say that we don't feel marvelous and look great at the end of the twenties. For many of us, this is actually the best physical period of our lives.

We may receive a few tangible signals, though, of the changes to come. Our joints may be a tad stiffer now after exercise. Our doctors may decide its time to start taking EKG tests at our checkups to keep tabs on our slowly aging hearts. Men will begin to see every extra ounce they eat settle along their belt lines, while women will see it on their thighs. We get more backaches.

On the job we find we can't abuse ourselves as freely as we once did. The all-nighters of the early twenties aren't fun anymore; our bodies rebel at the thought of being pushed that hard. They sense the need to husband resources.

BREAKING BAD HABITS

This is a prime time to change long-standing bad habits. Perhaps it's because we are entering the thirties and sensing that we have to nurture our bodies for the "long haul." It can also be because these bad habits, some of which date back to our teens, are beginning to take their toll.

It's not easy to toss off bad habits—major industries have developed around Americans' passions with dieting, trying to kick the smoking habit, and failure to exercise properly. But we *can* psyche ourselves up for a major overhaul. The four major "bad habits" in the United States are smoking, overeating, excessive drinking, and lack of exercise. Here are a few steps in the right direction:

Remove the source of temptation. If you smoke, stop carrying cigarettes around. If you don't exercise, stop taking the elevator to your office or the bus for those ten blocks to your home. Walk instead.

Exercise regularly. Make it a part of your life. We all complain that our schedules are too full to fit exercise in, but with a little innovation, you can make exercise a part of your day. How do you get to and from work? What do you do at lunchtime? Is there a half hour in the morning you could pull free for a workout? Give it a try, and commit yourself to doing it regularly.

Particularly with smoking and overeating, try to substitute some other pleasure for the bad habit. If you have to have something in your mouth, try diet sweets or diet colas. There are plenty of low-calorie munchies around—popcorn, fruit, for example—that can satisfy your cravings. If you can, substitute a walk around the block for your cravings.

Join a group to help you. Weight Watchers for overeaters. For smokers there are a number of programs, but the American Cancer Society sponsors free clinics on the evils of smoking that would scare the wits out of anyone. Your drinking might not classify you as an alcoholic, but Alcoholics Anonymous might be a good stop if you're beginning to worry about yourself. And finally, any YMCA or YWCA, and the occasional public school gym, has a fitness program for adults. Getting in with a group of peers can be just the trick for working out your problems.

THE IMPACT OF LIFE-STYLE

In addition to cutting down on bad habits, we should think seriously now about treating our slowly aging bodies more carefully. We can begin to feel how our life-styles are having a greater impact on our bodies than ever before. If we are serious outdoorsmen our bodies will begin to reflect that fact through ruddy skin and gnarled hands. Some of us might develop banker's paunch or salesperson's nervous ticks or executive's worry wrinkles. The kind of life we each lead begins to write itself on our bodies as the thirties unfold.

No life leaves our bodies pristine—even happy people get laugh lines. So we shouldn't think about changing our lives in search of a free lunch. But we might want to think of the life we have planned in terms of what it will do to our bodies. Will a high-stress existence furrow the face and chew up the stomach? Will physical labor put the body through its paces but allow the brain to wander about aimlessly? Will we be using many cosmetics, wearing tight clothes, standing up, sitting down, eating a lot, drinking a lot, traveling a lot? All of these factors will affect our bodies in the years ahead, depending upon what we do with them.

Realistically, the possible impact of our life choices is probably not a big enough factor to get many of us to change course abruptly.

But thinking about them can allow us to attempt preventive maintenance as we move through the thirties and forties.

If we know we are going to have to cope with a lot of stress we can begin now to read about the problem, to exercise in ways that reduce stress, and to eat foods that help keep stress levels low. Similarly, if our profession traditionally produces overeaters, we should start developing good dieting habits now. By thinking about the physical problems inherent in our lives we can head them off or blunt their worst effects.

For all of us there are some general tactics that will help our bodies best weather the slow shift into middle age:

Exercise.   It is simply a medical fact that the more a body part is used, the slower it wears out. By keeping our bodies widely active, we preserve them, keep them fresh and responsive. Besides, exercise in most forms is fun, and in today's fitness-conscious society it's a great way to make friends and business contacts.

Eat less.   Almost all of us have grown up eating too much. Now research links too much food, especially too much red meat to all kinds of health problems later in life. We should eat sparsely and make as much of our diet vegetarian as we can manage.

Keep up outside interests.   It may not sound like a health regimen, but all work and no play truly makes Jack a heart attack candidate. Pleasurable noncompetitive activity releases tension, which, if allowed to build up short circuits our circulatory system.

Get angry.   The closer anger comes to its initial cause the better. As we face the problems ahead we should get them out of our systems quickly. Bottled-up tension must find a resting place, and wherever in the body it rests will suffer.

Pay attention to our bodies' signals.   We should never go by other people's rules. Our bodies will tell us what is most unhealthy for us, and that factor will vary widely among individuals. What is a healthy and vibrant life for one person could literally kill another. We shouldn't fight our bodies. If we are constituted to live a quiet life, so be it. We shouldn't try to force ourselves to be high-powered. It isn't healthy.

FEELING WELL VERSUS FEELING PERFECT

During the twenties we had an arbitrary and not particularly fair standard for judging our health—perfection. If we didn't feel great we worried. When we were down or dreary or tired we felt there must be something wrong. Anything less than bursting vigor seemed unnatural.

During the third stage, we shift toward acceptance of the fact that adult reality operates on the principle of feeling well rather than feeling perfectly. Some days will be better than others. Our responsibilities will require that we plug along on the good ones and the bad ones. We can't expect to feel at our peak all the time; in fact, we will come to see peak days as a pleasant surprise. Most of the time we will feel well but not super, and will simply have to get on with business regardless.

That, of course, is easier said than done. I try to use positive reinforcement to get myself through the slow days. I'll promise myself a leisurely lunch if I get a personally set quota of work done in the morning. Also, I've gotten to know my pattern of ups and downs well enough that I can anticipate to some extent when I'll be slack; I set up my work schedule accordingly. For instance, late afternoon is habitually my worst time. I should probably live in a country with siestas. As a result, I never schedule crucial meetings or deadlines for late afternoon. I'll put the meeting in the morning and clean up the loose ends that result from it in the afternoon.

Other people have come up with their own strategems for handling the inevitable variety of moods and energies that comes with adulthood. It's a good subject to discuss with our peer groups.

We should always remember, though, that sometimes we are just plain sick or too distressed to get anything accomplished. When I was first starting out I used to fight against these situations. I would refuse to admit I was sick and I would force myself to sit at the desk when I was completely discombobulated. It never worked. Now I keep insisting I will come through right up to the last minute; I won't prejudge my illness or incapacity to function in the face of a problem until the moment of actually going to work. Then I pause and give myself a serious mental rundown. If I truly feel that the circuits aren't clicking,

I go back to bed or turn on the TV. I've found that I end up wasting more time trying to fight with my body than I do if I pay attention to it.

THE SHOCK OF MORTALITY

"I went into my twenties feeling like a bull," Bill Geffen recalls. "I just had so much energy . . . I was so strong . . . there was nothing I couldn't do. I didn't want to miss anything. Then I noticed a lump in my testicle. I tried to ignore it for a while. My girlfriend noticed it and she began to freak out. She kept after me until I made an appointment with the doctor, and sure enough, it was cancer.

"I had all the standard reactions to the cancer—it can't be; why me?; I want to die. But most of all I felt like my body had turned against me. Here I was thinking there was nothing my body can't do, and zap . . . it starts saying, 'There's lots you can't do. In fact, you may not even be able to just plain live.' Then, as I began treatment, I started getting philosophical. If I had wanted a test for my manhood, I couldn't have asked for a better one. Maybe I could have been dropped down in a minefield in Vietnam. That would have been about as good. But my illness was a real test of my independence. When you think you might die, no matter how many loved ones are around you, you're basically alone in your body.

"After a year of treatment I was announced cured. My girlfriend left—sickness didn't fit into her white-knight scenario. White knights don't get sick until they're seventy. After they've made a lot of money they die and leave you a big life insurance policy. I was terrified. What was going to happen to me. My work seemed a million years ago.

"Then I realized, Who cares, you're alive. What are you complaining about? Everything fell into a different perspective. I think I learned after being in the hospital that there is no such thing as failure in this life. There are people who try and people who don't try. All of a sudden, all of the tears and all of the things I thought would bring security were gone. What if I try something and it fails? What's the worst thing that could happen?

"As I saw it, the worst that might happen would be that I'd be out of a job. If you spend a year in and out of a cancer floor you don't know if you're going to live or die. I mean, a job seems pretty insignificant after that, you know."

The first signs of mortality are shocking. By the time we reach the end of our twenties, we no doubt have had some brush with the finality of life—either with ourselves or someone close to us. As in Bill Geffen's case, the encounter can bring about a range of emotions, from denial to acceptance, but most of all we find ourselves, as in much of the third stage, feeling the close bond between our inner selves and the flowing river of life.

What we do in reaction to these shocks also ranges widely. Some of us will take on a rigorous program of physical activity. We'll begin to work out, to watch our health carefully, in an attempt to prolong our good physical health.

Others will begin on a search for inner well-being. We may become more religious, more philosophical, more in tune with the spiritual well-being of ourselves and those around us.

In the midst of the great rebirth of the twenties, then, there is this note of sadness, of finality. What we are left with is a picture of life in its extremes. Most of us, though, refuse to live life in response to the limits posed by mortality, and instead move on, growing, changing, embracing the future. In both our physical and mental health, the intimations of mortality bring about a resolve to live life to the fullest. As we enter our thirties, we find ourselves determined to make the best of life.

Coming Full Circle

ONE DAY Penny Gregory was reprimanding her child when she was struck by a resounding realization. "I was so angry at her, I began yelling, and I said, 'If you insist on crying I'll spank you and give you a good reason to cry!' Then I stopped, startled, because I remembered that my mother used to use those same words when she was mad at me.

"Later on, when I stopped to think about it, I saw that I had become surprisingly like my mother in many ways. I was raising my child in a similar fashion the way she'd raised me. My views about the importance of family and good education were virtually the same as hers. Even the rhythm of our lives was similar to the pattern when I was growing up.

"It was truly startling to realize that, despite the women's movement, protest marches, Vietnam, recession, and everything else, I had wound up becoming my family's version of an adult. Then I looked in the mirror and thought, My God, I'm even starting to *look* like my mother!"

Many of us at the end of the twenties come to the sudden revelation that we are a lot more like our parents than we would have thought possible. Many of us see for the first time how our family characteristics are intrinsically established in our personalities, in physical habits and tastes, in attitudes and goals that were developed under our parents' roof, in hundreds of little ways.

We may be gradually becoming a new version of our parents.

224

Sleeker, better-educated maybe, more aware of family shortcomings, but still definitely a product of the old homestead. And no matter where we go or what we do, that fact will remain true for the rest of our lives.

For some of us who have had significant problems with our parents, that fact takes a great deal of getting used to.

THE RETURN OF CARING

Perhaps because we and our parents can see more of ourselves in each other now the end of the twenties is a time when we can begin to care about each other openly again. The battles of adolescence are past and the storms of the twenties have blown over. We are adults and they are adults. We have joys and problems in our independent lives and so do they. We need them, they need us. Now we should be able to smile like combatants after the shooting stops. We're still here and in one piece.

We can hug them and not feel as if we're endangering our independence. They can turn to us without feeling ridiculous. We're all in the same boat, and can now help each other along as best we are able.

Sher Watts found that her twenties experiences allowed her relationship with her parents to achieve a new level of warmth and friendship.

"I have a more adult relationship with my parents now, although we've always had a good relationship. There was never a lot of conflict between my parents and me as there is in other parent-child relationships. But there were always little problems, things I could never talk to my parents about—sex or men or drugs.

"Now they can accept the fact that I might not act like they acted when they were my age. But I can mention these issues to them and they can accept them without criticizing. We can talk about sex. That was a very hesitant thing, because I know it's very hard for a mother to accept a daughter's sexuality. I'm still a baby. But now my mother can admit out loud that her daughter is sexual and the world doesn't blow up. She's an adult, she can handle it. And she realizes that I'm an adult and will do certain things that maybe she wouldn't have done at my age, but that's okay. We can handle it.

"As a result I'm able to spend more time with them now than in any of the nine years before, and we have more in common. I'm becoming more like them.

"My life-style and values are changing; I don't care about staying out until four in the morning, as much as I might have earlier. Now at eleven o'clock, I'm tired too. I want to go to bed. I can spend the time with them on a weekend and just sit and talk or go to a movie with them or something; and we're doing it as a family.

"I know they're interested in my opinions. They'll talk to me just as they would talk to one of their friends. We still differ politically and in many other ways, but that's okay now. I don't have to worry about causing any waves. We'll never agree on certain points, but those aren't really all that important. I'm struck with the realization that I know I'm getting older and they're getting older too. I cherish the time that I have left to spend with them. Because they're obviously not going to be around forever."

OUR PARENTS' DEPENDENCE

Some of us find ourselves in the strange situation near the end of the twenties, where our parents are becoming dependent upon us. Barry Posen discovered that within a few years of becoming free of his parents he stood at the head of the family, helping to keep his parents' lives afloat:

"We're reaching a funny point where our relationship has shifted around. I used to rely on them for support and guidance—everything, from saying to my father, 'Gee, I need fifty dollars,' to calling up and talking about how I did well or poorly on a test. Now it has shifted from them providing it for me, almost to me providing it for them.

"There's been an unfortunate rash of illness in the last eighteen months. It's added a lot of pressure to my parents' lives. I've been the strong one who hasn't been there day to day, so I can come in and hear each side of the story without relating it to the other, or to act as the intermediary occasionally, when their day-to-day pressures are just too great. They need my presence to help get them through the crisis.

It's funny, in a paradoxical way. All through my twenties I worked hard to establish a physical distance away from them, while at the same time being very close emotionally. And now in the last eighteen months there have been times when I've had to go out to my folks' home two or three times a week. When they needed me my physical separation vanished. I found it draining occasionally, and irritating—I don't like being caught in the middle—but at the same time I see that they have real problems that I can't just ignore. I have to be there. I have that old sense of obligation that comes back in a weird way now that our relationship is changing.

"Where I used to rely on them, I think they're now starting to rely on me more and more. At first I wanted to reject it and say, 'I don't want anything to do with it.' But then we had a long talk and they said, 'Look, this is the way it is and you've got to accept your responsibility. It's not something you can shirk.' And they're absolutely right."

The realization that our aging parents may now need us more than we need them can be one of the most uncomfortable experiences of late twenties. It's a total turnabout of the relationship we may have had until then. And can come as a deep shock.

First of all, their mortality and age is a sign of our own vulnerability to time. We think a lot about time at the end of the twenties and its obvious effects on our folks can intensify the existential crisis we may be having anyway.

More importantly, our parents' increased need of us forces yet another reappraisal and adjustment of our relationship. But now, instead of forcing us to assert ourselves, we have to underplay our own lives and needs. We have to come back toward them across some of the hard-fought space we achieved during our twenties. We have to try to build them up, after using a decade to build ourselves up in relation to them.

But the end result of such a situation can be richly rewarding, as in Eric's case, by reestablishing the bonds of mutual need and trust that are unique to the parent-child relationship. The balance of need may have shifted away from us and toward them, but the fact that they can trust us—the adult in us—to help them, shows them and us that all the work they did when we were kids wasn't wasted and all the struggling we went through during the twenties allowed us to become confident enough that they are no longer a threat to us; we can slow down for them without endangering ourselves.

LINGERING CRISES

In a few cases, though, our ties with our parents may have proven too stiff and unyielding to be stretched and reshaped during the twenties. At the end of the decade we may be battling over the same ground we were on at our twenty-first birthday.

Ideally, says family problem expert Howard Halpern, parent-child crises should be resolved as early as possible, "but if you haven't resolved this by the early thirties, it doesn't mean you're doomed never to resolve it. You do get chances all along the way. People in their thirties and forties can still break loose."

The key to establishing adulthood in the face of stiff-necked, possessive parents, Halpern believes, is persistent patience. "Most parents can make the shift," he says, "but you've got to give them time. It's not easy."

Because if left to their own devices these parents would never let go, the responsibility devolves to us to set up a schedule for forcing them to accept our independence and to define the parameters of our adult relationship. The schedule should be based on our personal needs. For example, a woman tied emotionally to her mother and unable to establish a strong personal partnership because of that, may want to get her family problems cleared away before the end of the twenties so she has time to get married and have children by her mid-thirties, after which fertility may become a problem. A woman from an ethnic community where close parental ties don't interfere with traditional marriage, might have longer to work out her parental problems.

The form also should be based on our needs, because our parents' demands in this kind of situation are out of touch with reality. "Some people find it so unpleasant to be with their parents and still try to be adults that they can only see them on holidays or special occasions," Halpern states. If so, fine. Better to establish a separate adult identity and sacrifice time with parents, than to submerge our own lives for the sake of an outdated family arrangement.

In many cases, once the break is made we and our parents will be able to drift back together. The once-a-year visits may become semi-annual. We will be able to talk on the phone without engaging in shouting matches. The break, once cleanly made, will eventually heal. But if left untended it will fester and infect our lives. That is why, Halpern believes, it is essential to keep plugging away at establishing an adult to adult relationship with even the most recalcitrant parent. It's never too late.

DEATH OF A PARENT

"I had gone all the way out to the West Coast to get as far away from my father as I possibly could," James Thomas recalls. "He had stomped all over my personality when I was growing up and I felt as though I would never survive, never grow up at all unless I got far away from his overpowering personality.

"It worked. I felt more confident, more capable, and more grown up in Berkeley than I ever had before. I began to establish myself. I was proud of what I'd accomplished and was just about ready to come home in triumph, to meet my father adult to adult and hash out our problems.

"Then I got the phone call. My father, still in his fifties, had suffered a massive heart attack while on the road making his sales calls and was dead.

"I was furious. I was angry at him for all the problems he'd caused me. And I was even madder that he'd cheated me of my chance to show him I'd survived and prospered. I was feeling guilty, too, because I didn't feel as sad as I probably should have. Plus, I was scared; he'd died young of a heart attack. I had begun to realize how much like him I was in many ways. Did that mean I would have heart problems too?

"All told it was the most upsetting experience of my life. I went back home for the funeral and got the you're-the-man-of-the-family-now routine. I was glad to help my mother through the trauma, but I hated everything else about the trip. I hated myself. I hated life. I was miserable. I still get angry when I think about it.

"I know it's crazy. I know he didn't want to die. I know he didn't do it to spite me, but I can't help thinking, Why did the old bastard have to get me one last time?"

The shocking fact of death can interrupt the process of reconciliation with our parents at any time. It is especially shocking for us during the third stage of the twenties, because we are generally so concerned about impermanence and our own lost time. When a parent dies all our worst fears receive a tangible focus. They're all true. Life is cruel. It ends too soon. It has no regard for us or our feelings. Everything seems so purposeless in the face of a parent's death.

How can we cope with it? In essence, I believe this is one of the most totally personal experiences in life. It is intimately tied in with our relationship with our parents, our experiences, our religion, and dozens of other personal factors. No one goes through the experience in quite the same way.

However, to give some picture of what it's like, I'll relate my own experience. My father died a few months before my thirtieth birthday. We had not been close for years. When I last lived with him our mutual antipathy made any kind of normal conversation impossible. We were at loggerheads.

His death was sudden and distressingly impersonal. He lived alone, had a heart attack, and was found by police when his neighbors noticed he hadn't been out of his room for a long time. I had to work through the police to find his body and take care of funeral arrangements over the telephone.

The experience had a riveting effect on me. I found myself recalling with deep affection the early years of my boyhood, when my father and I had gotten along. I felt genuinely sorry that he was gone, which confounded me because I hadn't seen him in years. And I found myself thinking, at all hours, of what an unhappy man he'd been.

I began to see that his death was forcing me to confront the fact that I was becoming rather an unhappy man myself. I had recently taken a job that was supposed to be a major career improvement, but it was turning out to be a total flop. I wouldn't quit because I didn't want to disappoint my wife and cause us any financial hardship. But I hated it.

When my father died, my attitude toward the job solidified. I simply let it slide. It had no meaning for me at all. Eventually, the management, much to my relief, got rid of me.

Once I'd gotten the rotten job out of my system I was better able to view my feelings about my father's death. I realized that however unhappy his life might have been, it wasn't worthless or pointless. He had left me many good memories to go with the bad and he must have given me some worthwhile values because my own life had gone fairly well. If my father's very difficult life had worth and meaning, then I slowly became certain that mine would too. Through my children and my work and my marriage I would leave lasting impressions on people. That would be my meaning.

And I think, at the root, that is the message we must all find in the death of a parent: That while much of life is capricious and arbitrary, we *do* have some control and can make a difference. Our parents did—through us. We may make a difference through our children or through our work or the way we live, as examples to others. Life passes around us and through us. The power of death confirms the force each of us has in our lives.

Epilogue

LOOKING BACK TO my own twenties, it is incredible how different the world looked at twenty-one, twenty-four, and particularly at twenty-nine. It is almost as if I were three entirely different people: The brash, overindulgent, hyperactive postcollegian; the confused, deadly serious, volatile mid-twentian; the family-oriented, work-compulsive adult.

The same is true for most of us, I believe. I hope that no matter where you, the readers of this book stand in years when you first read it, you'll go back and read it again during later stages. During the early twenties the first chapters may seem richly alive while the end of the book will appear misty and unrealistic. Later on, however, the first chapters will seem self-evident while the problems and potentials of the final pages will take on the most important significance.

It is important to remember, too, at all stages, whenever you turn to this book, that none of us move through our twenties, indeed our lives, in the same manner. Even the broadest rules of human conduct don't apply universally. As a result, all the experiences in this book won't apply to any one person. Each of our situations is different, unique. And all the patterns explained here won't apply to everyone. You should take from the book what fits your life, and merely skim those sections that don't, as a source of information about what may be happening to your friends and peers.

I hope, though, that while everything in the book won't apply to each person, something here will touch each of you. We all will be able to find a bit of ourselves here, a reflection of our thoughts, fears, and expectations at each of the stages of the first adult decade. This turbulent time is one of the most serious, difficult and important struggles of our lives. It is excruciating trying to pull ourselves through this long series of tests, surprises, and startling lurches toward adulthood. And it has been severely neglected as a subject of study and explanation. Adolescence has garnered reams of attention. But the twenties, by comparison, were sold to us as an easy time, the calm after the storms of teenage days.

Nothing could be farther from the truth, especially in economically unstable times like these. To make a smooth, successful passage through the twenties takes all the help we can get. I hope this book can be a major component of that help, offering some comfort, some practical advice, and some forewarning of the problems that lie ahead.

I want the book to remind each of us that, as rough as things might seem, we are not alone, not abnormal, not on the road to ruin. We are simply facing the normal struggles of our age.

And, I can't overemphasize how crucial success in this struggle is for the rest of our adult lives. The experts stress how important the trials of this time are, how vital it is to grow during the decade. Both in love and work the twenties are essential for adult development. Unanimously, psychological experts state that to achieve true adulthood, true creativity, and, in fact, simple success in the real world, we must pass through these stages of growth during the twenties.

Psychologist Daniel Levinson, for example, points out that a person who fails to grow during the twenties, who fails to achieve intimacy, may end up isolated from the rest of life. The worker who fails to achieve some success, some work consolidation, may well be a failure in the rest of his/her career. These are not absolute, specific doctrines; psychologists aren't saying that if we want to be successful bankers we must immediately join banks and work eighty-hour weeks for the rest of our lives or that we should marry the first decent person we meet after passing age twenty-eight. But they are noting that generally, if we haven't made progress in our chosen direction, if we aren't in the process of getting there by the end of the twenties, we probably never will arrive.

During the twenties we establish the competence that carries us ahead in all areas of life during the adult decades. The growth we experience in intimacy, personal knowledge, and work skills are all intertwined. They meld to produce a person who can handle life. It is rare that a truly successful person has not also achieved some success at being personally intimate. And, conversely, the person who knows how to get close to other people, to achieve his/her own goals of intimacy is often very successful in his/her career. This overall capacity to face and cope with the situations adult life brings is what the trials of the twenties are all about, I believe.

I hope this book, if it does anything, provides a context for thinking and talking about the decade's momentous changes, huge swings of perception and unending challenges. I can't examine each person's life, but I hope I can present a tool that can help him/her understand it better.

I'd like it if the book encouraged us to talk with one another about the problems and opportunities of the first adult decade. I think peers are the greatest repositories of useful knowledge we can find. Only they are going through all this at the same time and under the same social circumstances as we are. They feel what we feel, suffer what we suffer, see what we see. They can be our best support and we should talk to them, lean on them, and allow them to lean on us. It makes the journey much easier and more enjoyable to have company.

The movement through the twenties is a growth process that doesn't stop abruptly on our thirtieth birthdays. Many of us will still be dealing with problems from the first adult decade as we move into the second. Even those who have moved into adult roles and feelings before the official end of the twenties don't stop growing. If one fact has emerged from the modern study of adult psychology it is that as long as we wish to, we can grow. Growth is a lifelong process. There is no deadline, no test, no limit. Growth and change may not be as intense, as impelling in later decades as they were in the twenties, but they are there. We should always look for ways to change, to improve our life situations or our inner selves. We have gone through a great deal of trouble during the twenties to learn how to do this. We shouldn't stop using these hard-won skills once that decade is past.